5d9

ANN CLARK'S

FABULOUS FISH

ANN CLARK'S

FABULOUS FISH

Easy and Exciting Ways to Cook and Serve Seafood

NAL BOOKS

NEW AMERICAN LIBRARY

NEW YORK AND SCARBOROUGH, ONTARIO

NAL BOOKS TRADEMARK REG. U.S. PAT. OFF. AND FOREIGN COUNTRIES
REGISTERED TRADEMARK—MARCA REGISTRADA
HECHO EN HARRISONBURG, VA., U.S.A.

SIGNET, SIGNET CLASSIC, MENTOR, ONYX, PLUME,
MERIDIAN and NAL BOOKS are published in the United States by
NAL PENGUIN INC., 1633 Broadway, New York, New York 10019,
in Canada by The New American Library of Canada Limited,
81 Mack Avenue, Scarborough, Ontario M1L 1M8

Design: Julian Hamer
Photography: Jerry Simpson
Stylist: Linda Cheverton
Food stylist: Ann Disrude

PHOTO CREDITS
Pottery by Richard Bennett, Great Barrington Pottery,
Housatonic, Mass.
Glassware by Simon Pearce, New York, N.Y.
Stainless flatware by Patino Wolf, D. F. Sanders, New York, N.Y.
Sterling silver by Georg Jensen, Royal Copenhagen, New York, N.Y.
Hand-painted backdrops by Jane Nelson, Unique Surfaces,
New York, N.Y.

Cover:
Flowers by Very Special Flowers, New York, N.Y.
Antique table by Pierre Deux, New York, N.Y.

Library of Congress Cataloging-in-Publication Data

Clark, Ann.
    Ann Clark's fabulous fish.

    Includes index.
    1. Cookery (Fish) 2. Cookery (Shellfish) I. Title. II. Title:
Fabulous fish.
TX747.C59   1987   641.6'92   87-5667
ISBN 0-453-00548-9

First Printing, August, 1987

1 2 3 4 5 6 7 8 9

PRINTED IN THE UNITED STATES OF AMERICA

*This book is lovingly dedicated to
my dear mother, my brothers, Steve and Mark,
my sweet sister, Merry, and to the memory
of my father, with fond recollections
of all the fun and laughter we had around
the dinner table in our childhood.*

ACKNOWLEDGMENTS

I am grateful above all to Shari Hamilton, Alana Dwyer, Clara Tread-well, Marilyn Caldwell, and Melissa Airoldi. These thoughtful, able, witty assistants and friends who tirelessly helped me in my classes and catering over many years have made my work all the more enjoyable.

To Melissa Airoldi, I owe a great debt of thanks for her apt sugges-tions, remarkable cheerfulness, efficiency, and steadfastness through-out the long and tedious process of deciphering my handwriting and typing and editing the manuscript. I much appreciated Alice Wight-man's help when the manuscript was in the final stages.

Many thanks to my sister Merry Clark who was a great and energetic source of information and moral support throughout the writing of this book.

Special thanks also go to many wonderful students and friends for their counsel and encouragement, in particular, Jane Koock, Roger Joseph, Sharon Watkins, Jennifer Ridgeway, Kate Clark, Linda Wooldridge, Julie Eskoff, Penni Wisner, JoAnn Williams, Phyllis Wald-ron, JoLynn Hoffman, Jan Fleming, Gay Gillen, and Audrey and Barry Sterling.

I wish to thank my wonderful agent, Nancy Love, for her enthusiasm and thoughtful assistance. And I am grateful to my editors Molly Allen and Irene Pink for their tremendous help; the final form of the book is due in large measure to their editorial input. I appreciate all the care they put into this project. Thanks are also due to Marie Simmons for her excellent suggestions and to Veronica Johnson for her sensitive, expert editing, which did so much to shape the book.

Contents

Introduction   xi

1. Some of the Basics: Ingredients and Equipment   1

2. On Cooking Fish and Shellfish   26

3. Fish Entrées   57

4. Shellfish Entrées   95

5. Cold Fish Dishes, Sandwiches, and Salads   119

6. Hot Hors d'Oeuvres, Sandwiches and Soups, and Brunch and Late-Night Supper Dishes   140

7. Grains, Vegetables, and Other Accompaniments to Fish Dishes   163

8. Fish Fumet, Court Bouillons, Marinades, Butters and Sauces, Coatings, and Shellfish Boils   196

LEXICON OF FISH AND SHELLFISH   239

INDEX   252

Introduction

It may seem odd for a person who has never lived on a seacoast or near any large body of water to be writing a book on fish, but it is a subject that fascinates me. I never cease to marvel at the incredible variety of seafood that is available, and wherever I have lived and traveled I have delighted in tasting unusual fish dishes, searching out the best seafood restaurants, and trying my hand at cooking whatever the local markets have to offer. Among these many wonderful fish dishes I clearly recall:

—Crunching the crispy, 4-inch-long, pan-fried sunfish or crappies caught on regular family expeditions to the rare small lake or slough in the South Dakota of my childhood. Just the right size for a little girl, I thought at the time.

—Reveling in my very first taste of just-caught boiled Maine lobster as a college student on the East Coast.

—Savoring octopus and potatoes fried in olive oil with a bottle of cold retsina one steamy summer night outside a tiny tavern in a questionable but colorful district of Athens.

—Breaking open and eating the roe of large purple-spined Pacific sea urchins on the pier in Santa Barbara, where divers on the fishing boats haul them up in large nets at sunset.

—Eating a gargantuan pile of succulent steamed mussels (150 per serving!) for lunch on a foggy Sunday in late November in Etretat, a bustling seaside town in Normandy.

—Trapping fresh spiny lobsters and grilling them over an open fire on the deserted (except for lots of iguanas) beach of an island off the coast of Yucatan.

—Being introduced to the pleasures of sushi and sashimi on a late-night chef's tour of the best Japanese sushi bars in San Francisco.

That a food so varied and delicious is also good from a nutritional standpoint is a very happy circumstance. Today fish figures more prominently in the American diet than ever before, which is not surprising given what we now know about its role in maintaining health and proper nutrition.

Fish is one of the most healthful foods available to us. It is low in fat and in calories. A 4-ounce portion of lean fish contains about 115 calories, of moderately fatty fish about 155 calories, and of fatty fish about 200 calories. Fish is high in protein. Four ounces of fish provide one third to one half of an adult's Recommended Daily Allowance of protein.

Fish is especially rich in A, D, and B vitamins and is an important source of the minerals phosphorus, potassium, iron, iodine, and selenium. Shellfish, especially oysters, are one of the richest sources of zinc, and many shellfish and canned fish with bones are high in calcium. Most shellfish is low in saturated fat. Crab, oysters, and lobster have much less cholesterol per serving than an average serving of egg. (Caviar, not an everyday food, has the highest cholesterol level of all fish.) Beef and pork contain between 25 to 35 percent more saturated fat per serving than fish.

The most exciting recent discovery pertaining to the healthfulness of fish centers on the oils found in some cold freshwater fish and in all cold saltwater fish, especially the deep-water varieties—herring, sardines, mackerel, and salmon. The beneficial polyunsaturated fats found in these fish oils, called the omega-3 fatty acids, are proving to be two to five times more effective in lowering blood cholesterol than the other major form of helpful polyunsaturated fats, the omega-6 fatty acids found in vegetable oils. The omega-3 fatty acids help to effectively flush cholesterol out of the blood, and make blood thinner and slower to clot, which may lessen the risk of heart attack and heart disease.

Recent tests point to further benefits from fish oils in the treatment of rheumatoid arthritis, eczema, psoriasis, and migraine headaches. Now we can say with confidence: For better health, eat fish more often!

Although we are advised to eat more fish, I have found in the course of teaching cooking during the past thirteen years at my school, La Bonne Cuisine, in Austin, Texas, and at others around the country, that most people are very wary of cooking fish and shellfish, and limited in their approach to them, both in the kinds of seafood they cook and in the ways they choose to cook and serve them.

I wrote this book to demystify the cooking of fish and to suggest exciting new taste alternatives that complement the wider range of fish available to an audience that is larger than ever before. But most of all, I hope to show how easy and pleasurable it is to cook and eat well every day.

There is, in fact, no mystery to cooking seafood—it is only unfamiliarity that makes it seem mysterious. Here are the most basic things you need to know, points that I will develop in greater detail in the next two chapters.

Fish is one of the most exciting foods to cook because of the wide range of seasonings that complement and enhance it. These are discussed in Chapter 1 and are reflected throughout the book in the recipes.

Fish is quick and easy to cook. The actual thickness of a whole fish, fillets, or steaks determines to a large extent the method and length of cooking. Fish can be cooked by many different techniques, none of them taking more than 10 minutes per inch of thickness of the fish. For a complete discussion, see Chapter 2.

Fin fish can be divided into three different types—lean fish, fatty fish, and moderately fatty fish. Fatty fish have more fish oil in them, which gives them more flavor and a few more calories. Don't be misled by the word *fat* as it describes fish; the fattest fish contain less fat then the leanest meat. Knowing which category a fish falls into helps determine how it should be cooked. A list of lean, fatty, and moderately fatty fish appears on page 28.

The texture of fish varies, so knowing the texture of a fish—fine, dense, or loose—also helps to determine the best cooking methods. The Lexicon of Fish and Shellfish on pages 233–51 describes the texture of the various fish used in this book.

Like fish, shellfish (oysters, scallops, mussels, clams, shrimp, and lobster) are quick and easy to cook and lend themselves to a wide variety of exciting preparations and seasonings.

Although my first love was regional French cooking, having lived and worked in France for six years, I am inspired today by many different ethnic cuisines—Thai, Mexican, Indian, and Moroccan in particular—and by the rediscovery of our regional American culinary heritage. Nowhere has this eclectic direction been more apparent than in California where imaginative young chefs and teachers have blended these varied influences into a culinary style distinctly their own. I felt this welcome inspiration from many talented chefs, colleagues, and friends in the wine industry when I cooked each autumn for three wonderful years at Iron Horse Vineyards in Sonoma County, California.

The excitement about good food has now spread all over the country. In 1987, we look to an imaginative reinterpretation of the melting pot of American cuisine by an impressive number of talented chefs, teachers, caterers, consultants, and writers. American food has come of age.

For me, cooking is not just the skillful and sensitive preparation of food, but more importantly, it is the anticipation of giving, and of receiving hospitality. Cooking and sharing food signify many things I value: the creative exercise of culinary skills, the warm offering of hospitality, the love of good food, and the joyful opportunity for thanksgiving.

Some of the Basics: Ingredients and Equipment

Before you ever start to cook fish, knowing some of the basics is very helpful. You will want to know how to select the freshest fish, how to choose the best seasonings for fish, and what are the most useful tools and cooking equipment. This basic knowledge will give you confidence in your approach to cooking fish.

BUYING FISH AND SHELLFISH

Fresh versus Frozen

Fresh fish has two important qualities that frozen fish lacks: delicacy of flavor and firm texture. Freezing alters the texture of fish and in thawing, much of the flavor in the juices is lost. Frozen fish, up until recently, has always been a poor second choice if good fresh fish has been available. Now for some fish, especially Pacific and Atlantic salmon, much better commercial techniques are being used to freeze whole fish. The best frozen fish are flash-frozen on the boat and coated with a glaze to prevent deterioration. When frozen this ideal way, as soon after being caught as possible, and cooked before completely thawed, these "frozen" fish are often fresher and in better condition than "fresh" fish that is in reality a number of days old. In general, however, if you have a good source of truly fresh fish, that is still your best bet.

Fresh Whole Fish

Buying fresh fish is a simple matter once you learn to recognize the qualities of freshness. The skin and scales of a fresh whole fish have a bright sheen, and the scales are firmly attached. The eyes should be rounded and clear, not sunken and cloudy; the gills should be a bright pink or red but not dark or slimy; and the flesh should be firm and elastic—it should spring back when pressed. If an indentation remains, it means the fish is a bit old. If health regulations do not allow you to touch the fish, watch the fish seller make this test for you. A fresh saltwater fish smells fresh, clean, and faintly salty, like a sea breeze. The slightest "fishy" or unpleasant smell or any hint of ammonia indicates the fish has started to deteriorate and should be rejected. (An exception to this rule: Shark and skate do give off a natural ammonia smell.)

Don't be shy about asking questions. Look carefully at the fish, ask to touch and smell it, and reject anything that does not please you. Whole fresh fish really look bright, plump, and pretty. Don't just ask if the fish is fresh, since the answer will always be yes! Always ask when the fish arrived in the market, where it came from, and if it has been frozen.

Coastal fishing waters are regulated by state agencies, and when those waters and the fish in them (mostly shellfish such as scallops, oysters, mussels, etc.) become polluted either by man-made chemical pollution or natural bacterial pollution, such as red or brown tides, commercial and sport fishing is prohibited until the situation improves. It is always a good idea to buy your fish only from a long-established, reputable market. When fishing and digging for clams yourself, inquire at the local health department for up-to-date information on safe fishing waters.

Fish counters in many large grocery chains are beginning to be staffed by employees who have some knowledge of fish. Specialty or gourmet grocery stores and chains have made big strides in displaying fresh fish and in providing better storage. On the one hand, it is cheering to finally see a wider variety of fish available, but it is discouraging to realize that in these large chains fish are often stored inappropriately and far too long to ensure maximum freshness. Fish should be displayed directly on the ice in a very cold refrigerated counter. If the glass surface of the display case is not very cold, you should question the freshness of the fish.

I have lived in landlocked parts of the United States where good fresh seafood has been hard to obtain. This has led me to a notion of the relativity of freshness; there seem to be three kinds of fresh:

Pristine Fresh: Fish just out of the water, which you catch yourself or buy from a fisherman off the boat.

Honest John Fresh: The recommendations of an honest fish seller, extremely helpful if you live far from a fish market and can rely on a telephone conversation to advise you of the availability of fresh fish on a particular day before you make a long trip to market.

Ever-Fresh: A lot of the fish sold in some big supermarket chains. It was fresh when it came in, it was fresh yesterday, and it will still be "real fresh" two weeks from today!

REMEMBER: Seek out the freshest source of fish in your area, regularly patronize that source, get to know the fish seller, and use your sense of sight, smell, and touch to assure that only the freshest fish come to your table.

Fresh Fillets and Steaks

It's easier to determine the freshness of whole fish than fillets and steaks, so if you want the freshest cuts, buy the whole fish and have it cut ("dressed") to your specifications. However, a good fish seller will fillet or steak only the amount of fish he can sell in a day. Precut fresh fillets and steaks should look plump, firm, and have a nice bright sheen. They should smell clean and fresh; reject any that smell unpleasant. If they have no luster, are gray or yellowish and dried out around the edges, or look soft and mushy, they are not fresh and will not taste very good. Be sure to buy fillets and steaks dressed that same day for optimum freshness.

Shellfish

Fresh oysters, clams, and mussels should be bought with their shells tightly closed. (Fresh scallops still in the shell are rarely seen in American markets.) If a few shells are opened slightly, tap them firmly, and if the shellfish is still alive the shells will close up quickly. Discard any shells that remain open. Oysters, clams, and mussels should feel quite heavy. Reject any light ones or any with broken and chipped shells, or any that do not smell fresh.

Fresh lobsters should be bought from a clean water tank and should be alive and kicking. If lobsters barely move or seem sluggish, they are likely to have been there too long to be "fresh from the sea."

Lobster tails sold in markets as fresh are most likely to have been frozen and thawed. Frozen lobster meat is watery when thawed and, when cooked, has a tougher texture.

Fresh crabs and crayfish are kept on ice and sold whole. They should also move in a lively manner to be really fresh. Crayfish tails are often available in frozen packages outside crayfish country.

Fresh crab (lump meat, back fin) and crayfish (tails) and fresh shucked oysters and clams are sold out of the shell in containers fresh or pasteurized, heated to 130° to 160° to kill bacteria. These pasteurized containers, when opened, will keep a week longer than the fresh. Be sure to buy them from a reliable market and check the expiration date of freshness on the containers. These forms are convenient and time-saving, and for most purposes just fine, but they are not quite as delicious as shellfish fresh from the shell. Fresh crabs, because they are so perishable, are also sold cooked whole (Dungeness), in claws (Florida stone crabs), and legs (Alaska king crab).

Bay and sea scallops are sold shucked and in their own juices and are usually sold out of gallon containers. Frozen scallops seem to suffer the least of all fish and shellfish from being frozen. All scallops have a thumbnail-sized piece of connective tissue which holds the scallop muscle to the shell. It is slightly tougher in texture when cooked, so it can be removed before cooking if desired.

Very little shrimp is sold fresh anymore. Keep asking and your fish seller will concede they are *fresh frozen*. Occasionally they do appear in the markets with heads and feelers still intact. They are beautiful! By all means buy them and cook them with heads on for superb flavor. The tiniest shrimp with heads on can be safely eaten whole—heads, shells, and all. Most shrimp of all sizes are sold headless, in the shell. All shrimp have a dark vein down the back. This is safe to eat, but may be gritty as well as unpleasant to look at, so devein shrimp if you wish although it is not strictly necessary.

If you must thaw any shellfish, do so gradually. The best method is to leave them in the package 24 hours in the refrigerator. If you cook them before they are completely thawed, they will have more flavor since flavor is leached out in the melting juices.

All fish and shellfish in all forms should smell fresh and pleasant. Any that do not should be rejected.

The Basic Cuts of Fish

Most whole fish are gutted as soon as they are caught to prevent the rapidly deteriorating innards from spoiling the whole fish, and are scaled at time of purchase or as they are brought into market. Skinning, boning, filleting, steaking, splitting, and other ways of dressing fish are excellent skills to know, but unless you have the correct tools and the time to perform these exact operations, it is better to ask your fish seller to prepare the fish the way you want it.

At a well-stocked fish market you will see fish in many forms. For the best methods of cooking, see the guide on page 30.

Whole Fish: A fish in the round, gutted and scaled, with head, tail, and fins left on.

Head-Dressed Fish: Same as above, but with head removed. I prefer to leave the head on; a fish looks unnatural to me without it.

Pan-Dressed Fish: Head-dressed fish with fins and tail removed.

Butterflied Pan-Dressed Fish: Fish cut in half lengthwise, with the backbone removed.

Steaked Fish: Slices of pan-dressed fish cut across the backbone, with skin and bone on. Steaks are thick slices, anywhere from 1 to 2 inches ideally, cut from large fish such as salmon, tuna, swordfish, halibut, and bass.

Filleted Fish: Long sections of skinned or unskinned fish cut off either side of the bone.

How Much Fish and Shellfish to Buy

Here is a guide to the amount of fish to buy per person:

Whole Fish: ¾ to 1 pound per person

Fillets: About ⅓ pound per person

Steaks: Depends upon size, but usually one 6- to 8-ounce steak per person

Shellfish: For almost all shellfish, I determine the amount by the piece: how many pieces per person for each recipe. Amounts will vary depending on preparation and appetites, and whether shellfish are served simply or in a sauce. For example 4 to 6 oysters per person as an hors d'oeuvre, 10 to 12 or more as a main course, for moderate appetites. For clams buy 10 to 12 per person as an hors d'oeuvre, 20 to 24 as a main course. If you are buying shelled fish, shrimp, crab, oysters, or scallops, count ¼ to ⅓ pound per person. Mussels, because they are so small, are a different matter. If they are to be served as a main course, I would normally buy 1½ pounds of mussels in the shell per person; as a first course or soup, about ¾ pound per person is adequate.

How to Store Fresh Fish and Shellfish

REFRIGERATOR STORAGE

Fish is extremely perishable, much more so than meat, and extra precautions need to be taken to protect its freshness. Be sure to ask your fish seller to wrap the fish with some ice around it to keep it really cold on your way home. Just 15 minutes at too warm a temperature will cause fish to deteriorate. If the temperature of fish goes up 10°, quality diminishes 10 percent.

When you get home, remove fish from market wrapping, wipe with a damp cloth or rinse quickly in cold water, if necessary, and pat dry. Then wrap it tightly in plastic wrap or foil, bury in a bowl or tray of ice, and cover tightly. This keeps fish at its coldest until you are ready to cook it.

All finfish are best cooked on the day purchased. If stored surrounded by ice, they will keep one day. Steaks and fillets are more perishable and should not be kept more than one day. The first time you buy fresh fish, do cook it the same day to taste it at its very best. The next time, leave it a day before cooking so you can notice the difference.

Oysters, clams, and mussels in the shell should be stored on ice in the refrigerator for not more than one to two days. Lobsters, crabs, and crayfish are best stored in a big paper grocery bag in the coldest part of the refrigerator. Ask for seaweed to be packed with them. Shucked or cooked shellfish should not be stored for more than one day.

FREEZER STORAGE

If you must freeze fish, use only the freshest fish. Do not freeze fish that have been sitting in your refrigerator for two days, for the flavor will be diminished. Do not freeze any fish that have previously been frozen. Clean the cavity of a whole fish, rinse quickly in coldest water, wipe dry inside and out, and wrap airtight using several layers of plastic wrap and foil. Seal in a plastic bag, label with the contents, the current date, and the latest date the fish should be consumed. (Lean fish should be frozen no longer than four months; fatty fish, which have stronger oils and flavor, do best frozen only three months.) Check to see that your freezer operates at a temperature not over 0° Fahrenheit.

Fish can also be successfully frozen in water; fresh shrimp and small whole fish freeze very well this way. Place the fish in a plastic container, fill with water to cover fish, seal, wrap well and freeze. Glaze larger fish with ice by dipping in cold water and placing on a tray in the freezer to freeze, then dipping a second and third time and freezing until a thick glaze or coat of ice completely encases the fish. Wrap well, label, and freeze.

HOW TO THAW

To thaw frozen fish, place still-wrapped fish in a bowl or on a tray in the refrigerator and let thaw slowly over a twenty-four-hour period.

To thaw more quickly, put wrapped fish under cold running water or in a large bowl of cold water until almost completely thawed. Take the fish that has been frozen in a block of ice and thaw under cold running water. When most of the ice covering has melted, put the fish in a plastic bag and continue to thaw under cold water. This will keep the flavorful juices from leaching out.

Frozen fish retain more moisture and flavor if cooked when not completely thawed. Once a fish has been thawed, cook it as soon as possible and never refreeze it.

SEASONINGS FOR FISH AND SHELLFISH

Practically all herbs and spices, aromatic vegetables, and other flavoring ingredients pair with fish in unique and exciting ways. There is no reason to fall back on hackneyed preparations (broiled fish fillet with melted butter, lemon, and paprika) when a world of seasonings is available to you. The following list of ingredients and references to recipes should spark your culinary imagination.

Herbs

Herbs are the aromatic green leaves of small woody plants. Fresh herbs are almost always preferable to dried herbs because their oils are still intact. Marjoram, thyme, rosemary, mint, flat-leafed parsley, dill, basil, and chives are easy to grow even in a kitchen window. As demand increases, different kinds of fresh herbs are appearing more regularly in the markets.

Bunches of fresh herbs keep well for a day or two in the refrigerator. Rinse, dry, place in a plastic bag with paper towels to absorb moisture. Some seasonal herbs such as basil freeze relatively well.

Place washed herb leaves in ice cube trays, cover with water, and freeze; or chop well, add olive oil (or make into pesto) and freeze in foil by tablespoonfuls for convenience. These frozen cubes of herbs can be added to simmering soups and stews.

Fresh herbs can also be used to make herb butters (see page 214). Keep herb butters on hand in the freezer, well-wrapped and labeled for quick use as sauces for fish.

When buying dried herbs, buy only whole-leaf herbs, and only in small quantities. Store in tightly sealed jars away from heat and light.

If you have space, store dried chives, dill, tarragon, and chervil in jars in your freezer or refrigerator. Because the aromatic oils of herbs are volatile, they lose flavor quickly in a dried state. Freezing gives dried herbs a longer life. Never use ground dried herbs; their flavor dissipates rapidly because so much surface is exposed to the air, and they tend to muddy sauces and soups.

A general rule for substituting dried herbs for fresh when fresh are not available is to use 1 dried to 2 fresh. Cut fresh herbs can be stored in the refrigerator in several ways: either trimmed of stems, washed, patted dry, and sealed in a plastic bag, or washed and put in a glass of water and covered with a plastic bag. I prefer the former method. Most fresh-cut herbs do not keep longer than two to three days.

Check your dried herb cupboard every few months. Dried herbs should be bright green and have a distinct aroma. If they smell vaguely of dried grass or straw, they will not have the power to flavor anything and should be replaced.

Most fresh herbs should be added to a dish at the last moment; if they are cooked too long they will lose their "fresh" quality.

Dried herbs, especially thyme, bay leaf, and fresh parsley, the base flavoring herbs, need to be added at the beginning of cooking. I like to get two levels of flavor by adding the dried herb to a sauce or stew at the beginning of cooking and then adding that same herb, fresh, chopped, just before serving.

An important thing to remember is that most herbs, spices, and aromatics give off a fuller flavor if they are added to a hot dish. The heat causes them to release their volatile oils.

For a concentrated herbal flavoring in wine cream sauces or marinades, make an infusion of herbs (thyme, rosemary, basil, mint, dill). To do so, crush ¼ cup of the fresh herb in a mortar, then cover with a small amount of water and simmer 10 minutes. Remove herbs and reduce liquid over high heat until only 1 to 2 tablespoonfuls remain. Add carefully to taste; only a small amount is necessary to flavor a sauce.

BASIL

A pungent herb that complements salmon, scallops, and halibut in particular. Basil has a more minty flavor when dried. It is excellent in butters and butter sauces, in marinades and vinaigrettes, and is marvelous with any tomato dish. Experiment with different kinds of basil: Italian, the small-leafed Oriental variety, bush basil, purple basil.

BAY LEAF
Look for imported or Turkish bay leaf (*Lauris nobilis*). Do not confuse this true bay with the harsher California bay with its long, sharply pointed, darker leaves. California bay can be used in tiny amounts in hearty Mexican dishes or stews but will ruin the fine flavor of most other dishes, especially stocks and sauces. It is normally used dried: fresh bay is slightly more bitter in flavor. Bay leaf, used a great deal in Mediterranean cuisines, is also an essential flavor in stocks, marinades, and court bouillons. Alternate bay leaves with pieces of swordfish on a skewer, marinate, and grill.

CHERVIL
One of the earliest spring herbs and difficult to grow, it's a close relative of parsley, has a delicate flavor, and is best used fresh. One of the classic *fines herbes* mixture (tarragon, chives, parsley, and chervil), it's excellent with delicately flavored fish, as a garnish, and in sauces. Fresh chervil is marvelous in soups, green sauces, and vinaigrettes for fish.

CILANTRO OR FRESH CORIANDER OR CHINESE PARSLEY
Cool tasting and pungent, this leaf of the coriander plant is an essential ingredient in and garnish for many Mexican, Indian, Moroccan, and Oriental dishes. It provides a cooling foil in combination with hot spices. As a garnish, I prefer whole leaves instead of chopped.

DILL
Associated with Scandinavian cooking and summer, the fernlike leaves of dill impart a delicate, refreshing taste when paired with fish. Use dill in butters, cold sauces, and marinades, and place it in the cavity of a whole fish that is to be baked. Fresh is infinitely better than dried for this cool-climate herb.

FENNEL
The edible bulb of fennel, chopped, or the ferny leaves, seeds, or dried stalks of ordinary fennel all subtly flavor fish with a delicate anise-celery taste. When using fresh fennel as a vegetable, cut off and dry out the green stalks to use later as a flavoring.

Put a few dried fennel stalks in the cavity of a fish for grilling, or toss them on hot coals to flavor-smoke fish, or tie the stalks in little bundles and flame with Pernod as a stunning presentation around a large grilled fish on a big platter.

Fresh fennel leaves have a sweet, rich bright taste which heightens the flavor of fish in stews, salads, grills, or when used as a garnish.

LEMON GRASS
A tall, coarse green stalk about ¼ to ½ inch in diameter much used in Southeast Asian cooking. It has a delicate, intriguing flavor and can be added to soups and marinades. If used frozen or dried, it is generally added in large pieces because it is too coarse to be eaten. This is a way to add lemon flavor without any acidity.

MINT
The sharp freshness of the fragrant leaves of the vigorous spreading mint plant enhances the richer fish (salmon, trout, mullet). Experiment with different varieties.

Wrap branches of mint around whole small fish to be grilled or baked, or use chopped in butter sauces, marinades, or in a rice pilaf with pine nuts and currants served hot or as a stuffing.

OREGANO
These small, intensely flavored leaves on long, thin stalks emit a strong direct flavor which is wonderful with clams and shrimp, or in Italian and Greek fish dishes, tomato sauces, and fish stews. Combines well with thyme, parsley, and basil. Makes an excellent flavored oil for grilling.

PARSLEY
Flat-leafed Italian parsley is prettier and more flavorful than the ubiquitous curly-leafed parsley. Parsley is one of the most useful, most readily available, hardiest herbs to grow and keeps a long time in the refrigerator. Essential in stocks, court bouillons, marinades, and vinaigrettes, with rice and potatoes, and in green sauces, it adds fine flavor to all kinds of fish. Use the stems to flavor stocks.

Parsley does not have to look banal as a garnish. Instead of whole sprigs of parsley, use whole leaves, or instead of chopping coarsely, mince finely and sprinkle on top of fish in diagonal lines or all around the outline of fish on a platter. Stuff the gills of whole poached fish with parsley sprigs to resemble a green collar.

ROSEMARY
This hardy aromatic shrub produces leaves that are sharp like pine needles, so when cooking with rosemary either crush the leaves in a

mortar or add branches that can be removed. Use sparingly in other preparations, as it is strong-flavored and will overwhelm the flavor of a delicate dish.

Use branches of rosemary dipped in olive oil or marinade to baste fish on a grill, or throw rosemary on hot coals for fragrant smoke.

SORREL
Often found growing wild, this dark green leafy plant looks like a spiky-leaved spinach and multiplies rapidly like mint in your garden. French cooks consider it one of the great herbs with fish. Its cool, clean, lemony taste accords perfectly with delicate-flavored lean fish and is a classic served with poached salmon.

Blanch about ½ pound of sorrel for 1 minute in boiling water, drain, press dry, chop, and add a little cream or butter to taste, and serve hot as a puree under poached fillets, or finely shred and add to a hot sauce.

TARRAGON
Recognize tarragon by its slender dark green leaves on a woody stem and its unusual tangy licorice flavor. If you are planting, be sure to get the true French tarragon, not the Russian variety that resembles it. The warm, sharp flavor of fresh tarragon marries well with lobster and is very good in butter sauces, in vinaigrettes, and with crème fraîche. Dried tarragon has a quite different and strong flavor. Fresh tarragon can be blanched and preserved in good-flavored white wine vinegar, or frozen in ice cube trays in water, broth, or oil.

THYME
The tiny, gray-green leaves of this woody shrub give off a warm rich flavor essential for court bouillons, fumets, soups, and stews. Use thyme branches in oil or a marinade to baste grilled fish or to throw on coals, or place branches in whole fish (trout, snapper, bass) to flavor while baking or grilling. One of the most useful herbs in your kitchen, thyme seems to go well with nearly all fish and all vegetables.

WATERCRESS
This fragile round-leafed water plant—with its spicy, tangy, refreshing flavor—makes an attractive garnish for fish, using leaves or whole stalks. It can be prepared and served like sorrel, but is excellent in cold sauces, added to salads, or as an ingredient in green sauces.

Spices

Spices are the hard, dried, aromatic parts of plants—seeds, bark, berries, etc. Many, but not all, come from the tropics. The best flavor comes from whole spices and seeds—nutmeg, allspice, cumin, sesame, peppercorns, dried red peppers, fennel seeds, cloves, cardamom, anise—which are lightly roasted (heated) in a dry skillet, then ground in a small electric spice grinder or pounded in a mortar with a pestle. A small fine grater is needed for nutmeg. Packaged ground spices such as ground cumin are convenient but do not have the sharpness of flavor of whole spices you freshly heat and grind yourself.

Whether whole or ground, spices have a longer shelf-life than herbs. Store in tightly sealed bottles away from heat and light.

Here's a suggestion for seasoning fish to be pan-fried: Mix a pinch of ground cumin, coriander seed, cayenne, fennel seed, or cinnamon with flour, salt, and ground pepper for coating fish.

CAYENNE

This medium-sized, hot, red chile, dried and ground, adds piquancy to shellfish dishes, fish soups, and tomato dishes. Use sparingly in marinades and in flour for coating fish. Other dried red chiles such as chile pequin, jap chile, and ancho can be ground and used as cayenne.

CORIANDER SEED

The pepper-like seeds of the coriander plant have a delicate spicy flavor, and are used crushed to season marinades and tomato sauces, ground for curries, or mixed with other herbs and garlic, then pressed into cuts of scored fish to be baked. Dried coriander seed has a subtle flavor and is generally used in combination with other herbs and spices.

CUMIN SEED

The small, brown, mildly hot seeds of the cumin plant are used ground in marinades and curries. Cumin's warm, stimulating, aromatic flavor is important in Middle Eastern, Moroccan, Indian, Mexican, and Southeast Asian cuisines. Cumin combines well with other spices and seasonings, especially coriander seed, garlic, sesame seed, and chiles.

FENNEL SEED

These small seeds of the fennel plant are often used in Provençal marinades for their delicate anise-like flavor.

GINGER

This gray-skinned, knobby root is indispensable in Asian cuisines, where it's always used fresh (usually minced or grated), but can be kept for months refrigerated if covered with dry sherry or 1 part sherry and 1 part water. Chop fine for a more pervasive flavor, or squeeze the juices of chopped ginger in cheesecloth for a pure ginger flavor without texture. Dried ginger is used in some curries, but there is no substitute for fresh ginger. The best ginger of all is the small, green spring ginger that appears in good local Oriental markets. Fresh ginger combines well with garlic, green onion, dark sesame oil, and soy sauce.

PEPPER

It's hard to imagine a kitchen without peppercorns. Never use packaged ground pepper; always grind your own. I use five or six pepper mills with different combinations of black, white, dried green, and dried red peppers such as japs or pequins. Add lightly crushed or whole peppercorns to marinades, stocks, and court bouillons. Since pepper becomes bitter with long cooking, use sparingly at first and add ground pepper to season at the end of cooking. Look for Tellicherry black pepper, which is considered the finest flavored of all. Malabar and Lampong peppers are two other excellent varieties. The Tellicherry, Malabar, and Lampong varieties are all quite pungent and full-flavored. The Sarawak, Ponape, and Brazilian are milder-flavored black varieties.

SAFFRON

This pungent bright orange-red threadlike spice is the dried stigmas of the flower *Crocus sativus*. Be sure to buy the threads, not ground saffron, which is usually not pure. Spanish saffron is generally considered the best. Beware of inexpensive Mexican saffron, which is not the true article. All pure saffron is expensive. Store well-sealed in a cool, dark place. Ask friends traveling to Spain to buy you a good quantity (⅛ pound); it will be cheaper than in the United States. To extract maximum flavor, pulverize saffron threads in a mortar and steep in a small amount of hot liquid. Saffron enhances the taste of shellfish and rice. Not only is its flavor important in bouillabaisse, paella, and risottos, but it adds its exquisite yellow color. Don't use too much (½ teaspoon for a dish for four to six) or its subtle flavor will turn bitter.

Aromatic or Flavoring Vegetables

THE ALLIUMS: THE ONION FAMILY

All members of the onion family (red, white, yellow, and green onions, leeks, pearl onions, shallots, garlic, and chives) bring out the

~

flavor of foods they are cooked with. Store onions, garlic, and shallots in a cool, airy place; keep green onions, chives, and leeks in the refrigerator.

> For a more varied and interesting onion flavor, use three or four different kinds of onions in place of just one kind. For instance, if a recipe calls for 2 cups of chopped onions, use one or two leeks, three or four green onions, a small red onion, and a couple of shallots. This gives a marvelous depth of oniony flavor. Wonderful in fish stews, tomato sauces, and stuffings, and with rice.

GARLIC

Buy heads of garlic with firm, tightly clustered cloves, never loose, soft, or discolored ones. Store in a cool, airy place, but don't refrigerate. *Always* remove the indigestible, bitter green sprout from the center of slightly old garlic cloves. I prefer to crush garlic to a paste in a mortar or with the tip of a chef's knife, or mash it with a fork, adding a little salt to absorb the garlic juices. The mashed garlic will disintegrate in cooking, but chopped garlic can be perceived as a distinct tiny piece in your mouth and give a sudden sharp flavor. It is also not as pervasive in flavor as mashed garlic, which is fuller in flavor because crushing releases the oils. If a more subtle garlic flavor is desired, blanch the garlic in boiling water for 10 minutes, then chop or puree to use. To remove skin of garlic, crush a whole clove with a sharp blow with the flat side of a chef's knife. Use only a stainless-steel garlic press, as aluminum presses give garlic an odd flavor. Garlic loses flavor if chopped too far ahead. Avoid using prepared garlic salt: make your own by mashing two cloves of garlic in a mortar with 1 or 2 tablespoons of salt.

There are three basic kinds of garlic available today: small, pale-purple-skinned heads, larger white heads, and the very mild, very large elephant garlic, sold in big pods or cloves.

> A roasted or grilled head of garlic, brushed with olive oil and roasted at 350° for 45 minutes or grilled for 35 minutes, spread on crisp French bread, is a nice accompaniment to a Provençal fish stew; it is best made only with the freshest heads of new garlic.

SHALLOTS

Not to be confused with scallions, shallots—small purple or gray bulbs—give their own subtle, distinctive taste to flavored butters, butter and cream sauces, marinades, stocks, stews, and vinaigrettes. Shallots are an essential seasoning in the French kitchen. Use them in place of scallions or other onions.

SCALLIONS

Scallions or green onions are simply young onions. They give a fresh sharp green taste and make an attractive garnish when the green tops are cut into thin strips.

Marinate whole cleaned scallions in basil-flavored olive oil, drain and grill for a superb taste.

LEEKS

The delicate, mild flavor of the white of leeks has no substitute. The dark green tops are too coarse in flavor and texture to be used. Leek is the French soup herb par excellence, and has a particular affinity for scallops, mussels, oysters, sole, and other fine-flavored fish. Leeks need careful cleaning to remove the grit between the leaves. Remove dark green tops, slice leek lengthwise to within 1 inch of root end, soak in warm water, and then rinse under running water, pulling back leaves to see if all dirt has been washed out.

CHIVES

Garlic chives and onion chives give a fine delicate onion flavor to sauces and salads. Use chives as well as chive flowers as an elegant garnish.

YELLOW, WHITE, AND RED ONIONS

Onions vary in sharpness of flavor according to variety and the type of soil they are grown in. On the whole, I use more yellow onions because they have a more distinct flavor than the white, but I favor red onions for grilling, salads, and sauces because of their color and flavor.

VEGETABLES WITH SEEDS

For a much finer flavor and a less watery dish, always remove the seed section of zucchini, cucumbers, and tomatoes by cutting the vegetable in half lengthwise and scooping out the center seed area with a small (demitasse) spoon. Cucumbers and zucchini make delicate accompaniments to fish dishes, especially salmon, when peeled, seeded, julienned, and steamed in butter. Season with fresh chives, parsley, chervil, and tarragon (*fines herbes*).

TOMATOES

Unless tomatoes are ripe and fragrant, they are not going to have much taste. Out of tomato season, it is better to use imported canned Italian plum tomatoes, which have at least been canned when fully ripe. In tomato season, buy extra red, ripe tomatoes to blanch, peel, and freeze whole in plastic bags. To use, defrost, drain, and chop. (See also Sun-Dried Tomatoes, page 20.)

Roasting tomatoes in a hot, dry skillet until the skin is browned all over is a great technique for bringing out a sweeter, richer, roasted flavor; they can then simply be peeled, seeded, and chopped as usual (see page 15).

Other Flavorings and Ingredients

BACON
I prefer to use a slab bacon with as little sugar or maple curing as possible. A quality butcher shop will carry this. I keep it on hand, in the freezer. (See also Pancetta.)

CAPERS
This flower bud of a Mediterranean bush adds a piquant taste to a number of dishes. I prefer the smallest capers, often called "nonpareil." Drain off the pickling liquid, rinse the capers, and place in a bottle with fresh white, tarragon, or champagne wine vinegar diluted with a little water (never use distilled or cider) and some herbs for a much better caper flavor.

For a spectacular and unusual garnish, deep-fry drained, dried capers until they open, and scatter them over sautéed fish. Seppi Renggli, chef at the Four Seasons restaurant in New York, devised this delicious garnish.

CHILI PEPPERS
The smallest and hottest fresh green chile is the 2-inch-long serrano. It has a sharp clean bite, and usually one or two serranos are plenty to give hotness to a dish for 4 to 6. The jalapeno is rounder in shape, about an inch long, and not quite as hot or fine-flavored as a serrano. The Anaheim is a 4-to-5-inch-long, lean, light green, mild chile. The poblano, a 5-inch-long, very dark green chile that looks like a twisted green pepper, has a special smoky depth of flavor and a subtle hotness.

CITRUS FRUITS
Lemons, limes, oranges, blood oranges, and grapefruits provide acidic flavors with their juices and grated or chopped peel. Lemons vary in flavor and sourness, so be sure to taste and adjust seasoning accordingly. Be very careful to avoid using the white of any peel since it is bitter, and be sure to wash the fruit well before using the peel. Lime peel can be rather bitter, so use it in small amounts. Grated citrus peel is excellent in flavored butters, butter sauces, with marinades, and in dipping sauces. Try a Hollandaise sauce flavored with lime or orange

instead of lemon. Orange juice combines with garlic, soy, ginger, and rice wine vinegar for an exotic marinade. Trout marinated in lemon juice for 10 minutes, then sautéed, is excellent. If fish sits in citrus longer than 1 to 2 hours, the acidity will cook the flesh—this is the ceviche principle.

Soak hard or unripe citrus fruits in boiling water for 10 minutes to soften and yield more juice.

CLAM JUICE
Bottled clam juice from cooked fresh clams is a useful product to keep on hand for making quick fish stock when you are in a hurry, but is not as fine-flavored as the real thing.

DAIRY
Use unsalted sweet butter for all recipes in this book. Some recipes call for clarified butter (see below). Cream means heavy cream or heavy whipping cream in most recipes. Crème fraîche is a heavy cream that is cured and thickened. It has a nutty flavor and can be used in place of heavy cream in any recipe. For instructions on how to make crème fraîche, see page 227. Milk is always whole milk—skim milk may be good for your diet, but makes thin sauces and soups. Light cream can sometimes replace heavy cream, especially in sauces for pasta.

To clarify butter: Slowly melt 8 tablespoons of unsalted sweet butter in a small heavy saucepan. Remove from the heat and let sit 10 minutes. Skim off the white foam at the top, pour off about 4 tablespoons of the clear liquid and leave the milky sediment in the bottom of the pan.

GRAPE LEAVES
Whether you use them fresh or in brine, soak these large distinctly flavored leaves in hot water for 30 minutes to soften, then wrap around small fish to keep from drying out and to flavor while grilling. You can also wrap them around small pieces of fish, tie in a bundle, steam, and serve with deep-fried lemon slices.

MUSHROOMS
Cultivated fresh: *White mushrooms* of all sizes are pretty bland in flavor but available everywhere. The large dark *shiitake* has a full-bodied flavor and could be used in any recipe that calls for fresh white mushrooms. *Oyster mushrooms* are pale-colored, delicate-textured, and delicate and buttery in flavor. *Enoki,* looking like a tiny cream-

colored button on a stalk, seem rather tasteless, but make a nice garnish for Oriental fish dishes or in salads.

Wild fresh: *Morels*, a dark, rich, and deep-flavored mushroom which grows wild in Wisconsin, Washington, Oregon, and California, is in season from mid-April to mid-June. *Chanterelles*, which look like small feathery orange umbrellas, are found in the Pacific Northwest as well as in parts of northern New England. *Cèpes*, *Boletus* mushrooms, or *Porcini* are forest mushrooms found in autumn. They are a rich, full-flavored mushroom.

All of the mushrooms listed above (except enoki) are sold in dried form. To use dried mushrooms, first place them in a colander and shake vigorously over a sink to remove all debris and dirt. Then, let them soak in warm stock or water until they are softened but *not* slimy. Soaking time will vary with each kind, usually 10 to 20 minutes. The flavor of dried mushrooms is a little more intense than the fresh. Store in a dry place.

OILS

Good-quality oils are expensive but go a long way in adding just the right flavor.

Extra-virgin olive oil, which is unrefined, has a distinctive, fruity olive flavor and color (greenish gold) and a balanced acidity. It is the product of the first pressing of top-quality olives. After pressing, it is usually filtered.

If you buy extra-virgin olive oil in large quantities, decant it into smaller containers for daily use. Store the remaining oil, well sealed, in a cool, dark place. To appreciate its fine flavor and aroma, use extra-virgin oil in salads, marinades, vinaigrettes, and sauces that aren't cooked for very long.

Oils from different countries have different flavors. Robust, fruity Tuscan oil and the more delicate, light French are my favorite extra-virgin olive oils.

All virgin olive oils (also labeled pure olive oil) have been refined— that is, olive paste from the first pressing is pressed a second time. Chemical additives and heat are then applied to extract a neutral and pretty tasteless oil. Sometimes a little full-flavored oil from the first pressing is added to give a better olive flavor. I prefer Sicilian and Greek virgin (pure) olive oils to Spanish and Italian virgin oils because they have a more characteristic olive flavor and heavier body. I use these mostly for sautéeing and cooking.

Of the vegetable oils, safflower is the lightest in flavor; French peanut is wonderfully flavored. I use both for sauces, sautéeing, and deep-frying. Corn oil I use the least. Store all vegetable and olive oils in a cool dark place, not next to your stove.

Nut oils such as walnut and hazelnut are excellent for flavoring cold sauces. As they are very perishable, buy them in small quantities and keep in the refrigerator.

Fragrant dark reddish sesame oil is used for flavoring but not for cooking, because of its low smoking point. Buy sesame oil at an Oriental market in small quantities and store in the refrigerator for use in Oriental dishes. Don't confuse dark Oriental sesame oil with the light-colored cold-pressed sesame oil in health food stores. The dark oil is pressed from toasted sesame seeds. Grapeseed oil is a French product pressed from grapeseeds and is primarily used for grilling.

Make your own grilling or basting oils by lightly heating olive or grapeseed oil and adding stalks of fresh rosemary, thyme, basil, fennel, oregano, tarragon, or mint. Let cool, pour into a jar, leaving herb in, seal and label.

PANCETTA
A lightly cured, delicate-flavored Italian "bacon" available at quality butcher shops and Italian markets. Bacon that has been parboiled for 1 minute can be substituted for this. (See also Bacon.)

SALT
Sea salt or coarse kosher salt has a more intense salt flavor than table salt, so be sure to use a little less of it than a recipe calls for.

SOY SAUCE
This liquid from fermented soybeans tastes dark, rich, salty, and savory. Though basic to the Asian kitchen, soy sauce may seem a little too salty for the Western palate and could be diluted with a little water.

There are many different kinds and qualities of soy sauce. When buying soy sauce, look for the words "naturally brewed" on the label and check to see that the only ingredients are soybeans, wheat, salt, and water. Chinese soy sauce is generally stronger and saltier in flavor. The Pearl River Mushroom brand, available in Oriental markets, has a rich, deep, fine flavor and is my favorite choice of soy sauce. Japanese soy sauces are a little less salty and lighter in flavor. The Kikkoman brand, available in most supermarkets, is an excellent soy sauce for all purposes and all the recipes in this book. Tamari, popular in the United States, is made without wheat and has a much stronger, saltier flavor. I don't use it at all.

STOCKS
Minor's professional-quality concentrated stock bases, in 1-pound containers at eight dollars each, come in many flavors, including fish and

lobster. Not available in regular markets; write to Flavour Base, Box 2515G, Dearborn, Michigan 48123 for information on ordering.

SUN-DRIED TOMATOES

These are tomatoes, usually plum tomatoes, sun- or air-dried to concentrate their flavor. It is not difficult to dry your own: use cherry or plum tomatoes, slice thinly, drain, and place on wire racks in a 100° oven until they are completely dried, about 10 to 12 hours.

VINEGARS

The amazing variety of flavored vinegars now available allows a wider scope for seasoning. Rice wine vinegar, used in Japanese and Chinese cooking, has a light delicate flavor with many uses beyond the Oriental kitchen. Stock French champagne wine vinegar, French or California tarragon wine vinegar, French red wine vinegar, full-flavored Italian balsamic wine vinegar, and Spanish sherry wine vinegar.

Use herb-flavored vinegars in vinaigrettes or in sauces calling for vinegar: beurre blanc sauce (see page 223) is wonderful with thyme or basil vinegar. Two vinegars I never use in cooking are distilled white vinegar and cider vinegar, both much too strong for the delicate flavors of fish. Substitute a good white wine vinegar for distilled white vinegar.

To make flavored vinegars, heat a good vinegar to a simmer, remove from heat, and add a handful of sprigs or stalks of fresh bruised or crushed herbs. When cool, pour in a bottle, and leave herbs in one week for optimal flavor. Then remove the herbs to keep vinegar from taking on a funny color.

Deglazing a pan with fine vinegar is an interesting way to flavor fish. Add 1 to 2 tablespoons of vinegar to the pan juices of sautéed fish, boil, scraping and stirring while vinegar cooks down and concentrates in flavor. Add fresh herbs. When only a teaspoon remains, add 1 to 2 tablespoons of butter, cream, broth, or water to round out the flavors and finish the sauce. White wine vinegar flavored with fresh sage is excellent for deglazing a pan in which trout has been sautéed with pancetta (see page 19). Raspberry wine vinegar is superb with salmon (see page 58). Fennel-flavored vinegar goes well with mullet and sea bass.

WINES

Generally speaking, the best wines for cooking and drinking with fish are light-bodied, flavorful dry white wines. Muscadets and Mâcon Blancs, generally in the five-to-seven-dollar range, are my top choices. Whatever wine you choose, keep a case of it on hand for convenience.

Don't forget that a light red wine—a Valpolicella, a Burgundy or a Beaujolais—goes well with some fish dishes such as Fish Braised in Red Wine (see page 70) and Salmon with Raspberry Wine Vinegar (see page 58).

BEFORE YOU BEGIN: NOTES ON EQUIPMENT

Tools and Utensils

If you are stocking a weekend kitchen near the beach or starting to cook fish for the first time, these are the most basic items you will need:

a 1½-quart saucepan

a 12-to-16-quart stockpot

a 12-inch skillet

a 10-inch steamer

a 12-to-14-inch baking dish

good-quality kitchen knives: a 5-inch paring and an 8-inch chef's knife

a spatula

a colander

large stainless-steel fine strainers for straining stocks and sauces

a 4-inch marble, wood, or ceramic mortar and pestle for crushing garlic, herbs, and spices

an oven thermometer to check the accuracy of your oven

a plastic ruler to measure thickness of fish

The additional items listed below will be helpful if you cook fish often and serve it in quantity:

fine-mesh stainless-steel skimmers for skimming stocks

open-mesh skimmers, wok tools, for stir-frying and lifting large pieces of fish out of deep fat

lots of colanders of all sizes

a deep-fat thermometer to ensure that fat stays at the proper temperature (375°) while deep-frying

an instant-reading thermometer to help determine doneness (about 135° to 145°) of a large fish, whether it's grilled, poached, baked, or baked in salt

a 10-to-12-inch wire-mesh circular spatter guard for frying pan

Chinese cleavers: a heavy one for chopping bones and fish heads, a lighter one for chopping vegetables. Japanese knives are specially honed; they are very sharp, superb for thin slicing or filleting

specialty heavy-duty knives for opening shellfish: oyster knives, clam knives, etc.

lobster and crab claw crackers

long picks of stainless steel, for picking lobster and crab meat out of the shell

a filleting knife with a thin flexible blade 7 to 9 inches long

a zester, for quickly obtaining thin, fine citrus peel

two 7-to-9-inch-long commercial stainless-steel spatulas with offset handles for lifting large fish out of baker/poacher or off grill and onto platter

sturdy, 12-inch stainless-steel spring tongs for lifting lobsters, seaweed, crabs, etc., out of deep pots or turning fish on grill

Pots and Pans

BAKING DISHES

Enameled cast-iron oval bakers or gratin dishes, especially the Le Creuset brand, have a tremendous advantage because you can cook on top of the stove, in the oven, or under the broiler and serve in the same dish. I have a stack of all sizes of these in white enamel. Oblong glass bakers will do, but the juices in the corners of a dish tend to evaporate or burn before the fish is done—oval is the best shape for baking fish dishes.

STEAMERS

Traditional Chinese bamboo steamers make attractive serving dishes for steamed fish dishes, particularly if lined during cooking with seaweed, greens, or fresh herbs. Designate one of your steamers for cooking and serving fish only, as you will never be able to completely remove a marine, but albeit pleasant smell from them. The best size bamboo steamer for two to four servings is 10 to 12 inches in diameter. An aluminum, stainless-steel, or enameled steamer 14 inches in diameter with two or three tiers is very useful to have for quantity cooking.

SKILLETS AND SAUTÉ PANS

I use all kinds: Teflon-coated, oval tinned-steel—perfect for sautéing trout—copper sauté pans, black cast-iron. But the one superb all-purpose performer is the Le Creuset heavy black-lined enameled cast-iron, 12-inch skillet. In it, food browns beautifully, cooks evenly, and does not stick. The pan cleans easily and the black lining does not affect the flavor of acidic sauces (tomato, lemon) the way a cast-iron skillet does. A skillet usually has slightly lower sloping sides; a sauté pan has higher, straighter sides, but both have same surface area.

POACHERS

The ideal kitchen would have a fish poacher of every size to match the variable sizes of fish to be poached. Unfortunately, the 17-inch standard-sized poacher always seems to be 3 inches too small and, for the number of uses, a little too expensive. So, for bigger fish, I improvise: I use an inexpensive 13-quart stainless-steel mixing bowl and lay the fish in, curved, on the bottom of the bowl. If a bit of the fish's head and tail peek out over the edges and out of the broth, it makes no difference. I also use a 17-quart stockpot and put the fish (wrapped in cheesecloth) in head first. Or at times, I take an old-fashioned oblong deep oven roasting pan, and position the fish diagonally to get the maximum length.

For lobsters, use a canner, or canning kettle, an inexpensive enameled pot 15 to 20 quarts or more which is perfect for boiling/simmering/steaming lobsters, crayfish, crabs, and shrimp in the shell in quantity. It's helpful to get one that has a built-in colander for easy removal of shellfish. Use it also for cooking and serving a fish stew for fifteen or more.

SAUCEPANS

Because of its size and heat-retaining quality, the 1½-quart enameled cast-iron Le Creuset wooden-handled saucepan is the perfect pan for butter sauces like the beurre blanc. Remember in making these delicate sauces to use the lowest possible heat and remove the pan from the heat when you feel it gets too hot.

Other Supplies

hemmed, washable 24-by-24-inch double cheesecloth for wrapping large whole fish for poaching (facilitates removal)

bamboo skewers (8 to 12 inches) for grilling small pieces of fish and for skewering across the stuffing of a fish

butcher's string

wide heavy-duty foil to cover an outdoor grill without a lid, or bake large whole fish in the oven

cooking parchment (also called baker's parchment) for steam-baking fish and shellfish en papillote; sold in small rolls at specialty cook-

ware stores or in larger quantities for less at restaurant- or com-
mercial-paper-supply stores.

Outdoor Cooking or Grilling

For more flexibility in outdoor cooking, I recommend a grill with a
lid, such as the Weber grill. There are many different kinds of grills,
all in different sizes and with special features. Choose one that is best
suited for your outdoor space and needs. Gas grills are another practical option. A covered Japanese ceramic grill, the unusual and beautiful green Kamado cooker, for example, works very well for slow
smoke grilling.

A hibatchi is useful for limited space on urban balconies or rooftops.
Basically, any kind of makeshift grill that can be raised about 4 inches
above the coals will do.

Portable hinged wire grills, in the shape of a fish or a shallow basket,
with long handles—used on top of the cooking grill—are helpful for
turning large fish and shellfish. Be sure to brush the grills with oil before
placing fish in them.

A portable metal chimney (a tin container device with a wooden
handle and a perforated bottom sold in hardware stores as a charcoal
starter) filled with paper in the bottom section and charcoal briquets
on top is the easiest way to start coals burning evenly and it eliminates
the need for liquid starter—and the resulting unpleasant fumes which
can adversely affect the flavor of grilled food.

CHARCOAL

Once you have grilled fish outdoors using unprocessed pure hardwood
charcoal, you will not easily return to chemically laden processed charcoal briquets or chemical starters, which adversely affect the taste of
grilled food.

Hardwood charcoal produces an intense heat that cooks the food
on the grill. It burns much hotter than hardwood chunks, which produce the smoke that gives grilled food a distinctively smoky taste. For
this smoky flavor to permeate the food, the wood chunks or chips
must be soaked in water 15 to 30 minutes before using to keep them
from burning, then placed on the white-hot charcoal. The grill must
be covered.

Hardwood charcoal does not give off a very pronounced flavor of
the wood it is made from, and it is appropriate to use it alone when
grilling more delicately flavored foods like chicken, lean fish, or vegetables. When a smoky flavor is desired for robust foods like pork,
lamb, game, and fatty fish such as salmon, swordfish, tuna, and trout,
soak and add the wood chips or chunks to the hot coals.

Of the three most common types of charcoal—mesquite, hickory, and oak—mesquite charcoal produces the hottest and longest-lasting fire. Because of the shower of sparks it throws out, it requires special care: a safe place to grill away from dry grass or leaves or wooden buildings. Always keep a gallon jug of water at hand.

Mesquite wood is inexpensive and readily available all over the Southwest. The best unprocessed mesquite charcoal on the market today (produced by the Yaqui Indians in Mexico) is available from Lazzari Fuel Company, P. O. Box 34051, San Francisco, California 94134. A 15-pound bag costs about $12, and they ship all over the country.

Wood chips or chunks made from mesquite, hickory, oak, maple, cherry, apple, pecan, and alder trees are available in gourmet shops.

To get added flavor, toss dried grapevine cuttings, dried seaweed cut into pieces, fresh herbs, especially bay leaves, sage, rosemary, thyme, fennel, and dill, whole garlic cloves, or chunks of fresh citrus rinds on the hot coals for a fragrant smoke.

Grilling Indoors

LE CREUSET (GRIDDLE) GRILL

A black, heavy, oblong ridged grill that fits over two burners on top of your stove. It heats to a very hot state, and quickly grills thick fish fillets or steaks leaving ridged grill marks on the fish. This practical, well-made piece of equipment makes grilling possible the year round. Use under a stove exhaust fan.

INDOOR ELECTRIC GRILL

A tabletop grill with an electric element, a hinged rack for easy turning, and a kebob rack and skewers. The Maverick electric grill features smokeless grilling, helpful if you do not have an exhaust fan over your stove.

CHAPTER 2

On Cooking Fish and Shellfish

Cooking seafood is not at all complicated once you understand that it is naturally tender in its raw state. A delicate, juicy form of pure protein, fish and shellfish do not need much cooking. When cooked even minutes too long, fish becomes tough and dry, and shellfish becomes rubbery.

FACTORS IN DETERMINING COOKING METHODS AND SEASONINGS

You need to consider three things to determine the best cooking method and seasonings for a particular fish: the fat content of that fish (lean or fat), its texture, (dense, fine, or loose), its degree of firmness of flesh (firm or soft), and its size (weight, length) and cut (whole, split, etc.).

Types of Fish

The fat content of a fish largely determines its flavor. Fatty fish with a higher proportion of oil or fat tend to be more distinctly flavored than lean fish, which are more mild and delicate in flavor. Compare, for example, mild-flavored veal, which has practically no fat, to a well-marbled T-bone steak, rich and flavorful. Fat contains much of the flavor of meat and the same is true with fish. In cooking, choose seasonings that complement the flavor and fat content of fish.

LEAN FISH (INCLUDING ALL SHELLFISH)

Lean fish, because they have only a small amount of internal fat, are best cooked in moist heat—either immersed in liquid or hot deep fat or surrounded by steam, which keeps the fish from drying out. Moist-heat methods appropriate for cooking lean fish are poaching, steaming, steam-baking (en papillote), deep-frying, braising, or cooking in soups and stews. Lean fish can be cooked in dry heat—baked, broiled, or grilled—if it is marinated or basted during cooking, or covered by a sauce or a vegetable mixture.

Lean fish marry well with all kind of herbs—dill, chervil, basil, thyme, tarragon, marjoram, oregano, parsley; with sauces made of butter, cream, wine, fish stock, citrus juices; with purees of spinach, sorrel, watercress, and lettuce. All of the onion family—shallots, leeks, scallions, red, yellow, and white onions, garlic, and chives—enhance the subtle taste of lean fish in sauces, stocks, or as basic flavorings. Other seasonings that compliment delicate-tasting lean fish are flavored vinegars (my favorites are champagne wine vinegar, raspberry wine vinegar, and rice wine vinegar)—used in poaching broths, marinade vinaigrettes, and sauces, and lighter French olive oils or hazelnut and walnut oils. Fennel and tomato, orange juice and orange zest, and Swiss and Parmesan cheese offer other flavors that are compatible with lean fish.

FATTY FISH

In general, the stronger-flavored fatty fish are best cooked in dry heat—sautéed, broiled, grilled, baked, or smoked—because their internal fat keeps them moist while they cook. Do not use fatty fish for soups, stews, or stocks, as their flavor becomes too strong when cooked in a broth. There are, however, exceptions to all recommendations. For example, salmon tastes wonderful cooked by any moist-heat method, mackerel is good poached and served in a wine-and-vinegar-flavored marinade, and large pieces of tuna braise exceptionally well.

Fatty fish, due to their larger proportion of oils or fat, tend to be more distinctly flavored. Mackerel, sturgeon, shad, and bluefish are all strongly flavored. Tuna, amberjack, salmon, sablefish, butterfish, whitefish, and trout are milder in flavor. All fatty fish stand up well to strong seasonings such as mustard, horseradish, vinegars, red wine, chiles, citrus juices, soy sauce, extra-virgin olive oils, cilantro, paprika, capers, sesame oil, and fresh ginger.

MODERATELY FATTY FISH

Because moderately fatty fish are in between lean and fat, they can be cooked by either dry- or moist-heat methods. The more distinctly flavored smelt, mullet, and swordfish can be seasoned with the stronger flavorings recommended for fatty fish. The rest in this category are excellent with the more delicate seasonings listed under lean fish.

The Lexicon of Fish and Shellfish (pages 239–51) lists commonly available fish and gives helpful descriptive information.

KINDS OF FISH

LEAN FISH*

black sea bass and	monkfish	scrod
freshwater bass	ocean and lake perch	sea trout (lean to
catfish	orange roughy	moderately fatty)
croaker/drum	pike	shark
flounder	pollock	sheepshead (fresh-
grouper	porgy	water)
haddock	redfish	sole
hake	red snapper	sunfish
halibut	rockfish	tilefish
lingcod	sand dabs	whiting

MODERATELY FATTY FISH

amberjack	pompano	swordfish
buffalofish	sheepshead (salt-	white sea bass
carp	water)	trout (moderately
dolphin or mahimahi	smelt	fatty to fatty)
mullet	striped bass	

FATTY FISH

bluefish	sablefish	sturgeon
butterfish	salmon	tuna
mackerel	shad	whitefish

* Includes all shellfish.

Texture and Firmness of Fish

I describe the flesh of a fish, first, in terms of how it feels when you press it, that is, whether it is firm or soft. However, the quality of texture of that soft or firm flesh can be further described as dense, fine, or loose, a quality that determines if it flakes when cooked, and if so, how.

Dense-textured fish, such as monkfish, shark, sturgeon, swordfish, and tuna, do not flake or hardly flake at all when cooked because their flesh is so firm and dense. They also take a little longer to cook because of that denseness.

Fine-textured fish, such as bluefish, mullet, sole, shad, flounder, sea trout, pompano, pike, trout, smelt, butterfish, mackerel, and sablefish, flake into the smallest pieces when cooked. Treat these fish gently and carefully. They are not a good choice for a soup or stew.

Loose-textured fish, such as cod, rockfish, grouper, lingcod, amberjack, orange roughy, pollock, and porgy, separate quickly into large flakes when cooked. They will cook in a little less time than fine or dense-textured fish because there is more space between flakes. These are good baked or braised with sauces. They can fall apart easily when sautéed or grilled.

Firm-fleshed fish, such as striped bass, redfish, red snapper, catfish, black bass, tilefish, and sheepshead, do not fall into flakes like loose-textured fish, but generally hold together very well any way they are cooked. They are especially good to use in fish stews because they won't disintegrate into the tiniest flakes as do fine-textured fish, or fall into a lot of large flakes as loose-textured fish would.

Soft-fleshed fish, such as sablefish, bluefish, butterfish, shad, smelt, sea trout, and flounder, deteriorate very quickly out of water, so be sure to test for freshness before purchasing. These are good grilled, broiled, or sautéed.

When you cook a certain kind of fish for the first time, make a note of these interesting differences in texture. You may refer to the Lexicon of Fish and Shellfish (pages 239–51) for further guidance in determining how to cook the fish you buy.

Size and Cut of Fish

The thickness of fish is also an important factor in determining the method of cooking. In recipes for braising, baking, grilling, deep-frying, or broiling, fish fillets of less than ¾ inch, like flounder or sole, would easily overcook. Fillets of this size are best poached, steamed, or quickly sautéed. Likewise, grilling a whole fish that is more than 3 inches thick at its thickest point is not a good idea because by the time the interior of the fish cooks, the outer parts closest to the intense heat of the grill are bound to be somewhat overcooked and dried out. A large 3-to 4-inch-thick, 4- to 5-pound whole fish is best baked wrapped in foil in the oven or poached in simmering broth. In either case, the fish remains moist from the steam in the foil or the broth in the poacher.

In the market fish appear in the following forms:

Whole, dressed: scaled, gutted.

Pan-dressed: scaled, gutted, with head, tail, and fins removed.

Fillets: fish cut in half lengthwise, with backbones removed (skin may or may not be left on).

Butterflied Fillets: the two fillets of a small fish, boned but with the skin left on, holding them in one piece.

Steaks: fish slices cut across the backbone or width of the fish.

Chunks: large pieces or cross-sections of a dressed fish (bone may be left in).

Here is a general guide to the cooking methods for various sizes and cuts:

Very small whole fish, *½ pound and under:* Pan-fry or deep-fry

Small whole fish *up to 1½ pounds:* Pan-fry, grill, sauté, poach, steam, braise, steam-bake, or bake

Medium whole fish, *1½ pounds up to 4 pounds:* Poach, bake, steam, steam-bake, braise, or grill if not thicker than 3 inches (and around 3 pounds)

Large whole fish, *including head, 4 pounds and up:* Poach, braise, or cook in smaller pieces in fish stews and soups

Pan-dressed whole fish, *usually ½ to 1 pound:* Sauté, pan-fry, steam, or bake

Fillets, no thicker than ¾ of an inch: Sauté, steam, or poach

Thicker fillets, up to 1 to 2 inches thick: Bake, braise, grill, steam, poach, deep-fry, broil, steam-bake, or cut in pieces to use in stews and soups

NOTE: Use skinned fillets for braising, poaching, baking, steaming, and steam-baking; the presentation is more attractive with the skin off. Use fillets with one side of skin on for broiling, grilling, or smoking fish because it helps to keep fish from falling apart.

Steaks, up to 2 inches thick: Steam, poach, broil, grill, bake, braise, or steam-bake

Larger chunks: Braise, poach, or use in stews

Here's a trick that seems to improve the flavor of fish which may not be pristine fresh. Cover the fish with fresh milk or buttermilk for 2 to 24 hours before cooking. Remove, drain, pat dry, and cook the fish simply: sauté, broil, bake, poach, steam, or steam-bake.

PREPARING AND COOKING FISH

An established general rule for cooking fish, from the Canadian Fisheries Board, holds true for almost all cooking methods: *Cook fish about 10 minutes per inch of thickness.* Remember, this is a general rule of thumb; some exceptions and variations are mentioned later on. If the fish is ice cold when it starts to cook, it will naturally take a little longer. Be sure to leave a larger whole fish at room temperature about 30 minutes before cooking.

When the fish is cooked, remember, too, that as long as it is hot it will continue to cook. A large whole fish baked or poached will continue to cook gently off the heat about 10 to 20 minutes, or until it cools down. Smaller fish or pieces of fish will not hold the heat as long, but will still cook until cool. Do keep this in mind when timing the cooking of fish. If you must hold the fish a few minutes to complete the rest of a dinner, slightly undercook the fish and finish cooking it in a 350° oven. Some fatty and moderately fatty taste better slightly undercooked; tuna, swordfish, amberjack, and salmon are more delicate in flavor and texture when left slightly translucent or rare at the center.

TESTING FOR DONENESS

Test whole fish for doneness by inserting the tip of a small paring knife at the top of the backbone at the thickest part and lifting up the flesh to see that it is opaque, milky white, and completely cooked through.

Test fillets with the tip of a small knife or a skewer or a fork in the center of the thickest part.
Cooked fish is opaque or milky white and tender, when done; uncooked fish is translucent or grayish white (the flesh is still attached to the bone of whole fish). Flakiness is not necessarily always the best test of doneness; the texture of many soft-fleshed fish is so delicate that the tines of a fork can push away or seemingly flake fish at any stage of doneness. When testing for doneness, always test at the thickest part.

PREPARING AND COOKING SHELLFISH

The Lexicon of Fish and Shellfish (pages 239–51) gives more detailed information on the varieties of shellfish and when and where they are available.

In buying shellfish, there are a few basic rules to help determine freshness.

The shells of oysters and hard-shell clams should be closed when bought, or should close when touched. Soft-shell clams are not completely closed since the neck of the clam protrudes somewhat.

The best test of freshness in a lobster is activity; if a lobster doesn't move around much and seems generally sluggish, select one of its livelier tankmates. The same holds true for hard-shell crabs which at their best wave their claws and sometimes seem to foam at the mouth. In the case of soft-shell crabs and scallops, you will have to rely on your fish seller's word that they are fresh.

Shellfish, especially the smallest forms—mussels, clams, and scallops—cook very quickly, so the 10-minute rule for fish does not apply here. Mussels and clams steamed in the shell are fully cooked when the shells open, about 3 to 5 or 6 minutes. Again, remember that the shells retain heat after being removed from the pot and continue to slightly cook the shellfish. Take special care in cooking shelled shrimp, clams, crayfish tails, oysters, scallops, and squid. Either steep them for 3 to 4 minutes in a hot savory broth or water just taken off a simmer, or fry or cook them at a simmer for just 1 to 2 minutes. Despite the descriptions on restaurant menus, shrimp, lobster, and crayfish cooked in the shell should never actually be *boiled* as it toughens them. Cooking them at a simmer in a flavorful broth or steaming them will ensure tenderness.

Broiling shellfish is risky since proximity to such high heat will tend to toughen them unless your timing is impeccable and brief. The best broiled dishes are those in which the shellfish are covered by a sauce. Shellfish, especially shrimp and scallops, are excellent grilled. The timing of the cooking will vary, depending on the size of the shellfish, the intensity of the fire, and the distance from the heat. Mussels, oysters, and clams can all be wrapped in foil packets and steamed open over the grill.

TECHNIQUES FOR COOKING FISH AND SHELLFISH

The descriptions and recipes that follow offer the basic techniques for cooking fish and should give you all the relevant information you need to know to cook fish, even if you have never cooked fish or used the techniques before. You learn by doing, so proceed with confidence!

For a wide variety of interesting dishes, use these basic recipes for cooking fish in combination with the marinades, stocks, sauces, and butters that appear in Chapter 8. The suggested combinations should spark your imagination.

Baking is the easiest of all the cooking techniques listed here, so if you are just beginning to cook fish, start with a recipe for baked fish fillets or a whole baked fish. Once you are familiar with the different techniques, they will all seem quite simple.

Baking

Baking fish keeps aromas in the oven, so if you have a small kitchen or small apartment and no overhead exhaust fan over your kitchen stove, using your oven for cooking fish will keep your whole apartment from smelling a little fishy.

Since baking surrounds a fish with a dry, even heat, care must be taken to keep the fish moist, either by marinating it and then basting while cooking or by covering the dish tightly with foil or a lid which creates steam, or by covering the fish with a sauce or with vegetables that are chopped and sometimes lightly cooked. Bake fish at 375° about 10 minutes per inch of thickness (including vegetables or toppings). All fatty fish bake especially well, because their inner fat bastes them.

When you bake a fish with a stuffing, you need to allow a little more time than the 10-minute rule because the stuffing insulates the fish from the heat so it takes longer for the heat to penetrate this barrier. Also, when you bake a whole fish or fillet covered with a sauce or with vegetables, you need to measure the fish *with* the topping to determine the correct cooking time. Again, the covering insulates the fish from the heat. Fish Fillets with Orange, Red Onion, and Fennel, page 85, is a good example of this technique.

Baking is also an excellent way to carefully finish the cooking of fish that are sautéed, grilled, or broiled. A whole 12-to-16-ounce trout takes very careful cooking to sauté through completely without over-browning the skin. It's better to sauté the trout on each side about 8 minutes per inch of thickness, then put it in a 400° oven for 5 to 8 minutes to finish cooking the fish through evenly.

The baking, braising, and steam-baking techniques (see pages 39–42) can all overlap a little—if you wrap a 3-to-4-pound whole fish in blanched lettuce, spinach, Swiss chard, or cabbage leaves, place in a shallow-sided baking dish, add an inch of broth with herbs and seasonings in the bottom of the pan, and bake uncovered, you are combining elements of all three techniques to produce a fine oven-baked dish.

Basic Baked Fish

Preheat oven to 375°. Place a whole fish, fillets, or steaks in a buttered baking dish. Add about ½ cup of fish stock, wine, marinade, sauce, or a flavored butter. Scatter herbs and perhaps finely chopped vegetables over the fish, and bake uncovered, basting occasionally for 10 minutes per inch of thickness of fish and toppings measured together.

Fish fumet and all court-bouillons (see pages 196–201) can be used to moisten fish while baking. Herbs such as fresh dill, thyme, fennel, rosemary, oregano, parsley, tarragon, or basil can be chopped and strewn over fish while it bakes.

The best vegetables that can be added to a simple baked fish are tomatoes, zucchini, carrots, broccoli, potatoes, mushrooms, or red and green peppers. Greens such as Swiss chard, lettuce, or spinach can be wrapped around fish fillets and baked with a little fumet, court bouillon, or wine poured over for moisture.

Baked fish offer vast possibilities for seasoning using fish stocks, marinades, sauces, or butters. Some combinations appear below; unless otherwise noted, recipes for the marinades, sauces, and butters appear in Chapter 8. You can also create your own combinations.

Fish and shellfish baked in a sauce:

Flounder with Minced Mushrooms and Shallots (Duxelles)
Lingcod with Tomato Sauce
Lobster with Tapenade
Mullet with Pesto (made with pine nuts)
Red snapper with Roasted Red Pepper Sauce
Scallops and shrimp with Pesto

Sauces to serve with baked fish and shellfish:

Chipotle Sauce with bluefish
Cilantro-Lime Butter with amberjack
Green Peppercorn Butter with pompano
Jalapeno-Cumin Butter with scallops

Lemon Butter and fresh dill with tilefish
Lime-Ginger Butter (page 96) with sea trout
Pecan-Cayenne Butter with catfish
Poblano Butter with black sea bass
Red Wine Butter with striped bass
Tomato Butter with scrod

Marinades for fish (baste during baking):

Bluefish in Hot Thai Marinade
Halibut in Buttermilk and Black Pepper Marinade
Mahimahi in Orange and Saffron Marinade
Redfish in Balsamic Vinegar and Basil Marinade
Rockfish in Garlic-Anchovy Marinade
Sea trout in Hot Pepper and Lime Marinade
Swordfish in Ginger-Soy Marinade
Trout in Juniper Berry and Gin Marinade
Tuna in Sesame-Sake Marinade

Stuffed Baked Fish

The cavity of a large whole fish can be stuffed with Duxelles (see page 232) combined with some toasted bread crumbs and a handful of parsley. Whole flat flounder are nice to stuff this way. Simply cut through the skin and flesh to the backbone, cut off both ends, and lift out backbone. Fill with stuffing.

Grilling

Grilled fish enjoy the spotlight of popularity today. Five or six years ago, California chefs began using special mesquite charcoal briquets made in Mexico to heat their grills. The intense heat given off by mesquite seemed to be an appropriate new way to flash-cook fish, the intense heat sealing the outside so the fish remained juicy. Grilling techniques can subject fish to 450° and 500° temperatures, so to be on the safe side, I usually count about 7 to 9 minutes' cooking time per inch of thickness. The closer fish is to the coals, the more quickly it cooks. Larger fish and thicker fillets need to be farther from the heat and cook more slowly.

Whether you use mesquite or other kinds of charcoal (see page 24), start your fire with a metal chimney. Place the briquets on the perforated rack and stuff lots of crumpled newspaper in the bottom half. The air holes in the bottom create a good draft for burning newspaper and the briquets sitting above the flame burn very evenly. The best reason for using the chimney is that it makes a liquid starter, which gives grilled food a funny chemical flavor, unnecessary.

To avoid the most common problems in grilling—undercooking, overcooking, and fish sticking to the grill—keep these tips in mind:

1. Before placing fish on the grill, be sure the fire is hot enough; start cooking when coals are uniformly covered with whitish-gray ash.

2. Be sure to spread the coals evenly so the heat radiates to reach every point on the grill above.

3. Using a stiff wire brush and lots of soap and hot water, clean the grill rack after each use. Oil the grill with a light vegetable oil and preheat to prevent fish from sticking to it. Lightly oiling the surface of fish fillets before placing them on a hot grill also helps to keep the fish from sticking.

4. The best fish for grilling are fatty fish—salmon, tuna, and swordfish in steak form are the easiest to turn and to get on and off the grill in one piece. A fillet with the skin still on one side is the next easiest. Place the skin side down first and more likely than not it will stick to the grill, which is fine, since skinless fillets make a nicer presentation. Simply slip your spatula just above the skin and scoop to turn your newly skinned fillet.

5. Move the fish as little as possible: with every move you increase the chances of the fish sticking to the grill. A hinged fish grill, well oiled, greatly facilitates the turning of the fish (see equipment section, page 24). Another interesting way to cook fish on a grill is to wrap it securely in heavy-duty aluminum foil, leaving a little space for steam to expand, along with a marinade and vegetables or herbs or other seasoning. Grill the packets 4 to 5 inches above medium-hot coals for about 10 minutes per inch of thickness.

6. Shellfish—particularly shrimp, prawns, and scallops—and firm-textured fin fish such as swordfish make excellent brochettes or kebobs. Cut the fish in about 1-inch cubes. I prefer to use disposable 8- or 12-inch wooden or bamboo skewers, which you should soak to avoid charring; on metal skewers the fish pieces tend to slip around.

Basic Grilled Fish

Use 1-to-2-inch-thick fillets for grilling. (If you wrap the fish in foil and cook on the grill, pierce the bottom of the foil in a few places for more smoke flavor and cook 10 to 12 minutes per inch of thickness.)

Prepare grill, place coals in top half of metal chimney, and crumpled newspapers in bottom half, and light. After about 20 to 30 minutes, when coals are uniformly covered with gray ash, spread them evenly in the bottom of a grill. Oil wire grill well, rub fish with oil or marinade, and place it directly on oiled grill raised about 5 inches from the coals. Grill fish about 7 to 9 minutes per inch of thickness, basting occasionally. Turn fish once. For easier turning and removal, oil and use a portable hinged wire grill in the shape of fish or a shallow basket.

Grilled Shrimp

Marinate large shrimp for 1 to 2 hours in any of the marinades listed in Chapter 8. Drain, skewer on soaked wooden skewers, and grill for about 4 to 5 minutes on each side.

Grilled fish and shellfish are excellent with the flavor of a marinade combining with that of smoke. Try some of the following pairings of fish with marinades. You can baste with the marinade to keep the fish moist. Recipes for the marinades appear in Chapter 8.

Bluefish with Hot Pepper and Lime Marinade

Catfish or sea trout with Buttermilk and Black Pepper Marinade

Flounder with Spicy Yogurt Marinade

Lingcod or grouper with Ginger-Soy Marinade

Mackerel with Mustard Seed Marinade

Mackerel, bluefish, or trout with Juniper Berry and Gin Marinade

Pompano with Mediterranean Marinade

Redfish with Hot Thai Marinade

Red snapper with Garlic-Anchovy Marinade

Shrimp with Orange and Saffron Marinade
Striped bass or orange roughy with French Mushroom Marinade
Swordfish or bluefish with Orange-Fennel Marinade
Swordfish or shark with Lime and Mint Marinade
Tuna with Sesame-Sake Marinade
Tuna or redfish with Greek Oregano Marinade

If you do not use a distinctively seasoned marinade and just grill your fish plain, the following butters (recipes appear in Chapter 9) go extremely well as a sauce to put directly on the hot fish as it comes off the grill. Some of my favorite combinations are:

Catfish with Pecan-Cayenne Butter
Mackerel with Grainy Mustard Butter
Mullet with Orange-Chive Butter
Perch with Poblano Butter
Pompano with Shrimp Butter
Redfish with Mango-Mint Butter
Red snapper with Cilantro-Lime Butter
Salmon with Anchovy Butter
Shrimp with Chipotle Sauce
Swordfish with Ancho Chile Butter
Tuna with Sun-Dried Tomato Butter

Other good accompaniments to serve with grilled fish are Creole Okra Relish and Papaya Corn Relish (see Chapter 8).

Broiling

Broiling is a technique I prefer to leave to the best restaurant kitchens with their finely tuned equipment—an eye-level salamander with many levels of adjustment from the flame. Home broilers vary enormously in quality and adjustability. Moreover, broiling often robs a fish of flavor by drying up the outside exposed to the flame, and marinades, sauces, or butters added to keep the fish moist can become slightly bitter or burned if too close to the intense heat. Because the heat from broiling is the driest heat of all, it quickly toughens fish if it is only slightly overcooked. Fish on a grill also cooks by an intense source of heat, but much more air circulates around the fish on an outdoor grill than in the small space of an enclosed oven broiler.

Basic Broiled Fish

Fillets ¾ to 1 inch thick are best for this method.

Preheat broiler 5 to 10 minutes. Place fish on a lightly buttered foil-lined broiler pan. Brush seasoned fish with marinade or melted butter or oil. Place fish about 4 inches under broiler and broil 7 to 9 minutes per inch of thickness.

Foolproof Broiled Fish

This method keeps the fish from drying out under the intense flame.

Preheat broiler 5 to 10 minutes. Place fish on lightly buttered foil-lined broiler pan about 4 inches under broiler and broil for 4 to 5 minutes per inch of thickness to sear or seal exterior and keep the juices in; then turn broiler off and let the heat of the oven finish the cooking for the remaining 5 or 6 minutes.

Broiled fish benefit from marinades that give them flavor and keep them from drying out. All of the marinades listed for grilled fish on pages 37–38 are appropriate for broiling.

Braising

Braising is an excellent method for cooking fish and one that inspires a creative sense of seasoning. It combines finely chopped vegetables with a flavorful broth, so that a lot of flavor is gently cooked into the fish. As an added bonus, it's hard to overcook using this method.

Experiment with different mixtures of vegetables and seasonings. A thick halibut steak braises beautifully on a bed of pureed spinach with fish fumet (see page 197) added. Braising a thick slice of tuna over sautéed onions, garlic, and lots of red and green peppers with a little dry white wine for the liquid is a classic method of the Basques in southwest France.

Braising obviously works best with larger pieces of fish, like big chunks of monkfish, 1- to 2-inch fillets or steaks or very large pieces of salmon, tuna, or swordfish, or a 2- to 3½-inch-thick whole fish that will take at least 30 to 40 minutes of cooking. Cooking the fish covered eliminates any smell of cooking and since the fish is already sauced, last-minute preparations are not necessary. Because a lot of people can easily be served with a large piece or pieces of fish, this technique is perfect for entertaining. Think of braising like slowly cooking a flavorful stew and create your own delicious combinations. Fish Braised in Red Wine, page 70, is a good example of this technique.

Basic Braised Fish

This works well with a 1-to-2-inch-thick fillet or steak, or a 2-to-3½-inch-thick whole fish.

Layer the bottom of a heavy casserole with a mirepoix of vegetables (finely chopped carrots, onions, and celery). Adding 2 tablespoons of butter to the mirepoix, gently cook it 4 to 5 minutes until the vegetables are soft. Place the fillet, steak, or whole fish on top of the vegetables, add herbs (thyme, parsley) and seasonings, pour in a small amount of flavorful broth (only an inch or two of liquid), cover tightly, bring to a simmer, and cook gently over a low flame or in a 350° oven at a simmer, allowing about 10 to 12 minutes per inch of thickness, or until done.

Use Fish Fumet, White Wine or Red Wine Court Bouillon (see Chapter 8) as the liquid for braising. A light chicken broth would also work, or water and ¼ cup of dry white or red wine. (See page 70 for Fish Braised in Red Wine.)

Steam-Baking

Steam-baking, or baking a fish en papillote (sealed in cooking parchment paper), is an easy technique with a dramatic and elegant presentation. The fish or shellfish bathe in aromatic steam with the vegetables and seasonings in a parchment enclosure. Be sure to fold the parchment firmly closed (see page 81), keeping all cut edges folded to the inside, or the steam will escape. Once the papillotes are hot, the steam causes the parchment papillotes to puff up about 3 inches and the high oven temperatures to brown them slightly.

A nice advantage of steam-baking is that the fish papillotes can be prepared 8 hours ahead and refrigerated until baked. Because the papillotes need to bake without overlapping, it is hard to fit more than six or eight papillotes in one oven or to serve more than six to eight people. I usually remove one papillote, slit it open, and test the fish for doneness before removing all the papillotes.

If cooking parchment paper is not available, regular aluminum foil can be used, but the packet won't puff up as much because the foil is heavier and seals tighter. In a pinch, wax paper can also be used, but it is the least desirable alternative because the paper is too fragile— the liquid will soak through if the papillotes are made ahead; the wax on the paper will also melt and smoke a little in the hot oven.

Steam-baking is a wonderful way to delicately incorporate flavors in a fish dish. Scallops en Papillote with Carrots and Lime-Ginger Butter, page 96, illustrates this perfectly. Use different vegetable combinations or flavored butters to create a wide range of exciting seasonings. Try the Fish en Papillote with Julienned Leeks, Carrots, Cucumber, and Zucchini, page 80. This is a good method for either firm- or loose-textured fish, but remember that the loose-textured fish will cook more quickly.

Basic Steam-Baked Fish

Begin by making the parchment wrappers for the papillotes. For one wrapper, fold a 15-by-15-inch piece of parchment in half and cut out a large half-heart shape, starting and ending at the fold. Open the parchment and butter well in the center of one side, using 1 teaspoon of butter for each papillote.

For consistent cooking, it is a good idea to use fish fillets about 1 inch thick. Cut fish fillets or 1-inch fish steaks diagonally into four to six pieces or strips about 1½ inches wide, or use shellfish such as shelled shrimp, scallops, or oysters.

Place fish and vegetables sufficient for 1 serving (about ⅓ pound of fish and ½ to ¾ cup of vegetables) in the center of each of the buttered parchment hearts. Dot with unsalted or flavored butter, sprinkle with 1 tablespoon of dry white wine, and garnish with fresh herbs. Salt and pepper lightly if desired.

Fold parchment over fish and vegetables, leaving a 1- to 2-inch space between the edge of the parchment and the fish. Starting at the top of the heart, crimp and firmly hold the cut edges to the inside so that no cut edge is exposed (which would allow steam to escape).

Arrange on a baking sheet so the papillotes do not overlap. At this point, the papillotes may be refrigerated. Bring to room temperature before baking or allow 2 to 3 minutes' extra time if baked directly from refrigerator.

Bake in a preheated 450° oven for 8 to 10 minutes per inch of thickness or at 425° for 10 to 12 minutes per inch. When done, the parchment will be puffed out and lightly browned. Remove one papillote and open to test for doneness.

To serve, take scissors and cut a large X in the parchment on top of the papillote, folding the flaps back, or remove the parchment and slide the fish and vegetables onto heated plates or platter. Serve immediately.

Basic Steam-Baked Shellfish

In cooking shellfish such as oysters or small shrimp or pasteurized crabmeat en papillote, it will only take 4 to 5 minutes at 450° or 6 to 7 minutes at 425°.

For steam-baked fish and shellfish, the possibilities of combining vegetables, herbs, and butters or sauces seem limitless. Try some of these intriguing combinations. (Recipes for butters and sauces appear in Chapter 8.)

Halibut with broccoli and Orange-Chive Butter / fresh chives
Lobster medallions with Caviar Butter / fresh chives
Mahimahi with Roasted Red Pepper Sauce / fresh oregano
Oysters with spinach or sorrel and Beurre Blanc / fresh spinach or sorrel
Pike with Green Peppercorn Butter / fresh parsley
Red snapper with Mango-Mint Butter / fresh mint
Salmon with zucchini and Poblano Butter / fresh cilantro
Shrimp with cherry tomatoes, Jalapeno-Cumin Butter / fresh cilantro
Sole with leeks and Herb (Chervil) Beurre Blanc / fresh chervil
Striped bass with Minced Mushrooms and Shallots (Duxelles)/fresh parsley

Steaming

Steaming is the best way to retain the delicacy of flavor and freshness of a particular fish. Steaming cooks fish without complications. Nearly all fish and shellfish, regardless of size or shape, can be successfully steamed.

Flavor can be added to a steaming liquid in many ways—use part broth and/or wine for the liquid, add chopped onions, shallots, fresh or dried herbs, or vegetables to the liquid. See, for example, Steamed Mussels with Orange, page 97, and Steamed Whole Fish with Ginger and Scallions, page 65.

With a tiered steamer, an entire meal can be prepared on one burner. Put 3 inches of water in the bottom of the steamer and bring to a boil. Fill the lowest tier with fish, the next tier with new potatoes, and the third with carrots, broccoli, or other vegetables. You may need to start the potatoes earlier if they are large and if the fish is not very thick so that all three tiers finish cooking at the same time, or you can simply remove each tier as its contents are done.

To facilitate the removal of steamed fish, filleted or whole, either wrap them in dampened cheesecloth or put them on a heatproof plate that fits in the steamer but leaves a good inch or two around the plate for the steam to circulate.

Save the flavorful juices that collect in the plate and pour them over the fish or add them to a sauce, but *don't throw them out!*

The 10-minutes-per-inch-of-thickness rule can be slightly abbreviated here—anyone who has ever carelessly lifted up a lid over a steaming dish and gotten a steam burn on the wrist can attest to the intensity of steam heat. Steaming seems to take less time for fish fillets—8 minutes per inch of thickness works well for me—but a large whole fish with a bone in may take 10 to 12 minutes per inch of thickness to steam.

Basic Steamed Fish

Over high heat, let 3 inches of water or other steaming liquid (water seasoned with crab or crayfish boil, page 237, or any of the court bouillons, pages 198–201) come to a boil in the bottom of a steamer. Place fish on a heatproof plate or wrap it in dampened cheesecloth, and set on the steamer rack.

～

Close steamer tightly and steam about 8 minutes per inch for fillets; 10 to 12 minutes for large fish with a bone. Test for doneness. Remove and serve immediately on a heated platter.

～

Steamed fish are generally not marinated but are often served with a sauce or flavored butter. Fish can be steamed over any of the stocks or court bouillons in Chapter 8 or simply over boiling water to which herbs or spices have been added to delicately flavor the fish in aromatic steam. Or herbs can be strewn over the fish while it is steamed.

Ivory Shallot Butter (page 223) with all its variations is a perfect accompaniment to steamed fish. Here are some other possible combinations (recipes appear in Chapter 8):

Catfish with Ancho Chile Butter
Halibut with Mango-Mint Butter
Monkfish with Green Peppercorn Butter
Redfish with Sun-Dried Tomato Butter
Salmon with Leek Beurre Blanc
Scrod with Aioli
Sea trout with Shrimp Butter
Sole with Tomato-Basil Beurre Blanc

Steamed or Boiled Live Lobster

Lobster is excellent when cooked by either method.

To steam a lobster, place the live lobster in the top section of a steamer over 4 inches of rapidly boiling, salted water. Fresh seaweed from the fish seller or dried seaweed from a health food store added with the lobsters imparts a special flavor. Steam covered 8 to 10 minutes for the first pound, and add 4 to 5 minutes for each additional pound.

To boil a lobster, place the live lobster head first in rapidly boiling, salted water. Boil lobster 7 minutes for the first pound, and add 3 minutes for each additional pound.

Steamed Clams or Mussels in the Shell

Allow at least 1½ dozen clams or 2 dozen mussels per person for entrée servings.

Scrub shells with a stiff brush under cold running water to remove sand and grit, and scrape off ("debeard") the hair-like beard on mussel shells. Discard any clams or mussels that do not close tightly when touched, or any that are excessively heavy and full of sand.

Place scrubbed clams or mussels in the bottom of a large casserole or stockpot and add about ¾ cup of boiling water and a pinch of salt. Cover and steam over medium-high heat just until the shells open, about 3 to 5 minutes. Discard any shells that have not opened. Strain flavorful steaming broth through a paper towel or cheesecloth and save it to add to sauces or soups or use as a court bouillon to boil or steam shrimp, crabs, crayfish, or lobster.

Steamed Shrimp

To steam shrimp, follow the instructions for Basic Steamed Fish, but cook only 6 to 7 minutes. For extra flavor, use Dark Beer Shrimp Boil (page 236) or Herb and Seed Boil (page 238).

Boiled Live Crayfish

Boiling, really simmering, is the best way to cook crayfish. For one serving, use about one dozen crayfish.

Soak crayfish in water before cooking, to rid them of any grit. Place crayfish in a large pot of rapidly boiling, salted water to which crab or crayfish boil (see Note, page 237) has been added. Cook about 5 minutes. Crayfish, like lobsters, turn bright red when cooked.

Steamed or Boiled
Live Hardshell Crabs

To steam crabs, place live crabs in the top section of a steamer over 4 inches of rapidly boiling, salted water. Sprinkle a dozen crabs with 2 tablespoons of salt and 2 tablespoons of crab boil (see Note), cover tightly and steam for 20 to 25 minutes, or until the crabs turn a bright orange.

To boil whole live crabs, bring a big stockpot of water to a rolling boil, add ¼ cup of salt and ¼ cup of crab boil for every 4 quarts of water, and add if desired 1 sliced lemon, 1 sliced yellow onion, 2 mashed cloves of garlic, and ⅓ cup of parsley stems. Plunge the crabs into the seasoned water and when it returns to a boil, cook crabs for about 8 to 10 minutes per pound. Thus, a dozen small (½ pound) rock crabs would take 4 to 5 minutes.

NOTE: Try the Ginger Dipping Sauce (page 230) for Crab; the Herb and Seed Boil (page 238), and the Spiced Shrimp, Crab, and Crayfish Boil (page 237).

Poaching

Poaching, like steaming, is among the healthiest ways to prepare fish. If your kitchen is minimally equipped, fillets and small fish are easier to poach than 4-to-5-pound whole fish, which necessitates a large metal fish poacher and some oversize utensils for lifting. See page 23 in the equipment section for using other pans as fish poachers.

It takes very careful attention to maintain the poaching liquid at a constant simmer, which occurs when the surface of the liquid just *shimmers*. The heat under a closed lid will normally build up and cause the liquid to come to a rolling boil. Delicate-textured fish simply break into pieces if this goes unnoticed for too long. For that reason, I usually poach fish with the lid of the poacher slightly ajar, which lets steam escape and prevents too much heat from building up. If you need your stove-top burners for other dishes, place the fish poacher in the oven; 400° should maintain an even simmer—check a couple of times during cooking to be sure.

If you are using a poacher with a rack and handles, you'll be able to remove the fish easily. Without a rack, you have two alternatives for removing the fish in one piece. One is to place the fish in the poacher wrapped in cheesecloth, twisting the ends to use as grips. The other is to use two 8-inch-long large commercial metal spatulas with offset handles, angle them underneath the fish, and simultaneously lift both to get the fish out without breaking off either head or tail.

Poached fish cooks perfectly by the 10-minutes-per-inch-of-thickness rule. Strain and use the poaching broth as a base for sauce or soup.

Basic Poached Fish

Prepare a poaching liquid, either water, a court bouillon, or a fumet (see pages 197–98).

Place hot poaching liquid in a fish poacher or a large stockpot or roasting pan, put fish into poacher on a rack or wrapped in cheesecloth, and bring liquid to a simmer (which occurs when the surface of liquid just shimmers or shivers). Never let the liquid boil because the big bubbles of a full boil break up the fish, especially fillets or steaks.

Cover, but leave lid slightly ajar, and poach about 10 minutes per inch of thickness. Test for doneness.

Carefully lift fish out of simmering liquid and let drain on a platter or in a colander.

Serve immediately. If you need to hold poached fish 5 to 10 minutes before serving, place on a heated platter, cover, and keep in a warm (250°) oven.

Poached Scallops

In a 3-quart saucepan bring 4 cups of White Wine Court Bouillon (page 198) or water or dry white wine to a simmer. Add scallops, cleaned and free from sand. Cover and simmer about 3 minutes for sea scallops, 2 minutes for bay scallops. Drain. Reserve cooking liquid for soups or sauces.

NOTE: This is the right amount of liquid for 1 pound of scallops (4

servings); adjust the amount of liquid if you are preparing larger or smaller amounts.

Poached seafood, like steamed, are not marinated. All of the court bouillons and the fumet in Chapter 8 are intended for poaching. Usually a sauce is served with the fish, or a flavored butter is placed on top of the steaming fish to melt and add flavor. The following combinations of poached fish and shellfish with sauces or flavored butters are very successful. (Unless otherwise noted, recipes appear in Chapter 8.)

Bluefish with Anchovy Butter
Halibut with Orange-Chive Butter
Lingcod with Sun-Dried Tomato Butter
Lobster with Tarragon Butter (see Herb Butters)
Mackerel with Horseradish Aioli
Monkfish with Basil Butter (see Herb Butters)
Orange roughy with Mustard Beurre Blanc
Pike with Red Wine Butter
Redfish with Roasted Red Pepper Beurre Blanc
Redfish with Salsa Verde (page 94)
Red snapper with Poblano Butter
Rockfish with Cilantro-Lime Butter
Salmon (served cold) with Cucumber–Dill Sauce (page 227)
Whole salmon with Mint-Flavored Herb Beurre Blanc
Scallops with Garlic, Shallot, and Parsley Butter
Sea trout with Pecan-Cayenne Butter
Shrimp (served cold) with Basil Aioli
Sole with Lime-Ginger Butter (page 96)
Striped bass with Caviar Butter

Sautéeing and Stir-Frying

Sautéeing and stir-frying are similar techniques. The point of both techniques is to continuously move or stir the fish so it doesn't remain on the hot surface or high flame for very long. *Sauté* literally means to jump: the pan is heated so hot the fish sizzle and jump about. Professional chefs jerk the sauté pan with a sharp, quick movement that makes the fish "jump" and keep moving. *Sauté* can also mean cooking at a fairly high heat in a sauté pan.

Stir-frying achieves the same result with a smaller surface area, the bottom curve of a wok, which requires less oil or fat. Since fish must be in small pieces for stir-frying, it is a perfect technique for shrimp and scallops. Hot and Crunchy Shrimp, on page 102, illustrates this technique well.

Basic Sautéed/Stir-Fried Fish or Shellfish

Heat a small amount of oil or clarified butter (see page 17) until very hot in a sauté pan or wok, add 1-inch pieces of fish or shellfish, and cook quickly, stirring or moving pan to keep fish moving. This usually takes under 8 minutes per inch of thickness. Or cook a 1-inch fillet or larger piece of fish such as trout over medium-high heat about 10 minutes per inch of thickness.

Sauces that are excellent with sautéed, stir-fried, pan-fried, oven-fried, or deep-fried fish are cold sauces, vegetable relishes, or salsas. With sautéed or deep-fried oysters, shrimp, or scallops, try Creole Okra Relish (page 233), Chipotle Sauce (page 228), or Papaya Corn Relish (page 233).

Often with fish that I cook in fat, I will use very little butter to cook the fish and will then add a little more of a special butter to flavor the dish. Some tempting combinations appear on page 52 (unless otherwise noted, the recipes for butters and sauces are all in Chapter 8).

Pan-frying

Pan-frying is a good way to cook small whole fish (½ pound or under) like freshwater bluegills, sunfish, crappies, bass, porgies, baby bluefish, small catfish, and trout. Because pan-frying uses quite a bit of cooking oil, it is a method I use very seldom.

Basic Pan-Fried Fish

Heat about ½ to 1 inch of vegetable oil, shortening, or clarified butter (see page 17) in a large, heavy skillet. Coat whole small fish or fish fillets in seasoned flour, fine crumbs, or cornmeal, or try cornstarch for a more delicate coating.

Fry over high heat until the fish is lightly browned and cooked through, about 3 to 4 minutes on each side. Drain on paper towels.

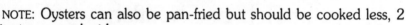

NOTE: Oysters can also be pan-fried but should be cooked less, 2 minutes on each side.

See page 52 for several good accompanying sauces and butters for pan-fried seafood.

Deep-Frying

The most important thing to know about deep-frying is that the oil must be kept constantly at the correct temperature—375°. Use a deep-fat thermometer to check the temperature of the oil. Do not deep-fry fish without an overhead exhaust fan, and take special care to place the pan of hot oil on a back burner to eliminate any chance of accidents.

If pieces of fish or shellfish, dipped in a dry mixture of crumbs, flour, or cornmeal and seasonings, or in a moist batter or coating (see pages 234–35 for coatings and batters) are placed in 375° oil and the oil remains at 370° to 375° during the cooking, the fried fish will have a crisp and dry crust when done, leaving very little oil when blotted on paper towels. Adding all the fish too quickly or adding too many pieces at once to the hot oil (i.e., filling the deep-fryer *more* than half full) causes the temperature of the oil to go down quickly and the fish and coating will rapidly absorb the oil. At 375°, the oil seals the fish and coating. At lower temperatures, the oil is not hot enough to seal and the fried fish become grease-laden, soggy, and unhealthy. You may need to turn the heat up or down slightly during cooking to maintain the correct temperature.

The most effective way to maintain the oil at a constant 375° is to heat it *very* slowly. Put at least 4 inches of oil in a 6-to-7-inch-deep metal pan, 10 to 12 inches in diameter. You need this depth so the oil doesn't boil over when the food is put in and this width to be able to cook in quantity. Deep-frying in a smaller pot would take a longer time.

Place over a low flame and slowly bring the oil to 375°. It should take at least 20 to 30 minutes. This slow heating helps to stabilize the oil at the proper temperature.

The oil used for deep-frying is a matter of choice. I prefer one that is very light in flavor, like safflower oil, but any pure vegetable oil such as corn or peanut oil can be used. Olive oil has a slightly lower smoking point and is fuller in flavor, but is widely used throughout the Mediterranean as the preferred oil for cooking fish.

Be careful not to let the oil heat to over 400° because at this temperature it begins to smoke and break down. If the cooking oil has not become too dark, it can be reused. Cool the used oil and filter it through a paper towel to remove any darkened bits of fish or breading, place in a tightly sealed jar, and store in a cool place.

To hold deep-fried foods for 10 to 15 minutes, spread pieces out on a wire rack in a warm (300°) oven. This allows air to circulate and keeps the coating dry and crisp. Deep-fried oysters are especially good. (Try the Fried Oyster Sandwiches on page 162.)

Basic Deep-Fried Fish
or Shellfish

One advantage of deep-frying is that it is one of the quickest ways to cook fish.

Half-fill a 4-quart, 10-to-12-inch-diameter saucepan with peanut, corn, or safflower oil. Place a deep-fat thermometer in the oil. Over low-medium heat, bring the oil *slowly* up to 375°; this will take 15 to 20 minutes. When oil is nearing 375°, but not before, quickly dip small pieces of fish or shellfish less than 1 inch thick into a batter or coating mixture and gently lower them into the oil. Do not fill fryer more than half full. Keep oil at a constant 375° by turning the heat up or down.

After about 1 to 3 minutes, when the fish is golden brown, remove it with an open-meshed skimmer, letting the excess oil drain back into the deep-fryer.

Shrimp, oysters, or 1-inch pieces of fish will be cooked in the time it takes the coating to brown—1 to 2 minutes.

So that the pieces do not steam and get soggy, spread them on paper towels, making sure they do not touch. Blot and serve immediately, or spread out on cooling racks in a warm oven to hold while deep-frying remaining pieces.

NOTE: See page 234 for recipes for coatings and batters for deep-fried fish and shellfish.

Oven-Frying

Fish can also be fried in the oven, which theoretically can be an easier and cleaner method. Be careful not to use too much oil or fat, however, or your oven will get spattered and smoke a little.

Basic Oven-Fried Fish

Brush fillets or very small fish on both sides with a small amount of oil or melted butter, season or coat, put in a good-sized baking dish so fish are separate and not touching, and place in a very hot 500° oven. Cook 8 to 10 minutes per inch of thickness.

NOTE: See page 234 for recipes for coatings and batters for oven-fried fish.

Sautéed porgy with Grainy Mustard Butter
Sautéed salmon with Red Wine Butter

Pan-fried catfish with Pecan-Cayenne Butter
Pan-fried oysters with French Salsa and Tomatillo Salsa (page 229)

Deep-fried rockfish with Lime-Ginger Butter (page 96)
Deep-fried scallops with Cilantro-Lime Butter
Deep-fried smelt with Chipotle Aioli
Deep-fried whiting with Anchovy Butter

Oven-fried perch with Garlic, Shallot, and Parsley Butter

Microwaving

Microwaving fish is a newer technique and produces good results if you take care not to overcook. However, since fish cooks so quickly by conventional methods, you save only a few minutes by microwaving.

Marinated fish or shellfish or lightly coated fish fillets ¾ to 1 inch thick work best for microwaving.

To thaw frozen fish in the microwave, place the fish still in its original wrapping in a shallow glass dish and microwave on defrost setting 10 to 12 minutes.

Basic Microwaved Fish

Place seasoned fish in a shallow 2-quart glass baking dish, cover dish with heavy-duty plastic wrap, and microwave at the highest setting for about 6 to 8 minutes, or less for ½ inch thick fillets. Remember to turn or rotate the dish once every 3 to 4 minutes for even cooking. Test for doneness at the minimum time. If the center of the fish is still translucent, put it back in the microwave for less than 1 minute and check again.

NOTE: Any of the butters or sauces suggested for poached or steamed fish can be successfully used with microwaved fish.

To Cook Squid

In general, the smaller the squid, the better they taste.

To clean squid, cut the tentacles off close to the head and save for cooking. Cut off the head and discard. With your fingers or a long-handled small spoon, pull out all the inside material, the viscera, the ink sac, and the flexible backbone or beak and discard. Turn empty body cavity inside out and rinse well. Turn it right side out and with a small, sharp knife lightly scrape off the purple skin, which comes away very easily. The squid is now ready to be cooked.

To blanch and use in salads, slice squid in ½-inch rings and cook in boiling salted water only 1 minute. Remove and place in cold water to stop cooking.

To deep-fry, pat dry squid rings, dust with flour or dip in a batter, and deep-fry at 375° about 1 minute, or until crisp and lightly browned.

To braise, cook squid, whole, sliced, or stuffed, in a flavorful sauce about 1 hour over very gentle heat

NOTE: See page 234 for coatings and batters for deep-fried fish and shellfish.

About the Recipes

This personal collection of recipes focuses on new and interesting, easy ways to prepare the varieties of fish and shellfish most commonly available throughout the United States.

No matter where you live, several types of freshwater or saltwater fish and shellfish, lean fish and fatty fish, will be available to you. Vast choice is not as important as freshness. Knowing how to select and correctly store really fresh fish, discussed in Chapter 1, is probably the single most important step in the preparation of fish for your table.

Understanding differences between lean and fatty fish helps you choose the cooking method and the type of seasoning for the fish you have chosen (see Chapter 2). Most lean fish can be used interchangeably, with some exceptions because of differences in texture and thickness. Fatty fish are more distinctly flavored, and seasonings and preparations may be particular to each fish. The suggested substitutions that appear with almost every recipe should give you an expanded sense of what fish will work in each context.

Try a new technique every time you cook fish and shellfish—in a few months you will be familiar with and comfortable cooking different kinds of seafood in many different ways.

I also want to introduce seasonings that are marvelous with fish but perhaps not much used in cooking fish at home: fennel, saffron, cumin, red pepper, chiles, raspberry wine vinegar, sesame oil, rice wine vinegar, walnuts, and pomegranate seeds.

The menus that appear with many of the recipes are suggested to guide you in choosing good combinations of texture, color, and taste, and to encourage new kinds of accompaniments beyond the banality of the steamed new potato. Chapter 7 is devoted to dishes that complement seafood meals, and when they appear on a menu they are highlighted with an asterisk. The suggested wines and beverages simply indicate a wide range of possibilities for you to explore and enjoy.

With a few exceptions, most of the recipes in this book take very little time to prepare and lend themselves to cooking for guests, too. In some cases, part of the dish can be made in advance and held, making last-minute preparation quick and easy; this will be indicated in the recipes and is marked with a ¶. Finally, all of the recipes can easily be doubled or tripled for entertaining.

I sincerely hope these recipes inspire you to cook fish more often and more creatively!

Fish Entrées

The many varieties of fish available in markets across the country today provide ample opportunity to explore different cooking techniques and seasonings for exciting new flavors. These fish entrées are designed for ease of preparation, whether you are cooking for two or for twelve, and most of the recipes take about half an hour from start to finish.

Salmon with Raspberry Wine Vinegar

SERVES 2

I enjoyed this intriguing dish several summers ago at the Restaurant Raphael in New York. This is my version from a memory of the wonderful play of tastes—soft raspberry fruit, tart vinegar, richness of salmon and butter.

2 shallots, finely chopped
2 tablespoons unsalted butter
⅓ cup plus 2 tablespoons raspberry wine vinegar
⅔ pound salmon fillet, ½ to ¾ inch thick, skinned,
    cut lengthwise into 2 pieces (see Note)
1 to 2 tablespoons crème fraîche (see page 227), heavy
    cream, or unsalted sweet butter
1 tablespoon fresh chives or chervil, finely chopped,
    for garnish
handful of perfect fresh raspberries (optional, but a
    very pretty garnish when in season)

Cook shallots gently in butter until soft, 2 to 3 minutes, in a medium-sized skillet. Add ⅓ cup of the raspberry wine vinegar and reduce over high heat until about ½ tablespoon of liquid remains. It will look like a glaze.

Add fillets, and cook 2 to 3 minutes on each side over medium-high heat. Remove fillets and cover with foil to keep warm.

Add 2 more tablespoons of raspberry wine vinegar to the pan. Reduce 1 minute over high heat. Add crème fraîche, heavy cream, or butter, stir until heated through, and pour over the fillets.

Garnish with fresh herbs and raspberries, and serve immediately.

NOTE: This would also be good with striped bass, red snapper, or redfish fillets.

MENU: Salmon with raspberry wine vinegar / Angel hair pasta / *Braised artichokes / Chocolate tart

SUGGESTED WINES: Chardonnay / Meursault / Beaujolais / Burgundy

Grilled Salmon
with Olive Butter

SERVES 4

The ultimate summer food—salmon and corn on an outdoor grill. The pungent, fruity flavor of the olives combines with the salmon for a hearty taste of summer. Spread the olive butter on the corn, too, then wrap corn in the green husks, and tie before grilling.

Olive Butter
1 cup imported French, Italian, or Greek black olives, drained, dried, pitted, and finely chopped
½ cup unsalted sweet butter
¼ cup chopped Italian parsley
¼ teaspoon freshly ground black pepper

1¼ to 1½ pounds salmon fillet or 1-inch steaks (see Note)
melted butter

Blend together olives, butter, parsley, and pepper in a mixer or food processor.

¶ This can be made a day ahead and refrigerated.

Oil the grill, brush the salmon with a little melted butter to keep it from sticking, and grill it about 10 minutes per inch of thickness.

Remove, place on a hot serving platter, spread with olive butter, and place in a warm oven to melt the butter.

NOTE: You can substitute ¾-to-1-inch-thick swordfish fillets (or 1-inch steaks) or any lean fish fillets, ¾ to 1 inch thick.

Fish can be grilled on the indoor grill as well as broiled or baked. Try Poblano Butter (page 222) in place of the olive butter.

MENU: Grilled salmon with olive butter / grilled corn on the cob, eggplant, scallions, red pepper, Anaheim peppers, yellow squash / *Couscous with tomatoes and cinnamon / Figs, blackberries, and nectarines in Grand Marnier

SUGGESTED WINE: California Chardonnay

Salmon Fillet Baked with Paprika and Walnut Sauce

SERVES 2

In this recipe, the thoroughly Hungarian play of flavors in the sauce is intriguingly different and very delicious: rich (walnuts), tart (lemon), mildly hot (paprika), and sour-creamy (sour cream).

Paprika and Walnut Sauce
1 tablespoon safflower or virgin olive oil
7 scallions, with green part, thinly sliced
1 large green bell pepper, chopped
1 heaping tablespoon Hungarian paprika, mild or medium-hot
⅓ cup large walnut pieces
½ teaspoon salt
¼ teaspoon freshly ground black pepper
8 ounces sour cream

1-pound salmon fillet, cut into 2 equal pieces (see Note)
juice of ½ lemon

Heat the oil in a small saucepan, add scallions and green pepper, cook over high heat, stirring, 2 to 3 minutes, or until onions and pepper are not quite cooked through. Add paprika and stir 1 minute. Remove from heat. Add walnuts, salt, pepper, and sour cream. Stir to mix well and taste for seasoning.

¶ This recipe can be prepared ahead up to this point and refrigerated overnight. Bring to room temperature and gently reheat to use.

Place salmon fillets in a small oiled gratin dish. Spread sauce over the salmon to cover, pour lemon juice over all, and bake at 400° 10 minutes per inch of thickness of fish and sauce, or about 15 minutes.

NOTE: Pike fillets or any ¾-inch-thick fillets of lean fish such as redfish, porgy, red snapper, or lingcod may be substituted for the salmon.

MENU: Salmon fillet baked with paprika and walnut sauce / *Spaetzle / Green salad / Chocolate torte

SUGGESTED WINE: Riesling

Roasted Salmon Feast

SERVES 10

A friend prepared this dish, inspired by a recipe of Seppi Renggli's, the chef of The Four Seasons restaurant, for a beautiful party in New York. The sharpness of the peppercorns combines nicely with the rich taste of the salmon. This is an elegant and impressive yet easy dish to prepare and serve. A roasted salmon is a spectacular sight on a buffet table. Roasting is much easier than poaching or grilling, and your kitchen stays cleaner. Plan your menu so that everything except the salmon can be made ahead and reheated.

> 5-to-6-pound whole salmon, gutted and scaled, with
>   head left on
>
> *Pepper Marinade*
> 1 teaspoon dried green peppercorns
> 1 teaspoon dried white peppercorns
> 1 teaspoon dried black peppercorns
> 1 tablespoon salt
> ⅛ teaspoon cayenne pepper
> ⅓ cup fresh lemon juice
> 2 tablespoons extra-virgin olive oil
> 3 garlic cloves, unpeeled
> 2 branches fresh rosemary, oregano, or fennel
> sprigs of Italian parsley, for garnish

Score the salmon on the top side, making diagonal cuts ½ inch apart down the length of the salmon, cutting about ½ inch deep with a very sharp knife. Mix the peppercorns, salt, cayenne, lemon juice, and oil together and rub this mixture into the cuts and over the bottom side of the salmon. Put the garlic and rosemary into the cavity of the fish and marinate in the refrigerator on a tray for about 1 hour.

Preheat the oven to 425°. Place the salmon on a rack that sits over a large baking pan. Roast uncovered about 10 minutes per inch of thickness or until the internal temperature, measured with an instant-reading thermometer, registers about 130 to 140°.

Remove the salmon from the oven, and put on a long, narrow, heated platter. Place sprigs of parsley all around the fish and serve.

MENU: Wild rice soup / Roasted salmon with *shallot confit / Scalloped corn with red peppers and goat cheese / Blackberry cobbler

SUGGESTED WINE: Meursault

Monkfish Braised with Leeks and Savoy Cabbage, with Tomato Beurre Blanc

SERVES 6 TO 8

Monkfish marries well with the earthy leek, cabbage, and tomato. An easy but refined dish.

> 4 tablespoons unsalted sweet butter
> 5 leeks, well rinsed, thinly sliced
> 1 medium head Savoy cabbage, washed, dried, thinly sliced
> ¼ teaspoon salt
> ⅛ teaspoon freshly ground white pepper
> ¼ teaspoon dried thyme, or 2 sprigs of fresh thyme
> 1½ to 2 pounds monkfish, rinsed in cold water and dried (thin dark outer membrane removed), sliced into ¾-inch pieces across the grain
> 1 recipe Tomato Beurre Blanc page 224

In a 9-inch skillet, melt the butter and gently cook leeks 5 minutes; add cabbage and cook another 5 minutes or until both vegetables are soft. Season delicately with salt, pepper, and thyme.

¶ The recipe can be made a day ahead to this point, refrigerated, and reheated.

Over medium heat, add monkfish on top of vegetables and simmer about 5 to 7 minutes or until monkfish is cooked through but still just a little rare in the center. The fish will continue cooking off the stove from the heat of the sauce, so for this reason it is best not to cook to the perfect point of doneness.

Remove the fish to a heated dish and cover with foil to keep warm. Cook the fish, leeks, and cabbage over a high flame for 2 minutes to blend and intensify the flavors. Meanwhile, put Tomato Beurre Blanc in a saucepan and gently warm. Remove the leeks and cabbage with a slotted spoon and place in a heated serving dish.

Place the monkfish on top of the leeks and cabbage and pour Tomato Beurre Blanc sauce over all, or serve sauce separately.

MENU: Monkfish braised with leeks and savoy cabbage, with tomato beurre blanc / *Crusty Persian rice / Salad of oranges and endive / Plum tart

SUGGESTED WINES: Mâcon Blanc / Chardonnay / Pinot Grigio

Roasted Monkfish in Five-Pepper Butter

SERVES 4

Peppers as spice combine beautifully and subtly with the flavor of monkfish in this very easy recipe.

> ¾-to-1-pound piece of monkfish, rinsed in cold water
> and dried, thin dark outer membrane removed
> (see Note)
> 1½ teaspoons mixed freshly ground peppercorn blend†
> 3 tablespoons unsalted sweet butter

Preheat the oven to 425°. Place an oval gratin dish not much bigger than the monkfish in the oven with the ground peppercorn blend in it, allow pepper to heat 2 to 3 minutes, then add all of the butter, return to oven, and let butter melt and bubble.

Remove the dish from the oven, and dip the monkfish in the pepper butter to coat all sides. Place fish in the gratin dish nicest side up and return to the oven for 20 minutes, or approximately 10 minutes per inch of thickness at the thickest point. After 10 minutes, cover loosely with foil.

Serve with pan juices poured over the fish.

NOTE: An equal amount of lobster, shark, or scallops may be substituted for the monkfish.

MENU: Roasted monkfish in five-pepper butter / Roasted red peppers / *Pommes de terre au diable / Poached pears in red wine

SUGGESTED WINES: Orvieto / White Rioja / Graves

† To make peppercorn blend, combine 1 teaspoon each of freshly ground peppercorns. Use two different varieties of black if possible (Malabar and Tellicherry, for example) plus white pepper and dried green peppercorns. To this mixture add ½ teaspoon of cayenne pepper and ½ teaspoon of salt. Store any leftover ground pepper for future use.

Baked Monkfish
with Walnut Pesto

SERVES 2 TO 3

Monkfish has a denser texture than most fin fish so it may take a little longer to cook than the 10-minute-per-inch rule. You could also slice it into ½-inch serving pieces, cover them with sauce, wrap individually in foil, and cook on a grill; or cook the fish as described below and then cut it into smaller pieces and serve on top of hot fettuccine tossed with the baking juices and black pepper.

Walnut Pesto
⅓ cup fresh basil leaves (about 12 large)
1 large clove garlic
⅓ cup fresh walnut halves
¼ teaspoon salt
grind of black pepper
¼ cup grated Parmesan cheese
¼ cup virgin olive oil

¾ pound monkfish (thin, dark outer membrane removed) in one piece cut from center, or 2 small tails of equal size (see Note)

Pound basil, garlic, walnuts, and salt in a mortar or quickly blend in a blender or processor. Mix in pepper, parmesan, and olive oil.

¶ Pesto can be prepared ahead and refrigerated overnight if necessary. Use at room temperature.

Coat monkfish with the pesto and place in a 9-inch oval gratin dish.
    Bake at 400° to 425° about 20 minutes, or about 10 minutes per inch of thickness.
NOTE: An equal amount of lobster, scallops, shrimp, or any lean fish fillets (¾ inch thick) may be substituted for the monkfish.

MENU: Monkfish with walnut pesto / *Bulgur with lemon and pine nuts / Salad of tomatoes, red onion, and goat cheese / Bitter chocolate cake and coffee ice cream

SUGGESTED WINES: Pinot Grigio / White Hermitage / Sauvignon Blanc

Steamed Whole Fish with Ginger and Scallions

SERVES 4

In this quintessential Oriental steamed fish all the flavors come through with bell-like clarity.

2 small whole fish, about 1½ to 2 pounds each, cleaned
    and scaled with the head and tail left on (see Note)
1 teaspoon salt
¼ cup fresh ginger, peeled and grated
8 to 10 scallions, thinly julienned in 3-inch lengths
8 fresh shiitake mushrooms, or 8 large dried shiitake
    mushrooms presoaked for 30 minutes in boiling
    water or chicken broth†
¼ cup soy sauce (preferably Pearl River mushroom
    soy sauce)
¼ cup peanut oil
5 to 6 sprigs fresh coriander, for garnish

Rinse the fish quickly and pat dry. Score by cutting two large X's ½ inch deep on both sides of fish. Rub with salt inside and out. Press all of the ginger and a quarter of the scallions into the cuts.

¶ The recipe can be prepared several hours ahead at this point.

Place fish on a heatproof plate in a steamer. Scatter the mushrooms on top. Close tightly and steam, allowing approximately 10 to 12 minutes per inch of thickness.

Remove the fish to a heated platter, sprinkle soy sauce evenly over both fish, and scatter the remaining scallions on top. Keep the fish covered with foil or put in a warm oven. Quickly heat the oil almost to the smoking point and pour over the fish. The scallions will sizzle and cook slightly. Garnish with fresh coriander and serve immediately.

NOTE: Small whole red snapper, sea trout, porgy, catfish, rockfish, perch, and flounder are all good for this recipe, as are thick fillets of firm-textured fish such as halibut, striped bass, or redfish.

MENU: Clear mushroom soup / Steamed whole fish with ginger and scallions / *Crusty Persian rice / Tangerine sorbet with almond cookies

SUGGESTED WINE: Blanc de Pinot Noir

† If neither are available, use regular large white mushrooms, thinly sliced.

Baked Whole Fish
à la Provençale

SERVES 4 TO 6

This is one of the easiest and most delicious ways of cooking a whole fish. In Provence in the summer the air is filled with warm aromas of wild thyme, rosemary, summer savory, fennel, oregano, and sage, all mingled with exquisite lavender, so the traditional Provençal seasoning mixture for fish always includes dried lavender. The herbal mixture here can be made up in large quantities and kept on hand or given to friends with instructions for making the marinade (simply add 3½ tablespoons of the mixed herbs and seasonings to the lemon juice and olive oil).

> 3-to-3½-pound whole sea bass, cleaned and scaled
>   with the head and tail left on (see Note)
>
> *Provençal Marinade*
> 1 tablespoon fennel seeds
> 1 teaspoon dried thyme
> 1 teaspoon dried rosemary
> 1 teaspoon dried summer savory
> ½ teaspoon dried basil
> ½ teaspoon dried oregano
> pinch of dried sage
> 2 teaspoons salt
> ½ teaspoon freshly ground black pepper
> ⅓ to ½ cup fresh lemon juice
> ½ cup extra-virgin olive oil
>
> sprigs fresh thyme, rosemary, oregano, sage, or pars-
>   ley, for garnish

Rinse the fish in cold water and wipe with a damp cloth. With a sharp knife, score the fish on both sides, cutting two or three large overlapping X's about ½ inch deep. Place the fish in a glass or metal baking dish— oval is best.

Crush the fennel, herbs, salt, and pepper together in a mortar. Add lemon juice and stir to dissolve the salt. Mix in the olive oil. Pour this marinade over the scored fish and turn to coat well. Refrigerate, turning once, for 1 to 2 hours.

Bake the fish uncovered at 425°, allowing 10 minutes per inch of thickness (measure at the thickest part), about 30 to 40 minutes. Baste fish several times with the marinade while baking. Test for doneness by inserting a small knife under the flesh at the backbone; if the fish is done, the flesh flakes easily and looks milky white, not gray and translucent.

To serve, place on a heated oval platter and, with a sharp knife and a serving spatula, make two or three vertical cuts across the fish. Slip the knife in at the backbone horizontally and slide the knife across the top of the bones from gills to tail to detach the flesh from the bones. Remove two or three neatly cut portions with the spatula. Detach the spine at the base of the head with one sharp cut and remove to another plate. Make two or three more vertical cuts through the flesh and skin, and serve, garnished with sprigs of fresh herbs.

NOTE: You can also use whole redfish, red snapper, pompano, porgy, drum, rockfish, or sheepshead. This dish is also good made with a large fillet of bluefish, or a thick tuna or swordfish steak.

MENU: Baked whole fish à la Provençale / *Zucchini gratin / *Roasted red pepper salad with garlic vinaigrette / Peaches in sweet white wine

SUGGESTED WINES: White Hermitage / Sancerre / Frascati

Fish with Walnuts, Red Onions, and Pomegranate Seeds

SERVES 2 TO 4

You will find variations on this combination of flavors with fish throughout the Middle East and in southern Russia. Pomegranates give a fresh, clean, tart taste and the fish looks like it is stuffed with rubies! Use citrus juices to replace the pomegranate seeds if they are unavailable.

> 1 3-pound whole fish, cleaned and scaled with head
>   and tail left on (see Note)
> 2 teaspoons salt
>
> *Stuffing*
> 1 cup chopped red onions
> 2 cloves garlic, mashed
> 2 to 3 tablespoons virgin olive oil
> 1 cup fresh white bread crumbs, soaked in ¼ cup milk
>   and then squeezed dry
> 1 cup chopped walnuts
> ¾ cup finely chopped parsley
> ½ teaspoon freshly ground black pepper
> salt to taste
> 1½ teaspoons paprika
> ⅓ cup pomegranate seeds, or if pomegranate is un-
>   available, 1 tablespoon fresh lemon or lime juice

Wipe the fish and sprinkle inside and out with the salt. Leave at room temperature while you prepare the stuffing.

To make the stuffing: cook the onions and garlic gently in the olive oil until soft. Add crumbs, walnuts, parsley, seasonings, and 3 tablespoons of the pomegranate seeds. Taste for seasoning.

Spoon the stuffing into the cavity of the fish and pat any excess on top of the fish. Place fish in an oiled baking dish and bake 45 to 50 minutes at 400° or 10 minutes per inch of thickness including the stuffing. Garnish with the remaining pomegranate seeds.

NOTE: Use red snapper, redfish, flounder, striped bass, porgy, rockfish, or sea trout. Or try this dish with thick fillets instead of whole fish. Put the stuffing on top of the fillets and adjust the baking time (allowing 10 minutes per inch of thickness including the stuffing).

MENU: Fish with walnuts, red onions, and pomegranate seeds / Spinach salad / Pound cake with apricot sauce

SUGGESTED WINES: Sauvignon Blanc / Mâcon Blanc / Frascati

Whole Fish Baked in Salt

SERVES 4

Although this recipe calls for a lot of salt, the fish does not taste salty at all, but is wonderfully moist and fresh-tasting. The moistened salt hardens to seal in juices and flavor.

> 4 to 5 pounds coarse or kosher salt
> 1 whole fish, 3 to 3½ pounds, cleaned and scaled with head and tail left on (see Note)
> 10 big sprigs one of the following fresh herbs: rosemary, thyme, dill, fennel, or mint (reserve 2 sprigs for garnish)
> 1 cup cold water

Line a baking dish with heavy foil. Cover the bottom with a layer of salt. Lay the fish on the salt. Put four sprigs of the herbs in the cavity of the fish and four on top of the fish. Cover the fish completely with salt. Slowly pour the water evenly over the salt-covered fish.

Bake at 400° for about 1 hour or until fish reaches an internal temperature of 140°. Check the temperature at thickest part of fish with an instant-reading thermometer.

When the fish is done, break the salt crust by tapping with a mallet or pestle, and place the fish on a heated platter. Remove the skin and wipe away any remaining salt.

Garnish with the remaining herbs and serve with a sauce or a flavored butter; Aioli with fresh basil (page 225) or Sun-Dried Tomato Butter (page 222) complement this dish nicely.

NOTE: Use whole redfish, red snapper, rockfish, drum, sheepshead, striped bass, or porgy.

MENU: Whole fish baked in salt / Spinach pasta / *Artichokes and Mushrooms in Madeira Cream / Fresh ripe pears and blue cheese

SUGGESTED WINES: Fumé Blanc / Mâcon Blanc / Pinot Grigio

Fish Braised
in Red Wine

Not only can red wine be served with many fish dishes, it is also a wonderful medium for cooking fish. One of the most unusual fish dishes I tasted in France was an old-fashioned Burgundian fish stew called a *matelote*: five or six kinds of freshwater fish simmered in a good red Burgundy wine with lots of fresh vegetables and herbs. The red wine sauce in the recipe that follows is a typical Burgundian sauce normally served with poached eggs; it results in a dish similar to matelote but somewhat easier to prepare.

> 1 tablespoon unsalted sweet butter
> 2 shallots, finely chopped
> 1 medium carrot, finely chopped
> 8 large mushroooms, finely chopped
> 1 to 2 strips thick-sliced bacon (without maple or sugar curing if possible), sliced in ½-inch strips or lardons
> ½ clove garlic, minced
> ½ teaspoon dried thyme
> 1 imported bay leaf
> pinch of salt
> grind of black pepper
> 1½ cups good Burgundy
> 2 whole brook or rainbow trout, about 10 to 12 ounces each, cleaned with head and tail left on (see Notes)
> 1 teaspoon butter
> 1 teaspoon flour
> ⅛ pound fresh oyster mushrooms, cépes, or chanterelles, washed, trimmed, and sautéed in butter for 6 to 8 minutes (optional)
> ½ cup tiny pearl onions, peeled, simmered in water until soft, and drained (optional)
> 1 tablespoon finely chopped parsley

Melt the tablespoon of butter in a small oval skillet large enough to hold both fish. Add the shallots, carrot, mushrooms, bacon, garlic, herbs, and seasonings and sauté about 5 minutes, or until mixture begins to brown.

¶ The recipe can be prepared ahead to this point and held refrigerated overnight. Reheat to use.

Pour in the red wine and simmer 15 minutes. Add the trout. Cover and simmer about 5 minutes; turn trout and simmer another 5 minutes. Remove the trout and cover with foil to keep warm.

Mix the butter and flour together on a shallow plate with the back of a fork, and add to the sauce; cook 1 to 2 minutes or until slightly thickened. If desired, add the optional ingredients and taste for seasoning. Add the parsley. Pour sauce over the trout and serve.

NOTES: As a variation, cook trout en papillote. Prepare the sauce and simmer for 20 minutes or until slightly thickened. Place the trout on a piece of parchment, spoon the sauce over the fish, and fold the parchment to seal (see page 81). Bake at 450° for 9 minutes. The optional chanterelles and pearl onions are especially good with this version.

For an unusual garnish make toasted herbed croutons by tossing cubed bread with melted butter and fresh chopped thyme; spread on a baking sheet to brown in a 350° oven for 15 minutes.

Other fish that could be cooked this way: a small whole coho salmon, or 1-inch-thick fillets of halibut, bass, redfish, red snapper, grouper, or rockfish.

MENU: Fish braised in red wine / *Spaetzle / Endive and chicory salad with walnut oil vinaigrette / Cold hazelnut soufflé with raspberry sauce

SUGGESTED WINES: Côte de Beaune / Pinot Noir

Brook Trout with Pancetta, Sage, and Champagne Wine Vinegar

SERVES 2

A wonderful combination of flavors—tart, herbal, and rich. Pancetta, a lightly cured Italian bacon, adds a special quality to this dish. It is quickly and easily made and, with the sage-leaf sauce, very attractive.

> 2 brook trout, 10 to 12 ounces each, cleaned with head and tail left on, boned or unboned
> salt
> grind of black pepper
> 12 leaves fresh sage
> 8 paper-thin slices pancetta, or if not available, 4 paper-thin slices prosciutto, or 4 pieces thinly sliced bacon (without maple or sugar curing if possible)
> 1½ tablespoons unsalted sweet butter or clarified butter (page 17)
> 2 tablespoons champagne wine vinegar
> 2½ tablespoons water
> ¼ teaspoon freshly ground black pepper

Sprinkle the cavity of the trout with salt and pepper and place four whole sage leaves inside each trout. Wrap pancetta around trout.

Heat the butter in an ovenproof skillet and brown the trout over medium-high heat about 7 to 8 minutes on each side, then place the trout in a 400° oven another 5 to 6 minutes to finish cooking. Test for doneness. When the trout is cooked through, remove and cover with foil to keep warm.

Add the champagne vinegar, water, and pepper to the pan along with the remaining four sage leaves, finely chopped. Stir and cook over high heat until the mixture is reduced to about 1 to 2 tablespoons.

Pour these pan juices equally over the two trout on a heated serving dish. Serve immediately. (It is also good cold.)

MENU: Brook trout with pancetta, sage, and champagne wine vinegar / *Polenta with Italian Parmesan / Escarole and mushroom salad / Warm cherry clafouti

SUGGESTED WINES: Orvieto / Chardonnay

Fresh Trout Meunière

SERVES 2

It's hard to beat the perfection of a simple dish like this, especially if you've just caught the trout yourself and are cooking outdoors! For a hearty breakfast, serve Trout Meunière with fresh hot biscuits, sautéed potatoes with chives, and cold pears poached in a good sauterne or red wine.

> 4 tablespoons clarified butter (page 17)
> 2 to 4 small whole trout, 10 to 12 ounces each (see Note)
> 2 tablespoons all-purpose flour
> ¼ teaspoon salt
> ¼ teaspoon dried thyme
> 1 to 2 tablespoons fresh lemon juice
> 2 tablespoons finely chopped parsley
>
> 8 to 10 sprigs watercress, well washed and dried, for garnish
> ⅓ cup thinly sliced almonds, sautéed in butter until golden (optional)

Heat the butter in a large ovenproof skillet. Dust the trout in flour seasoned with salt and thyme and place in the sizzling butter.

Cook over medium-high heat until fish is nicely browned on the outside, about 8 minutes on each side, then finish in a 400° oven. Test for doneness by inserting a knife at the backbone. If it's cooked through on the inside, the flesh will be milky white and will easily flake away from the bone.

Place the fish on a heated serving dish.

Heat lemon juice and parsley until warm in skillet the trout was cooked in, then pour pan juices over the fish. Garnish with sprigs of watercress, and almonds if desired, and serve immediately.

NOTE: You may substitute butterfish, sunfish, bluefish, catfish, sand dabs, and rex or petrale sole for the trout.

MENU: Fresh trout meunière / *Quick oven potatoes with rosemary / *Tomatoes à la Provençale / Hot apple tart

SUGGESTED WINE: Alsatian Riesling

Brook Trout with Wild Mushrooms, Fresh Herbs, and Crème Fraîche

SERVES 4

I started experimenting with this dish one summer in Germany, using an intriguing array of fresh wild mushrooms and fresh trout. Later, at Iron Horse Vineyards, in Sonoma County, California, where I cooked every autumn for three years for Audrey and Barry Sterling and their many guests, I added all the different fresh herbs which grow in profusion in their extensive gardens. This unusual and richly flavored dish cooks in 25 minutes, looks gorgeous, smells divine, and is a meal in itself.

> 4 tablespoons unsalted sweet butter
> 4 whole brook trout, 10 to 12 ounces each, cleaned
>   with bone in and head and tail left on (see Notes)
> pinch of salt
> grind of black pepper
> ¼ cup dry white wine
> ¼ cup crème fraîche (page 227) or, if not available,
>   heavy cream
> 6 6-inch branches fresh rosemary
> 6 6-inch branches fresh thyme
> 6 6-inch branches fresh marjoram
> 4 large leaves fresh sage
> 8 large sprigs fresh parsley, long stems removed
> ½ cup fresh chives sliced in 3-inch lengths
> 6 very large fresh mushrooms, field mushrooms, shi-
>   itake mushrooms, or oyster mushrooms, cut in
>   half, or 12 smaller mushrooms
> 6 large fresh chanterelles, cut in halves or quarters
> 4 large fresh cèpes
> ½ ounce dried cèpes, soaked in stock†
> ½ ounce dried morels, soaked in stock†

† *To clean dried mushrooms,* place in a colander and shake over the sink to remove sand, then rinse well under running water and soak in warm water or good stock until the mushrooms are soft. Soaking time varies from 20 mintues for thin mushrooms to 1 hour for thicker ones. Don't leave them in so long that they become so soft that they are slimy to the touch. Then drain and pat dry with paper towels. Strain and reserve soaking liquid for use in soups and stews if you wish.

Butter a large gratin dish or broiler pan, approximately 12 inches by 14 inches, with the butter.

Sprinkle the trout inside and out with salt and pepper. Place fish in the buttered pan, leaving some space around each. Pour the wine and crème fraîche evenly over the two trout. Scatter the herbs and mushrooms over the fish, and season well with salt and pepper. Cover tightly with foil.

Place in a 425° oven for about 20 to 25 minutes. Remove, arrange on a heated serving platter, and serve hot.

NOTES: Use other kinds of fish in place of trout—whole small bass or porgies, or large fillets of halibut, red snapper, or redfish.

You can use whatever mushrooms, dried or fresh, that are available, but try to use at least three or four different kinds. This dish could be made with a smaller selection of the fresh and dried mushrooms and fresh herbs listed, but, in any case, don't use dried herbs. If fresh parsley and chives are all that is available, use them. Use just one kind of mushroom if necessary, but do try to use dried mushrooms for the intense flavor they give.

MENU: Brook trout with wild mushrooms, fresh herbs, and crème fraîche / *Spinach timbales / Radicchio and oakleaf lettuce salad / Pear and hazelnut strudel with crème Anglaise

SUGGESTED WINES: Meursault / Graves / Chardonnay

Moroccan Fish
with Cumin

SERVES 4

This is adapted from a recipe for a typical Moroccan fish dish in Alan Davidson's *Mediterranean Seafood*. I prefer to sauté or bake instead of deep-fry the fish. You will love this combination of flavors. You can also use the marinade with large whole fish; prepare and bake it as for Baked Fish à la Provençale (page 66).

> *Marinade*
> 6 cloves garlic, peeled
> 1 heaping teaspoon salt
> 1½ teaspoons paprika
> 1½ teaspoons ground cumin
> ⅛ teaspoon cayenne pepper
> ½ cup packed finely chopped fresh cilantro
> juice of 1 lemon
>
> 1½ pounds redfish fillets, skinned, ¾ to 1 inch thick,
>   cut diagonally into 2-inch pieces (see Note)
> ⅓ cup all-purpose flour
> 1½ tablespoons extra-virgin olive oil
> 4 sprigs fresh cilantro, for garnish

Pound the garlic with the salt and spices in a mortar. Add the cilantro and lemon juice and stir until the mixture is well blended.

Cover the pieces of fish with the marinade and let stand for about an hour. Remove the fish and pat dry.

Dust the fillets lightly with flour just before cooking. Sauté in hot oil in a skillet until golden on both sides and cooked through.

Remove to a heated platter, garnish with cilantro sprigs, and serve hot or at room temperature.

NOTE: Other white fish can be used—halibut, flounder, haddock, cod, striped bass, red snapper, grouper, rockfish, porgy, drum, or lingcod.

MENU: Moroccan fish with cumin / *Couscous with chick-peas / Tomato and mint salad / Melon with cardamom cookies

SUGGESTED BEVERAGES: Gewürztztraminer / Dark beer

Grilled Swordfish with Sun-Dried Tomato Butter

SERVES 2

Swordfish, tuna, and salmon taste best just a little underdone. Cooked all the way through, these fish seem too dry. Don't be afraid to try it; the fish is not really "raw," just a little rare.

> 2 swordfish steaks (⅔ to 1 pound), ¾ to 1 inch thick
> (see Note)
> virgin olive oil or basil oil (page 19)
> 1 to 2 tablespoons Sun-Dried Tomato Butter (page
> 222)
> 1 tablespoon very soft unsalted sweet butter

Cook swordfish outdoors over hot coals or indoors on a heated ridged grill on top of the stove. Lightly oil the grill before cooking.

Heat the ridged grill or a heavy skillet for 5 minutes over high heat. Brush the pan lightly with a little oil and rub both sides of the swordfish with the oil to coat.

Place the steaks on the hot grill or in the skillet; turn after 2 minutes. They should take under 5 minutes to cook on a very hot grill. Leave a little underdone in center.

Remove and immediately put ½ tablespoon softened Sun-Dried Tomato Butter on each steak.

NOTE: Try amberjack, mullet, bluefish, mahimahi, or tuna instead of swordfish.

MENU: Grilled swordfish with sun-dried tomato butter / *Grilled polenta / Marinated zucchini salad / Peach crisp

SUGGESTED WINES: Mâcon Blanc / Pinot Grigio / Chardonnay

Tuna in Orange-Ginger Marinade

SERVES 2

An Oriental inspiration for fresh tuna. The exotic seasonings marry perfectly with the tuna, and fillets make an attractive, elegant presentation. The marinade can also be used as a dipping sauce for other fish: for example, with deep-fried scallops or steamed shrimp.

Marinade
¼ cup soy sauce
3 tablespoons rice wine vinegar
2 tablespoons sesame oil
3 tablespoons fresh orange juice
1 tablespoon grated orange peel
⅓ cup grated or minced fresh ginger

½ pound fresh tuna, sliced in ½-inch fillets (see Note)
2 teaspoons fresh clives, cilantro, or parsley, for garnish

Combine the marinade ingredients in a shallow dish. Add the tuna slices, spoon the marinade over them, and marinate 30 minutes to 1 hour.

Remove the tuna fillets from the marinade. Place in a sauté pan and cook over medium-high heat 1 minute on each side. No oil is needed as the tuna is moist from the marinade.

Garnish and serve.

NOTE: This dish is excellent also with swordfish, salmon, striped bass, halibut, and mullet.

MENU: Tuna in orange-ginger marinade / Steamed broccoli, scallions and snow peas / Cold mango mousse

SUGGESTED WINES: Gewürztraminer / Sauvignon Blanc

Ginger-Glazed Grilled Salmon

SERVES 2

The glaze in this quick-and-easy recipe gives salmon a rich, wonderful flavor. If mirin, an inexpensive and commonly available Japanese ingredient, proves hard to find, substitute 2 tablespoons of rice wine vinegar for it and add another ½ tablespoon of sugar to the recipe.

Ginger Glaze
2 tablespoons mirin (a syrupy Japanese rice wine)
2½ tablespoons soy sauce
1 tablespoon sake or dry sherry
½ tablespoon sugar
1 tablespoon squeezed juice of chopped fresh ginger†
1 tablespoon slivered shallot

2 salmon steaks or fillets, 1 inch thick, about 6 to 8 ounces each

Mix all ingredients except salmon to make a glaze. Brush the salmon with glaze on both sides and let sit at room temperature while coals burn down. Brush again and grill 5 to 8 minutes on each side. Brush again just before removing fish from grill.

MENU: Ginger-glazed grilled salmon / Fresh sautéed shiitake or other large mushrooms / Stir-fried spinach with sesame seeds / Cold orange pots de crème

SUGGESTED WINE: Gewürtztraminer

† Squeezed through a garlic press or cheesecloth.

Fish en Papillote with Julienned Leeks, Carrots, Cucumber, and Zucchini

SERVES 2 AMPLY, 4 MODESTLY

Perfect for an elegant dinner party, Fish en Papillote can be prepared well ahead, then just popped in the oven for 10 to 15 minutes of cooking. This can be prepared for up to six or eight people but for ease and speed of serving, shouldn't be made for more. It can be served with a beurre blanc sauce, such as Ivory Shallot Butter or its variations (page 223), a flavored butter, such as Lemon Butter (page 214) or Dill Butter (page 214) or nothing at all—it will still taste wonderful. Make your own combinations of fish, vegetables, and herbs.

> 5 tablespoons softened unsalted sweet butter
> 2 leeks, well rinsed, cut into matchstick slices 4 inches long
> 2 medium carrots, peeled, cut into matchstick slices 4 inches long
> 2 scallions, cut into matchstick slices 4 inches long
> 1 medium zucchini or yellow squash, peeled, halved, seeded, cut into matchstick slices 4 inches long
> 1 medium cucumber, peeled, seeded, cut into matchstick slices 4 inches long
> pinch of salt
> grind of white pepper
> 2 tablespoons finely chopped parsley
> 2 15-by-15-inch sheets cooking parchment or, if not available, lightweight foil
> 1 pound redfish fillet, ¾ to 1 inch thick (see Note)
> 2 tablespoons dry white wine
> 8 garlic chives or 1 scallion, cut into thin strips 5 inches long, for garnish
> 4 sprigs fresh thyme (optional)

Melt 3 tablespoons of the butter in a large sauté pan. Over medium heat, cook the leeks, carrots, scallions, zucchini, and cucumber, stirring for about 4 minutes, or until they "sweat," or just begin to release their juices in tiny beads on the surface. Stir in salt, pepper, and parsley.

Fold each piece of parchment in half and cut a large half-heart shape, starting and ending at the fold. Open the parchment and butter well in the center of one side, using 1 teaspoon of butter for each papillote.

Cut the fillets diagonally into four to six pieces or strips about 1½ inches wide.

Place half of the vegetables in the center of each of the buttered parchment hearts. Place an equal number of fillet pieces on top of the vegetables, dot equally with remaining butter, sprinkle each papillote with wine, and garnish with garlic chives or scallion strips and, if desired, two sprigs of thyme. Salt and pepper lightly if you like.

Fold the parchment over the fish and vegetables, leaving a 1-to-2-inch space between the crimped edge and the fish. Starting at the top of the heart, crimp and firmly fold the cut edges to the inside so that no cut edge is exposed (which would allow steam to escape).

Arrange the papillotes on a baking sheet so they do not overlap.

¶ The papillotes may be made ahead to this point the morning of the day they are to be cooked, and refrigerated. Bring to room temperature before baking or allow 2 to 3 minutes' extra time if baked directly from the refrigerator.

Bake in a preheated 450° oven for 8 to 10 minutes per inch of thickness, or at 425° for 10 to 12 minutes per inch of thickness. (These are two options for timing to facilitate serving.)

When done, the parchment will be puffed out and lightly browned. You might want to remove one and open to test the fish for doneness. Fillets should be opaque and milky white.

To serve, take scissors and cut a large X in the top of the parchment, folding the flaps back, or remove the parchment and slide the fish and vegetables onto heated plates or a platter. Serve immediately with a sauce or butter (see Chapter 8), or without any sauce at all.

NOTE: You can also use red snapper, sea bass, rockfish, flounder, sole, halibut, salmon, or monkfish. Scallops are also good prepared this way.

MENU: Fish en papillote with julienned leeks, carrots, cucumber, and zucchini / *Ivory shallot butter / Watercress and tomato salad / Blackberry tart

SUGGESTED WINES: Chardonnay / Chablis / Graves / Orvieto

Rigatoni with Eggplant, Tomatoes, and Sole

SERVES 4 TO 6

This makes a very satisfying meal that's not terribly difficult to or-
chestrate. While the oil is heating, bring water to a boil and cook the
pasta. Cook the tomatoes and eggplant while you deep-fry the sole.

> 1½ quarts safflower oil
> extra-virgin olive oil for skillet
> 1 large eggplant, unpeeled, cut into thinly sliced rounds
> pinch of salt
> grind of black pepper
> 4 large tomatoes, peeled, seeded, and finely chopped
> 1 tablespoon extra-virgin olive oil
> ¼ cup chopped fresh basil
> 12 ounces dried rigatoni or penne
> ¾ pound thin fresh sole fillets, cut into 4-by-1-inch
>   strips (see Notes)
> all-purpose flour
> pinch of salt
> grind of black pepper
> dried thyme
> ½ cup freshly grated Romano or Reggiano Parmagi-
>   ano

Begin to slowly heat the safflower oil for deep-frying the sole to 375°.

Brush a nonstick skillet with a small amount of olive oil, heat until
almost smoking, and quickly brown on both sides as many eggplant
slices as will fit in. Then cover to steam 1 minute. Remove and continue
until all eggplant is browned and soft. Slice the eggplant rounds into
thin 4-inch strips. Season with salt and pepper.

In a 1½-quart saucepan, cook the tomatoes in the tablespoon of
oil with 2 tablespoons of the chopped basil for 3 to 5 minutes.

Cook the pasta according to the directions on the package. While
the pasta is cooking, dip the sole pieces into flour seasoned with salt,
pepper, and thyme, and deep-fry in hot oil only a minute or two, until
fish is browned. Cook fish in two or more batches so as not to lower
the temperature of the oil. Remove to drain on paper towels.

Drain the rigatoni and toss with the cooked tomatoes, eggplant strips,
and the remaining basil. Place sole on top; sprinkle with cheese.

NOTES: This is also good with flounder, sea trout, smelts, cod, whiting, grouper, or catfish fillets.

Browning eggplant slices quickly in a very small amount of oil, then steaming it, is an excellent and healthful technique for cooking this vegetable.

MENU: Rigatoni with eggplant, tomatoes, and sole / *Mushrooms à la Grecque / Warm apple cake

SUGGESTED WINES: Soave / Sauvignon Blanc / Mâcon Blanc

Broiled Bluefish with Chipotle Aioli

SERVES 2 TO 4

This is a happy marriage of East Coast fish with West Coast flavor.

> 1 tablespoon virgin olive oil
> 2 tablespoons fresh-squeezed lime juice
> ½ tablespoon chopped fresh cilantro or Italian parsley
> ¼ teaspoon cayenne pepper
> 1¼ pounds fresh bluefish fillets (see Note)
> 1 recipe Chipotle Aioli, page 225

Combine the oil, lime juice, cilantro, and cayenne pepper, pour over the fillets, and marinate 30 minutes.

Remove the fish from the marinade, broil 4 inches from flame about 8 to 9 minutes per inch of thickness.

Serve immediately with Chipotle Aioli.

NOTE: Mackerel, trout, whitefish, sheepshead, mahimahi, mullet, redfish, red snapper, black sea bass, butterfish, and sablefish may be substituted for the bluefish.

MENU: Broiled bluefish with chipotle aioli / *Couscous / Sauté of red, green, and yellow peppers / Fresh ripe red pears and Roquefort cheese

SUGGESTED WINE: White Hermitage

Snapper Mexican Style with Sautéed Garlic and Lime

SERVES 2

Rick Bayless, a talented young chef and teacher, prepared this classic Mexican dish for me on a recent visit to Texas. He served it with thinly sliced green cabbage lightly dressed with a simple vinaigrette. An odd pairing, I thought at the time, but it was delicious.

>6 large cloves garlic, cut into medium-sized slivers
>2 tablespoons virgin olive oil
>¾ to 1 pound red snapper fillets, ¾ inch thick (see
>   Note)
>⅓ cup all-purpose flour
>pinch of salt
>grind of black pepper
>lime wedges

Heat the olive oil in a 9-inch skillet, add the garlic slivers, and cook very slowly and gently over low heat until the garlic is golden. If the garlic browns, it will taste very bitter. Remove the garlic when done and hold.

Lightly dust the fillets in flour seasoned with salt and pepper. Put fish in the hot oil and sauté over medium-high heat for 10 minutes per inch of thickness, or about 5 minutes on each side if 1 inch thick. Return the garlic to the pan at the last minute to reheat. Taste for seasoning and serve hot with lime wedges.

NOTE: Redfish, drum, sea trout, rockfish, sheepshead, grouper, halibut, porgy, or catfish can be used in place of the red snapper.

MENU: Snapper Mexican style with sautéed garlic and lime / Shredded cabbage salad vinaigrette / Fresh strawberries in orange juice and Cointreau / Cinnamon cookies

SUGGESTED BEVERAGE: Mexican beer

Fish Fillets with Orange, Red Onion, and Fennel

SERVES 2

The appeal of this unusual combination of colorful ingredients is its sharp, clean, fresh taste. It is fat- and dairy-free, and takes very little time and effort to prepare.

> 1 pound red snapper fillets, ½ to ¾ inch thick (see Note)
> 1 teaspoon virgin olive oil
> pinch of salt
> freshly ground black pepper
> 1½ tablespoons Pernod (see Note)
> 1 navel orange, peeled and sliced, each slice cut into quarters
> 1 large fennel bulb, rinsed and finely chopped
> 1 large red onion, halved root end to stem end and very thinly sliced
> ⅓ cup fresh fennel greens, rinsed and finely chopped

Slice the fish into two or four equal pieces and place in a small oiled baking dish. Season with salt and pepper, and sprinkle with Pernod.

Mix together the orange, fennel, and onion, and scatter evenly over the fillets.

Bake in a 400° oven for about 15 minutes or 10 minutes per inch of thickness including the vegetables. Test with fork to determine when the fish is opaque, milky white, and cooked through.

Serve immediately on warmed plates.

NOTE: Redfish, striped bass, halibut, grouper, rockfish, drum, porgy, lingcod, bluefish, or monkfish can be substituted for the red snapper.

Pernod, the anise-flavored aperitif much appreciated in Provence, reinforces the flavor of fennel. Use lime juice if Pernod is not available, although the flavor will be different.

MENU: Fish fillets with orange, red onion, and fennel / Wild and white rice with pecans / Spinach and avocado salad / Cold lemon mousse

SUGGESTED WINES: Chardonnay / Chablis / Pinot Grigio

Sole with Eggplant

SERVES 2 TO 4

This wonderful combination was adapted from a recipe for Sole à la Provençale in Alan Davidson's excellent *Mediterranean Seafood*. A perfect summer fish dish, easy to prepare, colorful, and fresh-tasting, this recipe is especially appropriate for thin fillets that are delicate in flavor and texture, like flounder or any of the soles.

> 1 pound sole fillets (lemon, rex, or petrale sole, or flounder), no thicker than ½ inch (see Note)
> ¼ cup extra-virgin olive oil
> 1 medium eggplant, peeled and sliced ¼ inch thick
> ¼ cup all-purpose flour
> 1 teaspoon dried basil
> pinch of salt
> grind of black pepper
> 2 tablespoons unsalted butter
> 4 large tomatoes, peeled, seeded, finely chopped, and drained
> 4 tablespoons chopped fresh basil
> ¼ teaspoon salt
> a few grindings of white pepper
> ¼ teaspoon dried thyme

Wipe the fillets with a damp cloth and set aside.

Heat 1 tablespoon of the olive oil over high heat in a nonstick skillet until very hot. Quickly dip both sides of the eggplant slices in the heated oil to coat, let brown lightly, turn, cover, and steam until soft, about 1 minute on each side. Cook in several batches, using more oil if necessary. Remove, season with salt and pepper, and keep in a warm (200°) oven.

Heat 1 more tablespoon of oil and continue cooking the remaining eggplant slices.

¶ The recipe can be prepared up to this point and held at room temperature for several hours.

Season the flour with the dried basil, salt, and pepper. Lightly flour the fish fillets, then shake gently to remove excess flour. Heat another tablespoon of oil in the same skillet. Add the fish and cook over medium-high heat 1 to 2 minutes on each side.

In a warmed, oiled baking or gratin dish, alternate layers of fillets and eggplant slices. Keep warm in the oven.

Melt the butter in a saucepan. Add tomatoes, fresh basil, salt, white pepper, and thyme. Cook over high heat until the tomatoes are heated through, then pour over the fish and eggplant.

Serve immediately.

NOTE: Other delicate-flavored white fish like cod, sea trout, redfish, red snapper, or striped bass could be used, as long as the fillets are thin.

MENU: Sole with eggplant / Marinated green beans with shallots and herbs / Lemon ice cream and pine nut cookies

SUGGESTED WINES: Sauvignon Blanc / Muscadet / Pinot Grigio

Steamed Halibut Wrapped in Swiss Chard

SERVES 2

Plain and simple, this flavorful dish makes a healthful and quick main course.

¾ pound fresh halibut, cut into 2 pieces, or 2 steaks
    (see Note)
pinch of salt
grind of white or black pepper
1 tablespoon unsalted sweet butter
½ teaspoon grated lemon rind
⅓ pound green or red Swiss chard, white rib removed,
    blanched 1 minute

Season the halibut with salt and pepper, dot with butter, sprinkle with lemon rind, and wrap with blanched leaves of Swiss chard.

Place on a steamer rack above 3 inches of boiling salted water, cover tightly, and steam about 8 to 10 minutes per inch of thickness. Remove to a heated platter and serve immediately.

NOTE: Rockfish, red snapper, or redfish fillets may be substituted for the halibut.

MENU: Steamed halibut wrapped in Swiss chard / *Potato soufflé / *Tomatoes à la Provençale / Mocha cake

SUGGESTED WINES: Sauvignon Blanc / Vouvray / Soave

Piccata of Mako Shark with Capers and Lemon

SERVES 2

A five-minute dish. Mako shark has a wonderfully delicate flavor and texture, and is excellent thinly sliced and prepared like veal scallopini. The Grand Central Station Oyster Bar in New York serves this delightful dish when mako shark is in season.

> 1 tablespoon virgin olive oil or unsalted sweet butter
> ¾ pound thin (¼-to-⅜-inch) slices of shark fillet (see Note)
> 1 small lemon, peeled and sliced, each slice cut into 8 to 12 pieces
> ⅛ teaspoon salt
> ⅛ teaspoon freshly ground white pepper
> 1½ teaspoons capers, well rinsed and dried
> 2 tablespoons finely chopped Italian parsley

Heat the olive oil in a skillet, add the shark fillets, and cook over medium-high heat only about 1 minute or a little less on each side. Remove to a heated platter.

Add the lemon pieces, salt, pepper, and capers to the skillet, and when hot, pour over the sautéed shark. Sprinkle with parsley and serve immediately.

NOTE: This recipe is excellent with many other lean, moderately fatty, and fatty fish. It works best with thinner fillets. Try it with: sole, flounder, orange roughy, catfish, salmon, trout, tuna, bluefish, red snapper, tilefish, porgy, ocean perch, rockfish, amberjack, and mahimahi.

MENU: Piccata of mako shark with capers and lemon / *Baked Ratatouille / Orange ice cream with bitter chocolate sauce and thin walnut cookies

SUGGESTED WINES: Chardonnay / Mâcon Blanc / Frascati

Braised Scrod with Leeks, Potatoes, Thyme, and Cream

SERVES 4

This is rather like a stew. It has a homey, satisfying quality with its simple, clear flavors.

4 leeks, carefully rinsed, trimmed, and thinly sliced
2 tablespoons unsalted sweet butter
1½ cups light cream
½ cup chicken broth
½ teaspoon dried thyme, or 2 tablespoons fresh thyme leaves
⅓ cup chopped fresh Italian parsley
¼ teaspoon salt
¼ teaspoon freshly ground white pepper
1½ pounds new potatoes, parboiled,† drained, and halved if large
1½ pounds fresh scrod fillets, cut into 1½-inch chunks (see Note)

Gently cook the leeks in the butter in a 4-quart heavy-bottomed casserole until the leeks are soft. Add the light cream, chicken broth, herbs, and seasonings, and simmer 10 minutes uncovered.

Add the potatoes, cook 5 more minutes, then add the pieces of scrod and stir so that the scrod is covered with the hot sauce. Cover and simmer gently 8 to 10 minutes or until scrod is cooked.

Place in a heated tureen and serve in large soup plates.

NOTE: Cod, haddock, pollock, hake, halibut, or catfish may be used in place of the scrod.

MENU: Braised scrod with leeks, potatoes, thyme, and cream / Toasted French bread / Fresh spinach and mushroom salad / Fresh blueberries with nutmeg and cream

SUGGESTED WINE: Chardonnay

† Cooked in boiling, salted water for 10 minutes.

Flounder in Tomato-Mushroom Sauce

SERVES 2

This is a quickly made, rather delicate sauce which goes very well with many fine-flavored fish fillets.

1 teaspoon unsalted sweet butter
1 medium leek, white and pale green stalk only, well
    rinsed, trimmed, and thinly sliced
1 large shallot, finely chopped
1 scallion, thinly sliced
½ pound fresh mushrooms, chopped
1 tomato, seeded and finely chopped
1 tablespoon chopped fresh parsley
1 tablespoon fresh thyme, leaves only, or 1 teaspoon
    dried thyme
½ teaspoon dried marjoram
2 tablespoons water
¾ cup light cream or crème fraîche (page 227)
¾ pound flounder or sole fillets, ½ to 1 inch thick, cut
    into 1½-inch strips (see Note)
pinch of salt
grind of white pepper
1 tablespoon chopped fresh parsley, for garnish

Place butter, leek, shallot, scallion, mushrooms, tomato, and herbs in a 9-to-10-inch skillet. Add water, and cook gently 5 to 8 minutes until vegetables are soft and liquid has evaporated.

¶ The recipe can be prepared ahead to this point and held overnight. Reheat to use.

Add cream to the skillet and bring to a very gentle simmer. Season the fish with salt and pepper. Place fish in the skillet. Spoon the sauce over the fish and cook 5 to 8 minutes, turning once. When the centers of the fish pieces are milky white, the fish is done. Remove fish to a heated platter, garnish with parsley, and serve.

NOTE: Redfish, red snapper, striped bass, rockfish, porgy, cod, halibut, salmon, trout, sole, shrimp, scallops, and oysters are also good prepared this way.

MENU: Flounder in tomato-mushroom sauce / *Champagne risotto / Fresh watercress and mushroom salad / Lemon sorbet and madeleines

SUGGESTED WINES: Chardonnay / Mâcon Blanc / Pinot Grigio

Baked Mackerel in Mustard-Scallion Sauce

SERVES 2

Mackerel, most often grilled or poached, is excellent baked. This distinctive mustard sauce perfectly complements its rich flavor.

2½ to 2¾ pounds fresh whole mackerel, head on or
     pan-dressed (see Note)
½ lemon
½ teaspoon freshly ground black pepper
½ cup crème fraîche (page 227)
2 tablespoons Moutarde de Meaux, or any other grainy
     French or Creole mustard
2 teaspoons lemon juice
4 scallions, finely chopped, including green tops
salt if desired

Score the whole mackerel on both sides, making two or three large X's ½ inch deep with a small sharp knife. Squeeze the lemon over the fish. Combine and stir the remaining ingredients. Cover the mackerel with all the sauce and marinate ½ hour. Turn once so the cuts in the mackerel are well coated with sauce.

Place mackerel in a small, buttered oval baking dish and bake at 375° 10 minutes per inch of thickness or until flesh is opaque. Serve from the baking dish.

NOTE: The mackerel can be grilled instead of baked; reserve part of the sauce to serve with the grilled fish, if desired.

Whole small bluefish, whitefish, mullet, trout, or coho salmon or mahimahi fillets may be substituted for the mackerel.

MENU: Baked mackerel in mustard-scallion sauce / Potato pancakes / Fresh spinach salad with goat cheese and balsamic vinaigrette / Rhubarb pie

SUGGESTED WINES: Mâcon Blanc / California Chardonnay

Sautéed Catfish
with Two Texas Butters

SERVES 12

These two butters go very well with the sweet flavor of catfish. Or use just one of them to simplify the preparation.

> 12 boned, skinned catfish fillets, about ½ pound each
> (see Note)
> 1½ quarts buttermilk
> 2 teaspoons freshly ground black pepper
> 6 tablespoons unsalted sweet butter for sautéeing
>
> **Pecan-Cayenne Butter**
> ½ cup whole pecans
> ⅛ teaspoon cayenne pepper
> 1 stick unsalted sweet butter
> ¼ teaspoon salt
>
> **Jalapeno-Cumin Butter**
> 1 tablespoon ground cumin
> 1 tablespoon fresh jalapeno chile, seeded and finely
> minced
> 1 stick unsalted sweet butter
> ¼ teaspoon salt

Marinate the catfish in buttermilk seasoned with black pepper for 2 to 24 hours. Drain and pat dry before sautéeing.

Prepare the butters:

For Pecan-Cayenne Butter, heat pecans in a skillet over medium-low heat, but do not brown (this can also be done in 350° oven for 7 to 10 minutes). Add the pepper to hot pecans and finely chop in a blender or food processor. Beat the butter in a mixer or blend in a food processor until soft and add all other ingredients. Hold.

For Jalapeno-Cumin Butter, heat the cumin in a small dry skillet until you smell an aroma. Combine all ingredients in a mixer. Hold.

¶ The recipe can be prepared ahead to this point and held overnight in the refrigerator.

Divide the plain butter equally in three 10-inch skillets and melt over high heat. Place the fillets in the foaming butter, lower heat to medium-high and sauté until lightly browned and cooked through—about 4 to 5 minutes on each side, or 10 minutes for each inch of thickness.

Melt each flavored butter in a small saucepan until hot. For best flavor pour each butter over opposite ends of the hot catfish fillet, so each serving is flavored with both of the butters.

Serve catfish on a heated platter.

NOTE: The catfish can also be oven-fried (see page 52). Whitefish, sea trout, and mullet may be used in place of the catfish.

MENU: Sautéed catfish with two Texas butters / *Scalloped potatoes with garlic and cream / Shredded red cabbage salad with vinaigrette / Peach pie

SUGGESTED BEVERAGE: Dark beer

Milk-Poached Halibut with Parsley Butter

SERVES 4 TO 6

Milk interacts in an interesting way with fish—it removes any odor and freshens and enriches the taste of mild-flavored fish. Like Mom's chicken soup, this is a homey, delicious recipe to make on a wintry evening.

> 1 recipe Milk Court Bouillon (page 201)
> 1½ pounds halibut fillets or steaks, 1 inch thick (see Note)
> 3 tablespoons parsley butter (page 214)

Prepare milk court bouillon, bring to a simmer, and place fillets carefully in liquid. Poach fish 10 minutes per inch of thickness. Test for doneness with the tip of a small knife. Remove to a heated platter when done and top with Parsley Butter.

NOTE: Cod, haddock, scrod, or hake fillets may be substituted for the halibut.

MENU: Milk-poached halibut with parsley butter / *Glazed carrots / *Spinach Bresse-style / Navel orange slices

SUGGESTED WINES: Mâcon Blanc / Soave

Grilled Tuna
with Salsa Verde

SERVES 4

The versatile Italian Salsa Verde, a thick parsley-, anchovy-, and lemon-flavored cold sauce, can be served with hot or cold fish dishes, cold roast beef or pork, or hot or cold poached chicken. I find it especially good with asparagus and steamed new potatoes.

Salsa Verde
1 cup packed fresh stemmed Italian parsley
1 large clove garlic, crushed
2 tablespoons coarsely chopped scallions
½ cup chopped fresh basil or, if unavailable, 1 tea-
    spoon dried basil
1 scant tablespoon anchovy paste
1 large hard-cooked egg, chopped
3½ tablespoons fresh lemon juice
¼ teaspoon freshly ground black pepper
salt
⅓ cup plus 2 tablespoons extra-virgin olive oil
1⅔ pounds tuna, cut about 1 inch thick (see Note)
1 to 2 tablespoons extra-virgin olive oil

Combine all the ingredients for Salsa Verde except the oil in a food processor. Gradually add the oil, a teaspoon at a time, and process until the sauce thickens, then add the remaining oil in a steady stream until it is all absorbed. The sauce should have the consistency of thick mayonnaise. Let stand 10 minutes before using.

¶ The sauce can be prepared 6 to 8 hours ahead and refrigerated. Serve at room temperature.

Cook the tuna outdoors over hot coals or on a heated indoor griddle-grill. Brush either grill lightly with oil, brush fish on both sides with oil, and grill 3 to 5 minutes on each side if 1 inch thick.
Serve fish with Salsa Verde on the side.
NOTE: Swordfish or salmon steaks, fillets of shark, redfish, red snapper, halibut, grouper, porgy, or rockfish can be substituted.

MENU: Grilled tuna with salsa verde / *Orzo with feta and tomatoes / Fresh blueberry-nectarine tart

SUGGESTED WINES: Sauvignon Blanc / Mâcon Blanc / Frascati

Shellfish Entrées

Shellfish lend themselves to distinctive seasonings such as ginger, garlic, sesame oil, and hot pepper—items which can easily be kept on hand. And since shrimp and scallops are almost always available, many of the following recipes using these shellfish are perfect choices for last-minute meals for family or entertaining. Shellfish cook quickly because of their small size, so if time is of the essence, the recipes in this section will be especially useful.

Scallops en Papillote with Carrots and Lime-Ginger Butter

SERVES 2

Freddy Girardet, the great Swiss chef, was one of the first to use this intriguing combination of ginger and lime with fish.

> ***Lime-Ginger Butter***
> 2½ to 3 tablespoons peeled and finely grated fresh ginger
> 2 large shallots, minced
> 1½ tablespoons fresh lime juice
> ¼ teaspoon salt
> ½ cup unsalted sweet butter
>
> 2 15-by-15-inch sheets cooking parchment or, if not available, lightweight foil
> ¾ pound sea or bay scallops, quickly rinsed and well cleaned of sand (see Note)
> 3 medium carrots, peeled and thinly sliced on the diagonal
> 2 tablespoons fresh chives that have been cut into 2-inch pieces on a diagonal, or chopped fresh parsley

Make Lime-Ginger Butter: Finely chop the ginger and shallots in a food processor. Add lime juice, salt, and butter, in small pieces. Process until well mixed. The recipe makes about 10 tablespoons, but for this dish, you need only 2 to 3 tablespoons. Wrap, label, and freeze the remaining butter.

Fold each piece of parchment and cut a large half-heart shape, starting and ending at the fold. Open the parchment and lightly butter the center of one side. Place half of the scallops on the buttered side of the papillote, add carrots, and dot with 1 tablespoon of Lime-Ginger Butter. Sprinkle with chives or parsley.

Fold the parchment over the scallops, leaving 1 or 2 inches between the crimped edge and the scallops. Starting at the top of the heart, crimp and firmly fold the cut edges to the inside so that no cut edge is exposed (which would allow steam to escape).

Arrange the papillotes on a baking sheet so they do not overlap. Place in a 450° oven for 6 minutes. When done, the parchment will be puffed out and lightly browned.

To serve, take scissors and cut a large X in the top of the parchment, or remove the parchment and slide the scallops onto heated plates.

NOTE: Fillets of sole, flounder, striped bass, redfish, halibut, red snapper, drum, or porgy, cut on the diagonal into 2-inch pieces and no thicker than 1 inch, could be used in place of scallops.

MENU: Scallops en papillote with carrots and lime-ginger butter / *Wild rice with scallions / Cold chocolate soufflé

SUGGESTED WINE: Sauvignon Blanc

Steamed Mussels with Orange

SERVES 4 TO 6

This variation on moules marinière has a wonderful subtle flavor.

    3 tablespoons unsalted sweet butter
    ¼ cup finely chopped scallions
    ¼ cup minced shallots
    1 red bell pepper, finely chopped
    ½ teaspoon dried thyme, or 2 teaspoons fresh thyme
    ¼ teaspoon dried basil
    2 teaspoons finely grated orange rind
    1⅓ cups dry white wine
    ½ cup water
    5 to 6 dozen fresh mussels, scrubbed and debearded,
        left in the shell
    ⅓ cup minced Italian parsley

Melt the butter in the bottom of a large stockpot or casserole. Gently cook the onions until soft, add all the remaining ingredients except the mussels and bring to a boil. Add the mussels, cover the pot, and cook over medium-high heat until the mussels open, about 3 to 5 minutes. Discard any mussels that have not opened. Remove mussels to a large heated bowl or platter, add hot broth and vegetables, sprinkle with parsley, and serve immediately.

MENU: Steamed mussels with orange / *Green beans with shallots / *Olive salad / Orange sorbet with almond cookies

SUGGESTED WINE: Mâcon Blanc

Brazilian Sautéed Shrimp with Coconut Milk, Peanuts, and Chiles

SERVES 4

This dish is a cousin to the great Bahiian dish, *vatapa*. The combination of coconut, peanuts, and chiles is also good with chicken.

4 tablespoons safflower oil
2 leeks, well rinsed and thinly sliced
2 scallions, chopped
1 yellow onion, chopped
1 red pepper, finely chopped
3 large ripe tomatoes, roasted (page 16), peeled, seeded,
 and chopped
¼ cup unsalted roasted peanuts
¾ cup chicken broth
1 cup coconut milk
6 serrano chiles, seeded and minced
1⅓ pounds medium shrimp, peeled
½ teaspoon paprika
⅛ teaspoon cayenne pepper
¼ teaspoon freshly ground black pepper
½ teaspoon salt
⅓ cup unsalted roasted peanuts, chopped, for garnish
2 tablespoons chopped fresh cilantro, for garnish
2 tablespoons chopped fresh parsley, for garnish

Heat 3 tablespoons of the oil in a large skillet, add the leeks, onions, and red pepper, and cook about 10 minutes over medium heat. Add tomatoes and cook another 5 minutes.

Take a third of the vegetable mixture and puree it with ¼ cup of the peanuts and all of the broth. Pour this into the skillet, add coconut milk, and continue to cook over medium heat, letting the sauce thicken a little, about 10 minutes.

¶ The recipe can be prepared a day ahead to this point, refrigerated, and reheated to use.

Meanwhile, gently cook the serrano chiles 2 to 3 minutes in a separate skillet in the remaining oil. Add the shrimp and all the seasonings to the serranos and sauté, stirring over medium-high heat until the shrimp are curled, 1 to 2 minutes.

Add the shrimp and chiles to the sauce and simmer to heat through. Garnish with the peanuts and herbs, and serve immediately.

MENU: Brazilian sautéed shrimp with coconut milk, peanuts, and chiles / Hot rice with cilantro / Hearts of palm and red pepper in vinaigrette / Cold lime mousse

SUGGESTED BEVERAGES: Lager beer / Sauvignon Blanc

Quick Scallop Sauté with Herbed Crumbs and Orange Wedges

SERVES 2

One of the simplest but tastiest ways to prepare scallops. Orange, bread crumbs, and herbs give a fine flavor and texture to the scallops.

¾ pound sea or bay scallops, lightly rinsed and cleaned
  of sand, and cut in half if very large
1 cup fine fresh or dried white bread crumbs mixed
  with ½ teaspoon each dried or fresh basil, thyme,
  chives, and marjoram and 1 tablespoon finely
  minced orange rind
½ teaspoon salt
¼ teaspoon freshly ground white pepper
2 tablespoons unsalted sweet butter
2 tablespoons virgin olive oil
2 tablespoons chopped fresh parsley, for garnish
8 peeled and sectioned orange wedges

Toss the scallops with herbed crumbs seasoned with salt and pepper just before cooking.

Heat the butter and oil in a skillet, add the scallops, and cook over medium-high heat until scallops and crumbs are golden on both sides, 5 to 7 minutes.

Garnish with parsley and serve with orange wedges.

MENU: *Watercress soup / Quick scallop sauté with herbed crumbs and orange wedges / *Marinated corn salad / Strawberry ice cream with raspberry sauce

SUGGESTED WINES: Sauvignon Blanc / Graves / Soave

Shrimp à la Provençale with Persillade

SERVES 8

This is a traditional dish from Provence originally made with crayfish. The "persillade" mixture—lots of finely chopped fresh parsley mixed with minced garlic—is an excellent and flavorful garnish for many other fish dishes: the garlic and parsley give off a wonderful aroma when added to a piping hot dish. The egg yolks could be omitted, but they give richness to the mixture of mushrooms, shallots, tomatoes, parsley, and garlic.

> 4 tablespoons extra-virgin olive oil
> 4 tablespoons unsalted sweet butter
> ¾ pound mushrooms, finely chopped
> 12 shallots, finely chopped
> 8 large tomatoes, peeled, seeded, and finely chopped
> 8 large cloves garlic, mashed to a paste with a fork
> 1 teaspoon salt
> ½ teaspoon freshly ground black pepper
> 2 teaspoons dried thyme
> 2 teaspoons dried oregano
> 2 pounds medium or large shrimp, peeled, with tails left on (see Note)
> 4 tablespoons brandy
> 1 cup dry white wine
> 4 large egg yolks, beaten, at room temperature
> 1 cup finely chopped fresh parsley

Heat 2 tablespoons of the olive oil and 2 tablespoons of the butter in a large sauté pan. Add the mushrooms, shallots, tomatoes, half of the garlic, salt, pepper, thyme, and oregano. Sauté over medium heat for 6 to 8 minutes. Taste for seasoning.

¶ The recipe can be prepared a day ahead to this point. Chill and reheat to use.

Heat the remaining 2 tablespoons of olive oil and 2 tablespoons of butter in another sauté pan. Add the shrimp, and cook over medium-to-high heat for 2 minutes only, until shrimp are curled.

Flame the brandy by cooking over high heat in a very small sauce-pan—when hot enough, the alcohol flames by itself—then pour the flaming brandy over the shrimp. Be certain your exhaust fan is not on when you flame the brandy. Shake the pan and when the flame dies, remove the shrimp and keep warm.

Add the wine to the pan, and simmer over high heat about 5 minutes to let the alcohol fumes evaporate and to concentrate the flavors of pan juices.

Then add this wine mixture to the mushroom mixture and cook over high heat about 5 to 6 minutes or until the mixture thickens.

Whisk the egg yolks in a small bowl, and slowly add, a tablespoon at a time, 6 to 8 tablespoons of the hot mushroom sauce to the yolks. Then slowly stir the egg yolk mixture into the remaining hot sauce. Add the shrimp to the sauce and stir, but do not heat above a simmer or the eggs will slightly curdle. Taste for seasoning.

Mix together the parsley and the remaining garlic and stir into the dish, leaving ¼ cup of the mixture for garnish.

Pour the hot shrimp and sauce onto a heated serving platter, sprinkle with the remaining persillade, and serve immediately.

NOTE: Crayfish can be used instead of shrimp.

MENU: Shrimp à la Provençale with persillade / Pecan rice / Fennel and orange salad / Cold apricot soufflé with thin chocolate cookies

SUGGESTED WINES: Blanc de Pinot Noir / Tavel Rosé / White Hermitage / Frascati

Hot and Crunchy Shrimp

SERVES 2 TO 4

This recipe was a Friday-night inspiration to satisfy a craving for something hot (spicy) and crunchy. At a roadside fish stand, I found the freshest and tiniest Gulf shrimp I had ever seen—so tiny and so fresh that I sautéed and ate them head, shells, and all. Delicious and nicely crunchy. Everything but the shrimp and cilantro can be kept on hand for this piquant dinner that takes only 10 minutes to prepare.

⅓ cup sesame seeds
4 tablespoons unsalted sweet butter, or 2 tablespoons
      unsalted sweet butter and 2 tablespoons virgin
      olive oil
5 to 6 large cloves garlic, finely mashed to a paste with
      a fork
⅓ cup peeled and finely chopped fresh ginger
¼ to ½ teaspoon dried red pepper flakes
½ teaspoon salt
⅓ cup slivered almonds
1¼ pounds fresh small shrimp, peeled but with tails
      left on
⅓ cup fresh cilantro leaves, for garnish

Toast the sesame seeds over low heat in a dry skillet, stirring constantly until the seeds are golden. Remove from the skillet and hold.

Heat butter/oil in a 9-inch skillet over a medium flame. Add the garlic, ginger, red pepper, salt, and almonds. Cook gently about 2 to 3 minutes, stirring frequently, until the garlic and ginger are soft but not browned.

Add the shrimp and stir for 2 to 4 minutes or until shrimp are pink and curled. Stir in the toasted sesame seeds. If the mixture is too dry, add 1 to 2 more tablespoons butter.

Taste for seasoning and serve immediately on a warmed serving dish garnished with fresh cilantro leaves and accompanied with rice and Major Grey's Mango Chutney.

MENU: Hot and crunchy shrimp / Mango chutney / Hot buttered rice / Cucumbers with cumin in yogurt / Fresh sliced oranges and kiwis

SUGGESTED BEVERAGE: Lager beer

Creamy Mustard Shrimp with Pasta

SERVES 2

Another 10-minute dish whose tart, creamy sauce perfectly accompanies any simply prepared pasta—fettuccine, linguine, angel hair, or the broad papardelle noodles.

1 leek, white only, well rinsed and thinly sliced
1 large shallot, finely chopped
2 tablespoons unsalted sweet butter
¾ to 1 pound medium shrimp, peeled
⅓ cup dry white wine
1 teaspoon dried basil, or 1 tablespoon finely chopped
     fresh basil
½ cup heavy cream or crème fraîche (page 227)
¼ teaspoon salt
¼ teaspoon freshly ground white pepper
2 teaspoons Moutarde de Meaux or other grainy pre-
     pared French mustard
1 tablespoon finely chopped fresh chives, dill, tarragon,
     or Italian parsley

Cook leek and shallot gently in a sauté pan in the butter until soft. Add the shrimp, cook about 2 minutes, stirring, then remove shrimp with a slotted spoon and hold.

Add white wine and basil and cook on high heat 1 to 2 minutes, for the wine to cook down. Add cream, salt, and pepper and cook until sauce is slightly thickened. Add the shrimp and mustard and cook gently to heat through, but do not boil or the mustard will become bitter-tasting.

Sprinkle with fresh herbs and toss, or serve with pasta.

MENU: Creamy mustard shrimp / Fettuccine / Mushroom, endive, and watercress salad / Apricot tart

SUGGESTED WINES: Chenin Blanc / Mâcon Blanc

Hot Scallop Mousse with Roasted Red Pepper Beurre Blanc

SERVES 8

Just a small portion of this creamy, rich, elegant French classic suffices. Jacques Pepin's Mousseline de Coquilles St. Jacques, as I saw him prepare it in a class, is the basis of this version. It can be prepared in individual 4-ounce metal baba or timbale molds or in a 6-cup fish mold.

> 1¼ pounds sea scallops
> 2 cups heavy cream or crème fraîche (page 227)
> 1 teaspoon salt
> ½ teaspoon freshly ground white pepper
> ⅛ teaspoon curry powder
> pinch of cayenne
> pinch of freshly grated nutmeg
> optional: green of leeks, blanched and sliced, or truffle,
>   thinly sliced, or carrot, cooked and thinly cut
> 1 recipe Red Pepper Beurre Blanc (page 224)
> watercress sprigs, for garnish

Clean the scallops carefully to rid them of sand, but try not to keep them under cold running water or you will wash away a lot of flavor.

In a food processor or blender, place scallops, ½ cup of the cream, and the salt, white pepper, curry powder, cayenne, and nutmeg, and puree.

Butter eight baba or timbale molds or one fish mold. Decorate the bottoms of the molds with diamond or crescent-moon shapes cut out of the blanched green leeks, truffle slices, or cooked carrots.

Beat the remaining cream until soft peaks form. Fold cream gently into the scallop puree, and taste for seasoning. Spoon into the molds, ¾ full, and top with small pieces of buttered waxed paper.

¶ Recipe can be prepared ahead an hour or so at this point. Keep in a cool place.

Place the molds in a baking dish and add simmering water to come halfway up the height of the molds.

Bake in a preheated 375° oven for 25 minutes. Remove from oven and let stand 10 minutes before unmolding. Place each mold upside down in a strainer to drain off excess liquid from molds. To unmold, turn out on individual plates or a platter.

Serve hot with roasted red pepper beurre blanc sauce spooned on top and garnished with watercress sprigs.

NOTES: For a very elegant variation, spoon some of the mousse into the bottom third of a mold, layer with a very thin slice of fresh raw salmon, continue alternating until the mold is full. Bake as directed above.

MENU: Hot scallop mousse with red pepper beurre blanc / *Braised artichokes / Radicchio and endive salad / Plum tart

SUGGESTED WINES: Chardonnay / Chablis / Muscadet / Champagne

Grilled Shrimp in Spicy Malaysian Coconut Sauce

SERVES 4 AS A MAIN COURSE, OR 6 AS AN HORS D'OEUVRE

This is a wonderful outdoor summer meal. The combination of flavors—coconut, chiles, peanuts, and lime—is very common in Brazilian cuisine. This recipe is appropriate for large shrimp, or prawns as they are often called. Rock shrimp, available on the Gulf Coast, are a fatter variety of medium to large shrimp with a hard gray-green shell and a distinctive lobster-like flavor.

> 1 tablespoon peanut oil
> 1 clove garlic, mashed
> 2 large scallions, chopped
> 1 stalk fresh or frozen lemon grass, finely chopped, or
>   if not available, use ½ tablespoon lemon juice
>   and ½ tablespoon lime juice
> 1 teaspoon minced serrano or jalapeno chiles, or ½
>   teaspoon cayenne pepper
> ¾ teaspoon salt
> ½ cup roasted unsalted peanuts, ground medium-fine
> ¾ cup coconut milk
> 1 tablespoon fresh lime juice
> ¼ cup minced fresh cilantro
> 1 pound large shrimp, rock shrimp, or prawns, peeled,
>   with tails left on

Heat peanut oil in a skillet and gently cook the garlic, lemon grass, and serranos until soft, about 2 minutes.

Add all the other ingredients except the shrimp and simmer 5 to 8 minutes to blend the flavors.

Cool to room temperature, mix well with the shrimp and marinate 1 to 2 hours in the refrigerator. Soak wooden skewers in water. Take the shrimp out of the marinade, skewer lengthwise through the back of the shrimp (allowing three to four shrimp per skewer) and grill over hot coals until cooked through, about 5 to 6 minutes on each side. Simmer marinade 5 minutes and serve as a sauce with the shrimp.

MENU: Grilled shrimp in spicy Malaysian coconut sauce / Fried rice with vegetables (carrots, onions, and bean sprouts) / Fresh mango tart

SUGGESTED BEVERAGE: Thai beer

New Orleans Barbecued Shrimp

SERVES 4

The ingredients in this recipe are similar to a recipe in the *The New Orleans Cookbook* by Rima and Richard Collin, but the technique and proportions are mine. Despite the name, barbecued shrimp is neither grilled nor barbecued, but it is good! In New Orleans, the shrimp is cooked in the shell, which makes peeling and eating with the sauce a messy but pleasurable experience. Have plenty of crusty French bread to sop up the sauce—you won't want to leave any.

    6 tablespoons unsalted sweet butter
    ¼ cup virgin olive oil
    8 scallions including green part, finely chopped
    3 large cloves garlic, mashed to a paste with a fork
    1 teaspoon dried rosemary, crushed
    1 teaspoon dried oregano
    1½ teaspoons dried basil
    2 imported bay leaves, crumbled
    ¾ teaspoon cayenne pepper
    ¾ teaspoon paprika
    ½ teaspoon freshly ground black pepper
    2 teaspoons fresh lemon juice
    1½ pounds medium shrimp, peeled, with tails left on
        (if larger shrimp are used, they should be butter-
        flied†)

Heat the butter and olive oil in a 10-inch skillet, add all the other ingredients except the shrimp, and cook gently 5 to 6 minutes.

Add the shrimp to the sauce and cook until the shrimp are curled, not more than 4 to 5 minutes.

Serve immediately, with bread to mop up the spicy sauce.

NOTE: If fresh herbs are available, chop and use twice the amount listed for the dried.

MENU: New Orleans barbecued shrimp / Crusty baguettes halved and warmed in oven / Avocado halves with chopped celery and Creole mustard vinaigrette / Cold rice pudding with brandy-flavored whipped cream

SUGGESTED BEVERAGE: Louisiana beer

† To butterfly shrimp, take a small sharp knife and cut the shelled shrimp down the middle of the back almost all the way through. Using your hand, a meat pounder, or the flat side of a cleaver, flatten the shrimp.

Stir-Fried Crab with Fried Noodles, Ginger, and Sesame Oil

SERVES 2

These pungent Oriental flavors are especially satisfying on a cold winter night. This colorful dish is very quick and easy to prepare.

> 2 tablespoons plus ⅓ cup peanut oil (if unavailable, use safflower or corn oil)
> 4 large scallions with green tops, thinly sliced on diagonal
> 2 leeks, white only, well rinsed and thinly sliced
> 3 small carrots, peeled and thinly sliced on diagonal
> ¼ cup peeled and minced fresh ginger
> 2 large cloves garlic, peeled and mashed to a paste with a fork
> ⅛ to ¼ teaspoon red pepper flakes
> 8 ounces fresh crab meat, lump or back fin (see Note)
> 1 tablespoon rice wine vinegar
> 1 tablespoon soy sauce
> 1½ teaspoons dark sesame oil
> 4 ounces dry vermicelli or angel hair pasta, cooked in boiling water 1 minute, well drained, cut into 2-inch pieces, and patted dry
> ½ cup fresh cilantro leaves for garnish

Heat 2 tablespoons of the peanut oil in a wok or skillet over high heat until almost smoking.

Stir-fry the scallions, leeks, and carrots for about 1 to 2 minutes. Turn the heat down to medium-high.

Add the ginger, garlic, and red pepper to the wok, and cook 1 minute, stirring constantly. Add the crab meat, and stir until hot. Mix together the vinegar, soy sauce, and sesame oil and add to the wok. Heat through.

Heat the remaining ⅓ cup of peanut oil in a 1½-quart saucepan, drop cooked, drained, and separated vermicelli into the oil, and cook for 2 to 3 minutes or until crisp.

Remove the noddles from the oil with a mesh skimmer. Drain the noodles on paper towels, toss to separate, and place in the center of a warmed serving dish. Spoon the hot crab mixture over the noodles, garnish with cilantro, and serve immediately.

NOTE: Cooked lobster, scallops, or shrimp, chopped in small pieces, or fillet of lean fish in small pieces could replace the crab.

MENU: Hot and sour soup / Stir-fried crab with fried noodles, ginger, and sesame oil / Watercress and red pepper salad with rice wine vinaigrette / Lemon sorbet

SUGGESTED BEVERAGES: Dark beer / Gewürtztraminer

Linguine with Garlic, Clams, and Cream à la Watkins

SERVES 4

Pasta has a true affinity for garlic, cream, and clams. This dish makes a perfect impromptu midnight supper, as my friend Sharon Watkins and I, craving garlic and pasta, discovered late one evening. Sharon's use of elephant garlic in this recipe is brilliant.

> 2 tablespoons virgin olive oil
> 3 to 4 large cloves elephant garlic, finely chopped (or
>   about ½ cup) (see Note)
> 1½ cups heavy cream
> 1 pint (about 30) fresh-shucked raw clams, chopped
> ½ teaspoon salt
> ¼ teaspoon freshly ground white pepper
> 1 pound linguine, cooked and drained

Heat the oil in a skillet and, over low heat, gently cook the garlic. Add the cream and cook over medium heat about 7 or 8 minutes or until slightly thickened. Add the clams, salt, and pepper to the sauce and heat through.

When the sauce is piping hot, toss with the cooked linguine and serve immediately.

NOTE: Elephant garlic is mild and delicate in flavor. If you use regular garlic, use only 2 to 3 medium cloves.

MENU: Linguine with garlic, clams, and cream à la Watkins / Hot crusty French bread / Escarole salad / Coffee ice cream and thin chocolate cookies

SUGGESTED WINE: California Chardonnay

Rice with Shrimp, Sausage, and Oysters

SERVES 8 TO 10

An easy and inexpensive dish with a Louisiana flavor for relaxed entertaining. This is my version of a traditional dish called Dirty Rice. I've removed the "dirty" elements by omitting the browned roux and the sautéed chicken livers normally used. Filé powder is a mixture of ground herbs, including sassafrass, that is sold in most grocery stores in the herb section. It originated in Louisiana and is used in gumbos, fish stews, and rice and seafood dishes.

3 tablespoons virgin olive oil or unsalted sweet butter
1 cup chopped yellow onion
1 cup chopped scallions
1 cup chopped celery
1 cup chopped green pepper or green and red mixed
4 large cloves garlic, mashed
1 tablespoon gumbo filé powder
2½ cups long-grain or Texmati rice
8 cups hot chicken broth
1 teaspoon cayenne pepper
½ teaspoon freshly ground black pepper
2 teaspoons salt
1 teaspoon dried thyme
1 pound ring sausage, spicy or plain
1 cup dry white wine
1 imported bay leaf
1 teaspoon dried thyme (additional)
½ teaspoon freshly ground black pepper (additional)
2 parsley sprigs
¾ pound small shrimp, unpeeled (see Note)
16 ounces oysters, fresh-shucked or in a jar, patted
　　dry on a paper towel
½ teaspoon cayenne pepper (additional)
½ teaspoon salt (additional)
4 tablespoons soft unsalted sweet butter
½ cup chopped parsley

Heat the oil or butter in a 3-to-4-quart heavy-bottomed casserole. Gently cook the onions, vegetables, and garlic about 8 to 10 minutes until almost soft. Add the filé powder and the rice, and stir to coat. Cook the rice 2 minutes, then add 5 cups of the hot broth and the cayenne, black pepper, salt, and thyme. Partially cover and simmer 20 minutes or until the rice is fluffy and dry.

While the rice is cooking, simmer the sausage in the remaining 3 cups of broth, with the wine and bay leaf, the additional thyme and black pepper, and the parsley sprigs for about 20 minutes. Remove the sausage and slice into ½-inch pieces. Cover with foil to keep warm.

Cook the shrimp in the shell in simmering water with oysters and the additional cayenne and salt, only 1 to 2 minutes. Remove, cool, shell, and chop the shrimp. Drain the oysters.

Place cooked rice in an attractive baking and serving dish, stir in the butter, parsley, sausage, shrimp, and oysters. Taste for seasoning and bake uncovered about 10 minutes at 350° to blend the flavors and heat through evenly.

NOTE: Crayfish tails may be used in place of shrimp.

MENU: Rice with shrimp, sausage, and oysters / *Green beans with shallots / Lemon cheesecake

SUGGESTED WINES: Sauvignon Blanc / Vouvray

Pasta Primavera with Mussels

SERVES 4 TO 6

A very nice meal for spring, and a colorful mosaic of gleaming fresh vegetables and succulent mussels mixed with green and white pasta.

4 tablespoons unsalted sweet butter
½ cup fresh new peas or snow pea pods
½ cup thinly sliced asparagus
½ cup sliced mushrooms
½ cup thinly sliced tiny carrots
1 cup heavy cream or light cream
4 pounds mussels, scrubbed and debearded
⅓ cup water
⅓ cup dry white wine
2 minced shallots
½ teaspoon salt
¼ cup plus 3 tablespoons minced fresh parsley
1 pound fresh green and white linguine
pinch of salt
grind of white pepper
¾ cup finely grated Italian Parmesan or Asiago cheese

Melt the butter and cook all the vegetables in it until barely tender, 2 to 3 minutes. Add the cream and cook 5 minutes or until the mixture is slightly thickened.

Place mussels in a large stockpot, add the water, wine, shallots, salt, and ¼ cup of the parsley, and bring to a boil. Remove and let cool. Steam the mussels over high heat until they open, 3 to 5 minutes. Remove mussels from the shells and hold.

Strain the juices through a fine mesh strainer. Add ⅓ cup of strained mussel-steaming juice to the vegetable sauce and reduce until thickened.

Cook the pasta according to package directions. While pasta cooks, add the mussels to the vegetable sauce and reheat just a few minutes.

Drain the cooked pasta and toss with the sauce; add salt, pepper, and remaining parsley.

Serve immediately on hot plates; pass grated cheese.

MENU: Pasta primavera with mussels / Watercress salad / Cold zabaglione with strawberries

SUGGESTED WINE: Soave

Indonesian Shrimp

SERVES 2 TO 4

These exotically flavored shrimp are excellent sautéed, broiled, or grilled over hot coals. The marinade can also be used as a dipping sauce for grilled or deep-fried fish.

Marinade

1½ teaspoons soy sauce (preferably Pearl River mush-
    room soy sauce)
1½ teaspoons fresh lemon juice
1½ teaspoons fresh lime juice
1 tablespoon rice wine vinegar
1 tablespoon water
1 tablespoon peeled and finely chopped fresh ginger
1 teaspoon ground coriander seeds
1 teaspoon ground cumin seeds
1 teaspoon brown sugar
1 large clove garlic, mashed to a paste with a fork
⅛ teaspoon cayenne pepper
1 pound very large shrimp (or, if you live in California,
    Monterey prawns), peeled and deveined, with tails
    left on or butterflied† (see Note)
1 tablespoon peanut oil
2 tablespoons fresh cilantro leaves, for garnish

Combine all the marinade ingredients and set aside while shelling and deveining the shrimp.

Cover the shrimp completely with marinade and refrigerate 2 to 3 hours.

Heat the oil in a heavy skillet until hot. Remove the shrimp from the marinade and sauté until they are curled and cooked through, a total of 3 to 6 minutes only (or broil or grill them for about the same length of time). Garnish with cilantro leaves and serve immediately.

NOTE: Smaller shrimp can also be used.

MENU: Indonesian shrimp / Fried rice / Steamed shredded zucchini in a vinaigrette / Crème caramel with poached pear slices

SUGGESTED BEVERAGES: Gewürztraminer / Dark beer

† See footnote, page 107.

Sautéed Soft-Shelled Crab with Ginger

SERVES 4

Late spring and early summer mark the height of the all-too-short soft-shelled crab season. Take advantage of their availability and fix them simply—dusted in flour and sautéed—or add the following exotic ingredients for a special dish.

½ cup cornstarch or all-purpose flour
½ teaspoon salt
¼ teaspoon cayenne pepper
½ teaspoon freshly ground white pepper
8 soft-shelled crabs, dressed, rinsed, and patted dry (see Note)
4 tablespoons unsalted sweet butter
3 tablespoons safflower or virgin olive oil
2 tablespoons minced fresh ginger
3 large cloves garlic, minced
¼ cup sesame seeds, toasted until golden
1 tablespoon mushroom soy sauce (preferably Pearl River)
1 tablespoon water
2 teaspoons sesame oil
⅓ cup fresh cilantro leaves, for garnish

Combine the cornstarch with the salt, cayenne, and white pepper. Dip the crabs into this mixture. Heat 2 tablespoons of the butter with 1½ tablespoons of the oil in a large skillet and when hot, add the crabs, undersides down, and sauté over medium-high heat 3 to 5 minutes or until browned. Turn and sauté 2 to 3 minutes more. Add more butter and oil if needed. Keep sautéed crabs on a heatproof platter in a warm (300°) oven.

Cook the ginger and garlic in the sauté pan until soft, scraping cooked bits, then add the sesame seed, soy, water, and sesame oil. When very hot, pour sauce over crab, garnish with cilantro, and serve immediately.

NOTE: To prepare soft-shelled crabs for cooking you need to do the following things (or have your fish seller dress them if you plan to cook the crabs soon after purchasing). (1) With a pair of kitchen scissors, cut off the eyes on the front of the head (this, as you might imagine, kills the crab). (2) Lift up the shell above the tail, or apron as it is called, on the underside of the crab and, with the point of a knife, scrape out the spongy-looking gills which are not to be eaten. (3) Cut off the tail or apron close to the body.

MENU: Sautéed soft-shelled crab with ginger / *Couscous with tomatoes and cinnamon / Shredded zucchini salad with rice-wine vinaigrette / Raspberry sorbet

SUGGESTED WINE: Sauvignon Blanc

Pasta with Crayfish

SERVES 4 TO 6

This very elegant dish has the flavors Louisianans use in their crayfish sauces—onions, green peppers, celery, and cayenne, but in a more delicate measure.

Crayfish Sauce
4 tablespoons unsalted sweet butter
2 tablespoons minced shallots
1 red onion, minced
2 tablespoons minced scallions
½ green pepper, diced
1 small rib celery, diced
½ tablespoon all-purpose flour
1 to 1½ cups light or heavy cream
¾ teaspoon salt
¼ teaspoon freshly ground black pepper
¼ teaspoon cayenne pepper
fresh lemon juice
pinch of dried basil
pinch of dried thyme

1 pound fettuccine, linguine, angel hair pasta, or
    papardelle
1 to 2 cups crayfish tails, precooked or raw (see Note)
2 tablespoons unsalted sweet butter
¼ teaspoon freshly ground black pepper
2 tablespoons chopped fresh parsley, for garnish

To make the sauce, melt the butter in a skillet and cook all the vegetables over medium heat until soft. Stir in the flour and cook 3 minutes. Add the cream and cook about 7 or 8 minutes over medium heat until the sauce has slightly thickened. Add the seasonings, lemon juice, and herbs.

¶ The recipe can be made to this point a day ahead, refrigerated, and reheated.

Just before serving, cook the pasta according to package directions.
While the pasta is cooking, reheat the sauce, add the crayfish, and cook 5 minutes for precooked crayfish and 10 minutes for uncooked.
Drain the pasta, toss first with butter and pepper, then with the crayfish sauce. Garnish with parsley and serve immediately.
NOTE: Crab, small shrimp, or scallops can be used in place of the crayfish.

MENU: Pasta with crayfish / Caesar salad / Fresh pears, grapes, apples, and walnuts

SUGGESTED WINES: Sparkling wine / Champagne

Pasta and Crab Meat Feast

SERVES 8 TO 10

This could be a spur-of-the-moment feast since all the ingredients are easy to find and the preparation is minimal. The taste is sensational—deliciously light with the play of flavors of the tomato, crab, and thyme.

> 2 to 2½ pounds green (spinach) fettuccine
> 4 tablespoons unsalted sweet butter
> 8 scallions, finely chopped
> 4 large red ripe tomatoes, peeled, seeded, and finely chopped
> ½ teaspoon salt
> ¼ teaspoon freshly ground white pepper
> ¼ teaspoon dried thyme or 2 teaspoons fresh chopped thyme
> 2 pounds crab meat, lump or back fin
> 1¼ cups heavy or light cream, at room temperature
> 1 large egg yolk
> ⅓ cup chopped Italian parsley

Bring a large pot of salted water to a boil. Add the fettuccine, and prepare the sauce while it is cooking, 5 to 10 minutes.

Melt the butter in a large skillet and gently cook the scallions 4 minutes or until soft. Add the tomatoes and seasonings and heat through.

Add the crab meat and toss to heat through. Add the cream well mixed with the egg yolk and stir, turning up heat. When the mixture is completely hot, stir in the parsley. Serve the sauce on top of a platter of green fettuccine or toss it with the pasta and serve.

MENU: Pasta and crab meat feast / *Zucchini gratin / Crusty sourdough bread / Pears poached in sauterne

SUGGESTED WINES: Chablis or Graves / California Chardonnay / Verdicchio

Grilled Red Pepper Shrimp

SERVES 2 TO 4

Shrimp takes well to all manner of spicy seasonings. For an easy party appetizer, increase the amount of marinade, and marinate and sauté shrimp in large quantities and serve cold.

> *Marinade*
> 2 large cloves garlic, mashed to a paste with a fork
> 1¼ teaspoons salt
> 1 teaspoon cayenne pepper
> 1 teaspoon paprika
> ⅛ to ¼ teaspoon red pepper flakes
> ⅛ teaspoon freshly ground black pepper
> 2 tablespoons fresh lemon or lime juice
> 3 tablespoons extra-virgin olive oil
>
> 1 pound large shrimp, peeled, with tails left on or butterflied† (see Note)

Prepare marinade: Pound the garlic and salt together in a mortar, add the cayenne, paprika, red pepper flakes, and black pepper to the mortar, and mix well. Stir in the lemon juice and slowly whisk in the oil.

Place the peeled shrimp in the marinade and mix well to coat. Let marinate 2 to 3 hours in the refrigerator.

Remove shrimp from the marinade and skewer on 8-inch wooden skewers through the back curve of the shrimp. This will hold it firmly on the skewer. Grill over glowing coals or sauté quickly in a hot skillet. Cook 3 to 6 minutes depending on the size of the shrimp and the heat of the coals or skillet. Shrimp are done when they are curled and firm.

Serve hot or cold.

NOTE: You can substitute crayfish tails or scallops for the shrimp.

MENU: Grilled red pepper shrimp / Red beans and rice / Cucumber and fennel salad / Green chile cornbread / Cold lime soufflé

SUGGESTED BEVERAGE: Dark beer

† See footnote, page 107.

CHAPTER 5

Cold Fish Dishes, Sandwiches, and Salads

Cold fish dishes are particularly practical for entertaining. Many of these recipes are great for lunches or picnics, such as Pan Bagnat; others, like Cold Fish Fillets Marseilles Style, are designed to be main courses, and some make a perfect complete meal salad, such as Saffron Rice and Shrimp Salad or Asparagus, Crab, and Potato Salad. The ingredients can be prepared ahead in almost all of these recipes.

Cold Crab
Wrapped in Lettuce

SERVES 6

Seasoned cooked crab meat wrapped in delicate lettuce leaves and tied with green onion is a healthful, unusual hors d'oeuvre that can also be served as a first course or a light lunch.

Marinade
1½ teaspoons soy sauce (preferably Pearl River mushroom soy)
1½ teaspoons fresh lemon juice
1½ teaspoons fresh lime juice
1 tablespoon rice wine vinegar
1 tablespoon water
1 tablespoon peeled and finely chopped fresh ginger
1 teaspoon ground coriander
1 teaspoon ground cumin
1 teaspoon brown sugar
1 large clove garlic, finely chopped
⅛ teaspoon cayenne pepper

1 pound fresh crab meat, lump or back fin, or pasteurized crab in containers (see Notes)
8 scallions, chopped
¼ cup chopped cilantro (optional)
12 leaves Boston lettuce, washed and dried
12 6-inch-long scallion strips, or 12 long fresh chives

Combine the marinade ingredients in a small bowl. Mix the crab meat, scallions, and cilantro together with 3 tablespoons of marinade.

Place equal amounts of the crab mixture on each lettuce leaf, roll up and tie with scallion strips, and chill until ready to serve. Use the rest of the marinade as a dipping sauce if you wish.

The dish can be held for 2 to 3 hours, covered tightly with plastic wrap. It may also be steamed 10 minutes and served hot.

NOTES: You can mix any delicate cooked, flaked, lean white fish such as catfish, redfish, tilefish, lingcod, scrod, or flounder, or cooked scallops, lobster, or shrimp with the crab.

MENU: Cold crab wrapped in lettuce / Cold Oriental noodles with peanut sauce / Pineapple ice cream

SUGGESTED WINE: Sauvignon Blanc

Salade Niçoise

SERVES 6 TO 8 AS A MAIN COURSE,
OR 10 TO 12 AS PART OF A BUFFET

This whole meal in a salad makes a good cold picnic dish or luncheon or buffet offering. All the separate ingredients can be prepared a day ahead and held to be assembled just before serving. Arrange the ingredients on a large white platter with an eye to attractive contrasts in colors and shapes.

Vinaigrette
¼ cup red wine vinegar
½ teaspoon salt
¼ teaspoon freshly ground black pepper
1½ tablespoons small capers, rinsed and dried
⅔ cup extra-virgin olive oil

Salad
8 small new potatoes, jackets left on, cooked and sliced
    or cut in wedges
½ pound small green beans, cooked
½ large red onion, halved and very thinly sliced
½ pound fresh tuna, grilled a little rare, cut into 1-inch
    chunks, and marinated with 1 tablespoon dress-
    ing, or 7 ounces tuna fish canned in oil, drained
8 anchovy fillets, rinsed and dried
3 tomatoes, peeled or unpeeled, cut in wedges
2 roasted red peppers (see page 187 to make yourself,
    or buy already roasted in jars), sliced in 1-inch-
    wide pieces
⅔ cup black olives (imported Niçoise)
4 hard-cooked eggs, cut in wedges
4 large sprigs fresh rosemary or fresh thyme, for garnish
    (optional)

Combine the vinaigrette ingredients and mix well.

Arrange the salad ingredients side by side in an attractive way on a large white platter; do not toss. Just before serving pour the vinaigrette over the salad and garnish with fresh rosemary or thyme, if available.

MENU: Salade Niçoise / Crusty French or sourdough bread / Fresh peach tartlets

SUGGESTED WINES: Chardonnay / Sauvignon Blanc / Verdicchio

Bay Scallop Gazpacho with Roasted Tomatoes, Basil, and Avocado

SERVES 4 TO 5

A refreshing meal in itself. This version of the classic cold summer soup will intrigue you with the subtle taste of roasted tomatoes. (Roasting is an easy technique widely used in Mexican cooking.). Basil, avocado, and scallops enhance the gazpacho with their wonderful flavors and textures. A perfect summer lunch, everything in it is healthful and low in calories, and it can be made ahead.

1 large clove garlic
½ teaspoon coarse salt
¼ teaspoon freshly ground black pepper
2½ tablespoons Spanish sherry wine vinegar (or, if unavailable, red wine vinegar)
3 tablespoons virgin olive oil
4 large ripe tomatoes
¾ cup strained juice from roasted chopped tomatoes, or canned tomato juice
8 ounces bay scallops, quickly rinsed clean (see Note)
¼ cup chopped parsley stems
pinch of salt
½ large red bell pepper or pimiento, finely chopped
1 small cucumber, peeled, seeded, and finely chopped
2 large scallions including 2 inches of green stalk, finely chopped
1 cup ice cubes
½ large avocado, coarsely chopped
4 thick slices day-old French bread, cut in ½-inch cubes
8 large basil leaves, julienned
⅓ cup coarsely chopped Italian parsley

Mash the garlic and salt in a mortar and transfer to a large 3-quart bowl. Mix in the pepper, vinegar, and oil.

To roast tomatoes: Place the whole tomatoes in a very hot, dry skillet and toss until lightly browned on all sides; this takes only 10 minutes. Remove the tomatoes, peel, seed, and finely chop them over a sieve set over a bowl to catch the juices. Reserve the juice; add with the tomatoes to bowl.

Place the scallops in lightly salted boiling water to cover with the parsley stems. Cover and remove from heat. Drain after 1 minute. Chop in half. Add to bowl.

Add all the remaining ingredients to bowl and taste for seasoning— you should be able to taste the vinegar—and serve immediately. If serving later, combine everything except the avocado, bread, basil, and parsley, which you will add just before serving, and chill up to 6 hours.

NOTE: Use the larger ocean scallops if bay scallops are not available, and cut them into small pieces.

MENU: Bay scallop gazpacho with roasted tomatoes, basil, and avocado / Fresh sweet corn soufflé / Peach shortcake

SUGGESTED WINES: Chilled Beaujolais / Sauvignon Blanc

Belgian Shrimp and Endive Sandwiches

MAKES 4 LARGE OPEN-FACED SANDWICHES

This recipe is based on one in Nika Hazelton's excellent *The Belgian Cookbook.* Belgium is a country that takes food and drink seriously. The large number of independent breweries and variety of beers, the superb restaurants and bakeries, and the fabulous Brussels markets displaying an incredible variety of produce from the far reaches of the world all attest to this fact. I first ate sandwiches like this, accompanied by Greuzes, the oddly sweet local beer, with Belgian friends in Brussels pubs.

> ¼ pound small shrimp simmered in the shell 1 minute, then peeled and chopped (or use 1 recipe Dark Beer Shrimp Boil, page 236)
> 3 large heads Belgian endive, finely chopped
> ⅓ cup finely minced scallions with tops
> ⅓ cup finely chopped Italian parsley
> ⅔ cup very thinly sliced celery
> ½ tablespoon chopped fresh tarragon, or if not available, a pinch of dried tarragon
> 2 large hard-cooked eggs, finely chopped
> ¼ cup mayonnaise (preferably homemade)
> ½ teaspoon tarragon or champagne wine vinegar
> pinch of salt
> grind of white pepper
> 4 large slices firm, dense bakery or homemade bread (pumpernickel, country or German light rye, flaxseed bread, dense whole wheat)

Combine all the ingredients in a bowl, and taste for seasoning.

¶ This recipe can be made a day ahead to this point.

Spread on thin slices of firm bread just before serving.

NOTE: Serve this delicious sandwich as part of an afternoon tea, an elegant office brown bag lunch, or as an open-faced canapé. Without the bread, it's a fine cold salad—serve on a large radicchio leaf and garnish with a little dollop of caviar.

MENU: *Cold tomato soup / Belgian shrimp and endive sandwiches / Baked apple with honey and cinnamon

SUGGESTED BEVERAGE: Belgian beer

Provençal Summer Sandwich (Pan Bagnat)

SERVES 6

A salad in a crusty roll, these sandwiches are sold in kiosks on the beach along the Riviera. *Pan Bagnat* is a Provençal word for "bathed bread"; the bread is brushed or bathed with olive oil. This makes a perfect picnic lunch.

> 6 large crusty French bread rolls or round kaiser rolls, sliced in half horizontally
> 2 large cloves garlic, cut in half
> about 6 tablespoons extra-virgin olive oil
> 6 teaspoons Spanish sherry wine vinegar or red wine vinegar
> salt
> freshly ground black pepper
> 6 paper-thin slices red onion
> 6 large tomato slices
> ½ pound grilled fresh tuna, sliced, or a 7-ounce can albacore tuna, drained and flaked
> 8 radishes, thinly sliced
> 1 green pepper, sliced in thin rings
> 6 anchovies, rinsed, drained, and patted dry
> 6 large basil leaves or sprigs of Italian parsley
> optional additions: imported black olives; 2 hard-cooked eggs, sliced; 10 ounces cooked artichoke hearts, sliced; 1 stalk celery, sliced; 6 pieces lettuce; sliced roasted pimientos

Place the cut rolls in a 350° oven for 10 minutes to slightly dry out, then rub with cut clove of garlic. Brush each half with olive oil, sprinkle each with 1 teaspoon of vinegar, and sprinkle lightly with salt and generously with pepper.

Layer ingredients in the exact order listed above, distributing evenly among the rolls. Cover with other bread half, and press down to firmly combine all ingredients. Wrap tightly and keep cool until served. Pan Bagnat will keep about 4 or 5 hours.

MENU: Pan bagnat / *Marinated black-eyed pea relish / Fresh strawberries and brownies

SUGGESTED WINES: Tavel Rosé / California White Zinfandel

Cold Fish Fillets Marseilles Style

SERVES 4 TO 6 AS AN APPETIZER, OR 3 TO 4 AS A MAIN COURSE

This is one of my favorite dishes and, since it needs to be made ahead, a perfect one for summer entertaining. The piquant sauce is typical of Provençal cooking. Don't be put off by the long list of ingredients—assembling them is the hardest part of this otherwise easy recipe. This dish is also good served hot.

Tomato Sauce
2 tablespoons extra-virgin olive oil
1 medium red onion, sliced into thin rings
1 large clove garlic, crushed
1 pound imported canned peeled tomatoes, with juice,
    chopped, or 1 pound fresh tomatoes, peeled,
    seeded, and chopped
½ teaspoon black peppercorns, crushed
⅛ teaspoon cayenne pepper
1 teaspoon dried thyme
½ teaspoon dried basil
1 tablespoon fresh minced parsley
1 imported bay leaf
salt and freshly ground black pepper to taste
½ teaspoon coriander seeds, crushed (optional)
½ teaspoon cumin seed, crushed (optional)
½ cup dry white wine
2 tablespoons fresh lemon juice, or to taste
½ cup minced fresh parsley (additional)

¼ cup all-purpose flour
pinch of salt
grind of black pepper
½ teaspoon dried basil
1 pound firm redfish fillets at least ½ to 1 inch thick
    (see Note)
¼ cup extra-virgin olive oil

Heat 2 tablespoons of the olive oil in a heavy skillet. Add the onion, cook gently until soft, then add the garlic, tomatoes, seasonings, wine, and lemon juice. Simmer about 30 minutes. Add the additional parsley.

Combine the flour with salt, pepper, and basil. Dust the fillets with seasoned flour. In another skillet, heat the remaining ¼ cup of olive oil until hot. Add the lightly floured fillets and sauté over medium heat until almost cooked through—3 to 4 minutes on each side. Remove the fish and place in the hot tomato sauce, spoon sauce over the fish, and turn off the heat.

Let the sauce cool. Refrigerate until cold. When chilled, arrange the fillets and sauce on a large white platter and serve.

NOTE: Red snapper, rockfish, striped bass, halibut, lingcod, grouper, porgy, tilefish, whiting, scrod, catfish, or cod fillets can be used instead of the redfish.

MENU: Cold fish fillets Marseilles style / Caesar salad / Hazelnut torte

SUGGESTED BEVERAGES: Sauvignon Blanc / White Hermitage

Cold Normandy Mussel Salad with Mint, Cider Vinegar, and Crème Fraîche

SERVES 4

A refreshing spring lunch with the special flavors of Normandy.

¼ cup minced shallots
¼ cup roughly chopped fresh mint
1¼ cups dry white wine
1 tablespoon cider vinegar
5 dozen fresh mussels in the shell, scrubbed and debearded
1½ cups crème fraîche (page 227)
⅓ cup fresh mint, minced (additional), reserve 1 tablespoon
1 tablespoon cider vinegar (additional)
1 to 2 tablespoons strained cold mussel steaming liquid
salt and freshly ground white pepper to taste
12 fresh mint sprigs, for garnish

In the bottom of a 5-to-6-quart stockpot or casserole, put shallots, mint, wine, and cider vinegar and bring to a boil. Add the mussels, cover, and steam about 6 to 8 minutes or until the mussels open. Remove the mussels and let cool. Take off top half of the shell and discard. Strain the broth through a sieve lined with dampened paper towel, and reserve.

Combine crème fraîche, cider vinegar, 1 to 2 tablespoons of broth, and salt and pepper. Chill.

To serve, arrange the cold cooked mussels in half shells on a large platter, and spoon a little cold crème fraîche sauce over each mussel. Sprinkle with the reserved minced mint and garnish with fresh mint sprigs.

MENU: Cold Normandy mussel salad with mint and crème fraîche / *Pommes de terre au diable / Plums poached in red wine

SUGGESTED WINE: Muscadet

Thai Squid Salad with Hot Green Chiles and Mint

SERVES 4 TO 6

This dish offers so much flavor for so few calories that it should be called a "free" salad (the way some diets list foods that are so low in fat and calories that any amount you eat is permissible). This salad will keep for a week in the refrigerator.

1¼ pounds fresh squid, cleaned, sliced into ¼-inch rings (see Note)

Sauce
3 tablespoons fresh lime juice
3 tablespoons Nam Pla, Nuoc Mam Thai, or Vietnamese fish sauce (Squid brand is excellent)
2 cloves garlic, minced and mashed
¼ large red onion, thinly sliced
2 scallions with green, minced
1 12-inch stalk lemon grass, minced (optional)
1 tablespoon chopped fresh cilantro
½ teaspoon cayenne pepper
1 small serrano chile, seeded and minced
1 bunch fresh mint, leaves only, chopped (about ½ cup packed)

1 head lettuce, washed, patted dry, and very thinly sliced or shredded
2 limes, thinly sliced or in wedges, for garnish

Cook squid rings in boiling salted water 1 to 2 minutes, then remove and put under cold running water to chill.

Combine all sauce ingredients and toss with the drained squid. Store in the refrigerator until ready to serve.

Put the lettuce on a serving dish, arrange the salad on top of the lettuce, garnish with lime wedges, and serve cold.

NOTE: Small shrimp can be substituted for the squid.

MENU: Thai squid salad with hot green chiles and mint / Fried rice / Compote of three melons with pecan cookies

SUGGESTED BEVERAGE: Thai beer

Poached Fish Salad Chiffonade with Walnut Oil Dressing and Dill

SERVES 6 TO 8

An elegant make-ahead dish designed to be served cold. Long, thin shreds of lettuce—or sorrel or spinach—called a "chiffonade" from the French word for rags, make an especially attractive bed or garnish for cold fish and shellfish salads. A chiffonade can also be quickly sautéed in butter and served warm for a delicious and unusual accompaniment to poached fish.

> 2 recipes White Wine Court Bouillon (page 198)
> 3 to 3½ pounds whole redfish, red snapper, sea trout, or striped bass, cleaned, head and tail left on (see Note)
>
> **Walnut Oil Vinaigrette**
> 4 tablespoons Italian balsamic or Spanish sherry wine vinegar (or if unavailable, red wine vinegar)
> 1 teaspoon salt
> ½ teaspoon freshly ground black pepper
> 4 to 6 tablespoons French walnut oil
> 8 to 10 tablespoons virgin olive oil or safflower oil
> ½ medium red onion, very finely chopped
>
> 1 to 2 heads red-tipped Boston, romaine, or oakleaf lettuce, washed and dried
> 1 cup fresh dill sprigs, for garnish

Simmer the court bouillon for 30 minutes and cool slightly; add the whole fish and simmer for about 30 minutes or 10 minutes per inch of thickness.

Remove fish from the liquid and, while still warm, peel off the skin with your fingers or a small knife. With a sharp knife, make 3 to 4 diagonal cuts on the top side of the fish through to the bone, then remove fillets by sliding knife along bottom. Sever the backbone at the head and remove. Cut the remaining fillet into three to four diagonal pieces.

Combine all vinaigrette ingredients and mix well.

Make the chiffonade by stacking the lettuce leaves and thinly slicing across the rib of the lettuce. Spread sliced lettuce on a long platter and drizzle 2 to 3 tablespoons of the vinaigrette over all.

Crab, Lettuce, and Tomato Sandwich on Toasted Cornmeal Brioche

Pasta with Crayfish
Marinated Corn Salad
Grilled Swordfish with
Sun-Dried Tomato Butter

Fish Soup with Corn and Zucchini
Baked Whole Fish à la Provençale

Thai Squid Salad with
Hot Green Chiles and Mint
Hot and Crunchy Shrimp

Cold Tomato Soup
Saffron Rice and Shrimp Salad

Arrange the poached fish attractively on the lettuce.

Pour the remaining vinaigrette over the fish, and garnish each piece of fish with four or five small sprigs of fresh dill.

NOTE: Other fish such as halibut, drum, cod, lingcod, or rockfish can be substituted. If whole fish is not available, use about 2½ pounds of fillets.

MENU: *Mushrooms braised with garlic and herbs / Poached fish salad chiffonade with walnut oil dressing and dill / Cassis sorbet

SUGGESTED WINES: Chardonnay / Chablis / Mâcon Blanc / Soave

Scallop Ceviche with Orange and Avocado

SERVES 12 AS A FIRST COURSE, OR 8 AS A MAIN COURSE

A more colorful and highly seasoned version of a deservedly popular South American dish.

> 2 pounds fresh sea or bay scallops, well cleaned of sand, patted dry, and cut into 1-inch pieces (see Note)
> 1 large red onion, halved and sliced very thin
> 1 tablespoon champagne vinegar, Spanish sherry wine vinegar, or red wine vinegar
> ⅓ cup virgin olive oil
> ⅛ to ¼ teaspoon red pepper flakes
> ¼ teaspoon dried oregano
> ¼ teaspoon ground cumin
> ½ teaspoon black peppercorns, crushed
> 1 imported bay leaf
> 2 tablespoons fresh lemon juice
> 1 cup fresh lime juice
> 1 large orange, peeled and sliced, each slice cut into quarters
> 1 ripe avocado, coarsely chopped and dipped in lemon or lime juice
> 1 cup corn, either fresh off the cob or frozen, cooked and drained
> 1 red pepper, chopped
> 12 leaves Boston lettuce, red cabbage, or radicchio, washed and dried
> 2 tablespoons chopped cilantro or Italian parsley leaves, garnish
> 8 lime slices or wedges, for garnish

Place prepared scallops in a glass bowl or plastic container. Mix together the onion, wine vinegar, seasonings, and lemon and lime juices, pour over the scallops, mix well, cover tightly, and refrigerate for at least 6 hours, stirring scallops and seasonings from time to time.

Carefully mix in the orange pieces, avocado, corn, and red pepper.

Serve on large Boston lettuce leaves, or on a chiffonade of lettuce, (see page 130) or spoon into large cupped leaves of red cabbage or radicchio. Garnish with cilantro or parsley and serve with lime wedges.

NOTE: Ceviche can also be made with tuna, swordfish, red snapper, striped bass, or halibut—only be sure the pieces of fish are no more than 1 inch thick. The fish can also be lightly sautéed and then marinated.

MENU: Scallop ceviche with orange and avocado / Black bean soup / Fresh ripe mangoes

SUGGESTED BEVERAGES: Beer / Chilled Spanish sherry (Fino or Amantillado)

Lobster, Kiwi, and Orange Salad With Tomato Vinaigrette

SERVES 6

An elegant but simple combination, very colorful and low in calories.

2 lobster tails, cooked, chilled, and cut crosswise in ¼-inch slices (see Note)
4 kiwis, peeled and sliced or cut in wedges
2 large oranges, peeled in sections, pith removed
1 head curly endive (dark tops removed), escarole, or Boston lettuce, well washed and dried (use tender inside leaves)

Vinaigrette
1 tablespoon lemon juice or lemon and lime juice mixed
½ teaspoon salt
⅛ teaspoon freshly ground white pepper
2 teaspoons tomato paste, or 1 small tomato, peeled, seeded, and finely chopped
½ teaspoon Dijon mustard
3 to 4 tablespoons virgin olive oil or safflower oil
1 tablespoon heavy cream

Prepare all the salad ingredients. Make the vinaigrette dressing.

¶ Recipe can be made ahead and held a day at this point.

Toss the lettuce with half of the vinaigrette and arrange on a large platter. Arrange the lobster tail slices, kiwis, and orange sections attractively over the lettuce and spoon the remaining vinaigrette over the salad.

NOTE: Try this recipe with cooked crayfish tails, shrimp, crab, or scallops.

MENU: Lobster, kiwi, and orange salad with tomato vinaigrette / *Pecan biscuits / Strawberry Bavarian cream

SUGGESTED WINE: California Chardonnay

Saffron Rice
and Shrimp Salad

SERVES 8

This delicious, colorful salad can be a filling main course for a summery meal. It also looks fabulous as part of a buffet of summer salads.

1 heaping teaspoon Spanish saffron threads (do not use powdered or Mexican)
3 cups hot water
1½ cups long-grain rice
1 teaspoon salt
¾ pound medium shrimp, cooked and peeled
12 imported black olives, pitted
½ pound large mushrooms, sliced
1 small jar pimiento slices, drained
1 large green pepper, halved, seeded, and sliced
1 large red bell pepper, halved and seeded, and sliced
¼ pound imported Italian salami, thinly sliced and chopped (optional)

Vinaigrette
2 tablespoons red or white wine vinegar
½ cup extra-virgin olive oil
¾ teaspoon salt
½ teaspoon freshly ground black pepper
⅓ cup chopped scallions

Dissolve the saffron in the hot water. Add the rice and salt, and cook about 15 to 20 minutes or until done. While the rice is cooking, combine the vinaigrette ingredients in a small bowl.

Cool the rice quickly by spreading on a large baking sheet. While still warm, toss with three quarters of the vinaigrette.

Toss the shrimp, olives, vegetables, and salami with the remaining vinaigrette.

¶ This salad can be prepared 1 to 2 days ahead and stored, well covered, in a large bowl in the refrigerator.

Arrange the rice and all the other ingredients on a large platter (or toss together in a big bowl) and serve cold or at room temperature.

MENU: *Cold tomato soup / Saffron rice and shrimp salad / Honeydew melon halves sprinkled with lime juice

SUGGESTED WINE: Sauvignon Blanc

Asparagus, Crab, and Potato Salad

SERVES 6

This elegant but filling salad is perfect in springtime when asparagus and new potatoes are in season.

Herb and Mustard Sauce
3 tablespoons finely chopped parsley
¼ cup chopped watercress leaves
¼ cup fresh snipped chives
2 tablespoons fresh tarragon or dill
2 tablespoons fresh chopped and blanched sorrel leaves
2 tablespoons chopped fresh chervil, if available
1 cup crème fraîche (page 227) or sour cream
2 tablespoons lemon juice
1 teaspoon salt
¼ teaspoon freshly ground white pepper
1 tablespoon Dijon mustard

12 ounces crab meat, back fin or lump
1 head Boston lettuce, washed and dried
1 head curly endive, green tops cut off and discarded,
    white stalks washed and broken in pieces
1 pound fresh asparagus (stalks peeled if thicker than
    a pencil), cooked and drained
1 red bell pepper, evenly chopped
1 pound scrubbed new potatoes, cooked and sliced

Combine all the sauce ingredients, reserving 2 tablespoons of mixed herbs for garnish. (If tarragon, sorrel, and chervil are not available, simply increase the amount of the other herbs.) Taste for seasoning and adjust accordingly.

¶ The recipe can be prepared to this point the night before and refrigerated, to be assembled at the last minute.

If fresh crab is used, sauté for 4 minutes in butter; if pasteurized or precooked crab is used, simply remove it from the container.

Arrange the Boston lettuce on a serving platter and place the curly endive on top. Place the asparagus with tips on the outside, like the spokes of a wheel. Scatter half the red pepper on the asparagus, and mix the rest in with the sauce. Combine ½ cup of sauce with the crab and potatoes, mix well, and place in the middle of the platter. Sprinkle the reserved herbs on top and serve the remaining sauce on the side.

MENU: Asparagus, crab, and potato salad / Brownies and fresh raspberries

RECOMMENDED WINE: California Chardonnay

Lobster Sandwiches with Tapenade

SERVES 2

These make à wonderful picnic lunch for the beach or an elegant outdoor lunch.

> 2 to 4 pieces lightly toasted light French country rye bread, sourdough bread, or Cornmeal Brioche (page 194)
> ½ cup Tapenade (page 231)
> ½ pound boiled or steamed lobster meat
> 6 slices ripe red tomatoes
> 6 leaves fresh basil, or ½ teaspoon crumbled dried basil
> 2 leaves Boston lettuce, washed and dried

Spread toasted bread with tapenade and top with a layer of lobster meat, tomato slices, basil, and lettuce. Press down top slice, cut in half, and serve.

MENU: Lobster sandwiches with tapenade / *Roasted green pepper salad / Blackberry ice cream

SUGGESTED WINES: Champagne / Sparkling wine

Smoked Fish for Sunday Brunch or Supper

SERVES 10

The ultimate in classy entertaining—and it entails no cooking! This is a northern European combination of foods which works well in any season and is especially practical to serve as a buffet for a large number of people. All the smoked fish, breads, and salads can be purchased. I like to serve at least five varieties of smoked fish, three good hearty salads, and a wide assortment of light and dark country French and German rye and pumpernickel breads accompanied by cold tart sauces, good mustards, and flavored butters like Tomato Butter (page 217), Green Peppercorn Butter (page 218), or any of the herb butters on page 214.

SMOKED FISH

You need about ½ pound per person. For a good selection, choose five of the following varieties of smoked fish. Buy 1 pound each for a total of 5 pounds to serve 10 people.

Salmon	Whitefish	Mackerel
Trout	Sturgeon	Herring
Sablefish	Eel	

SAUCES

One recipe of each of the following: Horseradish Sauce (page 230); Cucumber-Dill Sauce (page 227); Chipotle Aioli (page 225)

SALADS

Choose three salads to have a variety of taste, color, and texture. You will need about 1½ to 2 quarts of each.

Warm Potato Salad with Tarragon and Shallot Vinaigrette (page 186) / Beet salad with fresh dill and sour cream / Cucumber salad / Chopped hard-cooked egg salad with lemon mayonnaise and fresh thyme and parsley / Mushrooms à la Grecque (page 180) / Finely shredded red cabbage with caraway seed and balsamic vinegar

DESSERT

Hot apple tart

SUGGESTED BEVERAGES: Dry Mosel / Reisling / Dark beer, especially Belgian

Oysters on the Half Shell with Five Spicy Sauces

SERVES 10

This feast for oyster lovers appears as the cold first course of a simple, hearty hot meal (see Menu).

OYSTERS

You will need 1 to 1½ dozen fresh oysters per person. If you buy them in the shell, be sure you have oyster knives and at least two people helping to shuck. You should set up a shucking area near the kitchen sink with plenty of clean dish towels and large trays of crushed ice nearby for the oysters.

To serve: Open the oysters and place them in the half shell on a bed of crushed ice in a very large shallow dish or tray. Sink bowls of the sauces in the ice, with accompanying small long-handled spoons to spoon the sauces onto the oysters.

SAUCES

French Salsa (page 229)
Tomatillo Salsa (page 229)
Chipotle Sauce (page 228)
Creole Okra Relish (page 233)
Roasted Red Pepper Sauce (page 227)
NOTE: You may want to double the smaller-yield recipes to be sure to have enough.

MENU: Oysters on the half shell with five spicy sauces / Jalapeno cornbread / Spinach soufflé / Rhubarb pie

SUGGESTED BEVERAGES: Muscadet / Sauvignon Blanc / dark Mexican beer

Hot Hors d'Oeuvres, Sandwiches and Soups, and Brunch and Late-Night Supper Dishes

Quick-and-easy Oyster-Parmesan Popovers, Tomato Crab Cream over Pecan
Biscuits, Fried Oyster Sandwich, Cream
of Scallop Soup with Saffron, and Crab
Cakes Southwestern Style with Lime and
Chiles—these hot savory dishes are among
my favorite recipes. The recipes in this
section evoke comfort and hominess, if
not elegance, and are perfect for suppers
or brunches, as first courses or hors
d'oeuvres.

Oyster-Parmesan Popovers

MAKES 6 POPOVERS

It takes only 10 minutes' preparation and 20 minutes in the oven to prepare this delicate dish. Bake and serve in individual ramekins or soufflé dishes for a great brunch or lunch dish, a hot first course, or a late-night savory supper.

    4 large eggs
    ¾ cup whole milk
    ¾ cup all-purpose flour, sifted
    ¼ cup finely grated Italian Parmesan cheese
    ¼ teaspoon salt
    2 tablespoons fresh snipped chives, chopped basil, or
        chopped parsley
    2 tablespoons unsalted sweet butter (for greasing ra-
        mekins)
    ⅓ cup Italian Parmesan cheese, finely grated (addi-
        tional)
    big pinch of cayenne and freshly ground black pepper
    1 10-ounce jar fresh oysters, drained and patted dry
        (cut very large oysters in half if necessary) or 6
        large freshly shucked oysters

Combine the eggs, milk, flour, ¼ cup of Parmesan cheese, salt, and herbs in a mixer and mix well. Fill six well-buttered 4-or-5-ounce individual ramekins, custard cups, or soufflé dishes three-quarters full (about ½ cup).

Combine the ⅓ cup of Parmesan and the peppers, roll the dry oysters in the mixture, and place one large oyster in the middle of each ramekin.

Place the ramekins on a thin baking sheet (if using a heavy sheet, be sure to increase the oven temperature 25°) and bake in a preheated 450° oven about 20 to 25 minutes or until popovers puff high and are crusty brown on the outside. Or turn the oven down to 400° after 10 minutes if the popovers brown too quickly.

The oysters make the popovers a little more moist: all the more delicious.

MENU: Oyster-parmesan popovers / Mixed green salad with sliced beets / Orange cake

SUGGESTED WINE: Chardonnay / Muscadet / Orvieto

Provençal Onion and Anchovy Tart (Pissaladière)

SERVES 6 AMPLY FOR LUNCH, OR 8 TO 10 AS AN APPETIZER

The name *pissaladière* comes from the old Provençal word for anchovies: *pissalat*. Resist calling this a pizza; it's a dish unique to Provence, and cheese is never added. The easy-to-make crust is a kind of modified brioche (with butter or egg), which can also be used for other kinds of cooked vegetable tarts or quiches. The olives should be flavorful—French Niçoise olives or Greek Kalamata—*not* canned American olives.

Crust
1 cup all-purpose flour
pinch of salt
3 tablespoons unsalted sweet butter
1 large egg
1 package active dry yeast, dissolved in 2 tablespoons
    warm water
2 to 4 tablespoons all-purpose flour

Filling
4 medium yellow onions, very thinly sliced
3 to 4 tablespoons extra-virgin olive oil
2 large tomatoes, seeded and finely chopped, drained
1 to 2 tablespoons tomato paste
½ teaspoon salt
¼ teaspoon freshly ground black pepper
2 teaspoons dried thyme
1 imported bay leaf
2 garlic cloves, mashed to a paste with a fork

Toppings
25 large (or about 1 cup small) imported black olives,
    pitted
12 to 15 anchovies, rinsed, drained, and sliced in half
    lengthwise

To make the crust, cut or rub the butter into the flour. In a small bowl, combine with a mixer, or with your hand, the egg, yeast, and water, then mix in the flour and butter.

Knead the dough for a few minutes, sprinkle with extra flour to keep from sticking. Cut an X 1 inch deep on top of the dough ball (this allows a greater surface area to be exposed to warm air), cover loosely with plastic wrap, and leave in a warm place to rise 15 to 30 minutes.

To make the filling, slowly cook the onions in the oil in a large skillet until very soft, approximately 30 minutes. Add the tomatoes, tomato paste, seasonings, and garlic and cook over medium heat until all the liquid has evaporated and the mixture is quite dry. Remove the bay leaf.

Press the dough into a buttered 10-inch tart pan with a removable bottom. Spread the filing evenly on the dough and make a crisscross pattern on top with the anchovies and olives.

Bake in a preheated 375° oven for 40 to 50 minutes.

Remove from the oven, let cool slightly, cut with a sharp knife into serving pieces, and serve at room temperature.

MENU: Provençal onion and anchovy tart / Caesar salad / Pistachio ice cream

SUGGESTED WINES: Tavel Rosé / Côtes du Rhone

Crab-Filled Omelets

SERVES 2

A great late-night dish, luxurious and satisfying but simple to prepare. Or for a perfect brunch, serve the omelets with fresh hot popovers, sautéed zucchini with fresh rosemary, and pecan tartlets for dessert.

> ¼ to ⅓ pound fresh or pasteurized crab meat, lump
>   or back fin (see Note)
> juice of 1 lime
> 3 tablespoons unsalted sweet butter
> 1 red or green bell pepper, seeded and finely chopped
> 1½ teaspoons virgin olive oil
> 4 tablespoons chopped fresh parsley
> pinch of salt
> grind of white pepper
> 5 large eggs
> 1 large egg yolk
> 2 tablespoons heavy cream
> ¼ teaspoon salt
> ⅛ teaspoon freshly ground white pepper
> pinch of dried basil or thyme
> 1 tablespoon fresh chives (cut into 1-inch lengths), for
>   garnish

If crab meat is fresh, sauté in butter for 4 minutes; if precooked or pasteurized, use as is.

Sprinkle the lime juice on the crab meat and cook gently in 1 tablespoon of the butter for 2 minutes. Remove from heat.

Sauté the bell pepper in oil until soft and mix with the crab and parsley. Season lightly with salt and pepper.

In a separate bowl, mix together the eggs, egg yolk, cream, and seasonings.

Melt 1 tablespoon of the butter in a 7-inch well-cured or Teflon-coated omelet pan. When the butter foams, swirl it around the sides of the pan and discard the excess.

Pour half of the egg mixture into the omelet pan. Cook over medium-high heat, lightly stirring so that all of the egg mixture is lightly set, but not browned. Warm the crab mixture a few minutes in a pan over medium heat. Place half of the warmed crab mixture in a strip in the middle of the omelet. Then roll the omelet out of the pan, folding the top half over the filling and into a roll, onto a warmed plate; garnish with chives.

Repeat with the rest of the egg mixture and crab for a second omelet.

NOTE: You can use lobster or crayfish instead of crab meat.

MENU: Crab-filled omelets / Hard rolls and basil butter / Olive salad / Strawberry tart

SUGGESTED WINES: Champagne / Chardonnay

Tomato Crab Cream over Pecan Biscuits

SERVES 2

A wonderfully delicate and delicious combination for brunch, lunch, or a light late-night supper. It takes only 20 minutes to make the biscuits and sauce. Or use the sauce over rice, with the addition of hot chiles.

2 tablespoons sweet unsalted butter
2 tablespoons chopped scallions
1 large tomato, seeded and chopped
6 ounces fresh or pasteurized crab meat, lump or back
    fin, flaked with a fork (see Note)
½ teaspoon salt
grind of black pepper
dash of cayenne (not more)
⅓ to ½ cup heavy cream or crème fraîche (page 227)
1 tablespoon finely chopped fresh parsley
2 large Quick Buttermilk Pecan Biscuits (see page 195)
    or 4 large pieces French bread, toasted

Melt the butter in a hot saucepan and gently cook the scallions until soft. Add the tomato and cook 2 to 3 minutes, then add the crab meat, seasonings, and cream and heat through. Taste for seasoning and serve hot over halved biscuits.

NOTE: Lobster or scallops can be substituted for the crab.

MENU: Tomato crab cream over pecan biscuits / Watercress salad / Fresh pears and bleu cheese

SUGGESTED WINES: Chardonnay / Mâcon Blanc / Orvieto

Fish Soup
with Corn and Zucchini

SERVES 8 TO 12

Keep bottled clam juice and canned tomatoes on hand to make this delicious and healthful soup often. It's a perfect dish to serve easily to a large group. You use only one big pot for cooking. Ladle the soup from the pot, soup-kitchen style, placing soup bowls and piles of crusty sourdough bread in the kitchen and letting guests serve themselves. If all the fresh herbs in the recipe are not available, use as many fresh as you possibly can. Poblano peppers, if available, can be added; their smoky chile flavor will give this fresh, clean-tasting soup a Mexican touch.

¼ cup extra-virgin olive oil
3 large cloves garlic, mashed to a paste with a fork
2 cups yellow onion, finely minced in a food processor
¾ cup dry white wine
2 cups bottled clam juice
6 cups canned peeled Italian plum tomatoes, pureed
    with juices, or ripe fresh tomatoes, peeled, seeded,
    and pureed
2 to 3 zucchini or yellow squash, sliced ½ inch thick
1 or 2 poblano peppers, roasted, peeled, seeded, and
    chopped (optional)
2 to 3 ears of sweet corn, cut into 2-inch pieces
1 10-ounce package frozen corn
salt and freshly ground black pepper to taste
1 teaspoon chopped fresh chives, or ½ teaspoon dried
1 teaspoon chopped fresh oregano, or ½ teaspoon
    dried
1 teaspoon chopped fresh thyme, or ½ teaspoon dried
1 teaspoon chopped fresh basil, or ½ teaspoon dried
1 teaspoon chopped fresh rosemary, or ½ teaspoon
    dried
1 pound medium shrimp, shelled with tails left on (see
    Note)
1 pound sea scallops, well cleaned of sand, cut in half,
    or bay scallops, left whole (see Note)
½ cup chopped fresh Italian parsley

Heat the olive oil in a 6-quart or larger heavy-bottomed casserole. Add the garlic and onions and gently cook about 8 to 10 minutes or until soft. Add the wine, turn the heat up, and cook briskly 5 minutes. Add the clam juice and tomatoes and simmer for 15 minutes.

¶ The recipe can be prepared ahead at this point, cooled and refrigerated overnight. Gently reheat and proceed with the following steps.

Add the zucchini, peppers, corn, salt, pepper, chives, and herbs and cook 5 to 7 minutes.

Stir in the shrimp and scallops, and cook only 3 to 5 minutes or until shellfish is done. Taste for seasoning.

Stir in the parsley just before serving.

NOTE: This soup is excellent hot or cold, or leftover as a sauce for pasta. Fresh lean fish fillets cut in pieces or other fresh shellfish such as mussels, oysters, or crab may be used in addition to or in place of the shrimp and scallops.

MENU: Fish soup with corn and zucchini / Avocado and spinach salad with mustard vinaigrette / Crunchy sourdough bread / Pecan pie

SUGGESTED WINES: Chardonnay / Sancerre / Frascati

Shrimp Bisque

SERVES 6

A rich, finely flavored classic soup that can be made a day ahead. Its superb taste makes it worth a little more effort in the preparation.

6 tablespoons unsalted sweet butter
mirepoix: 1 peeled carrot, 1 yellow onion, and 1 stalk
    celery, all finely chopped and mixed together
4 large ripe tomatoes, peeled, seeded, and finely
    chopped
salt and freshly ground white pepper, to taste
1½ pounds medium-large shrimp, unpeeled (see Note)
3 tablespoons brandy
1½ cups dry white wine
⅓ cup long-grain rice
3 cups Fish Fumet (page 197) or bottled clam juice
1 cup homemade chicken broth
1 imported bay leaf
2 tablespoons coarsely chopped fresh parsley
½ teaspoon dried thyme
dash of cayenne pepper
1 cup heavy cream
1 tablespoon dry or Sercial Madeira (optional)
2 tablespoons finely chopped parsley

Melt 2 tablespoons of the butter in a saucepan. Add mirepoix and cook until soft. Add tomatoes and simmer slowly until the liquid evaporates and sauce thickens, about 10 minutes. Season with salt and pepper. Set aside.

Heat 2 tablespoons of butter in a large, heavy-bottomed casserole. Add the shrimp, in their shells, and cook, stirring, 3 to 4 minutes. Add brandy, heat, and flame (see page 100). Remove shrimp when the flames die down and set aside. Transfer shrimp with a slotted spoon to platter; when cool enough to handle, remove the shells. Reserve shells and shrimp separately.

Pour white wine into shrimp liquid and bring to a simmer. Add rice, fish fumet, chicken broth, bay leaf, parsley, thyme, and cayenne to the wine and simmer 20 minutes.

The procedure in this paragraph can be omitted, but it adds a more intense shrimp flavor to the soup. Melt the remaining 2 tablespoons of butter in a small saucepan. Add the shrimp shells and cook over medium heat 2 to 3 minutes. Place the shells and butter in a blender or food processor and blend until very finely chopped. Press this mixture through a strainer to remove shell bits and add sieved butter to the soup.

Puree twelve shrimp in a blender or food processor with a little added stock and set aside. Chop the remaining shrimp in ½-inch pieces and set aside for garnish.

¶ The recipe can be made a day ahead to this point; ingredients should be well wrapped and refrigerated.

Add the mirepoix to the soup, then add the cream. Heat to a simmer, add pureed shrimp, mix well, and adjust the seasonings. Add the Madeira, garnish with chopped shrimp and parsley, and serve immediately.

NOTE: Lobster or crayfish may be substituted for the shrimp. A cup of fresh minced mushrooms may be added to the mirepoix.

MENU: Shrimp bisque / Crusty French bread / Spinach salad with goat cheese / Fresh peach ice cream

SUGGESTED WINES: Chardonnay / Graves / Champagne

Acadian Catfish Court Bouillon

SERVES 12

Clara Treadwell of Menard County, Texas, shared this recipe with me from Mrs. Theo Melancon of Mamon, Louisiana, deep Cajun country where they pronounce the name of this dish as "koo-be-yon." I've adapted and altered the recipe to produce this version of Cajun catfish stew.

⅔ cup safflower oil
1 large yellow onion, finely chopped
½ cup chopped scallions
2 cloves garlic, mashed to a paste with a fork
1 cup finely chopped celery with leaves
1 cup chopped red or green bell pepper
28 ounces canned imported plum tomatoes, pureed
2 tablespoons tomato paste
1 cup water, chicken bouillon, or bottled clam juice
¼ cup chopped fresh parsley

Cajun Catfish Seasoning
1 teaspoon cayenne pepper
1 teaspoon freshly ground black pepper
½ teaspoon paprika
1 teaspoon dried marjoram
½ teaspoon dried thyme
½ teaspoon dried basil
1 teaspoon salt

3 pounds fresh catfish fillets (see Note)
½ cup all-purpose flour
8 cups cooked buttered long-grain rice

Heat ⅓ cup of the oil in a heavy-bottomed 6-quart casserole or saucepan. Cook all the vegetables except the tomatoes in the oil over medium heat until soft, about 8 minutes. Add the tomatoes, tomato paste, water, and parsley and bring to a simmer, stirring to mix all the ingredients.

Mix Cajun catfish seasonings together. Rub all the fillets with this mixture, then roll in flour and lightly brown in the remaining ⅓ cup of oil. Remove the fish and drain on paper towels. (The catfish is not completely cooked through.) Cut into pieces approximately 2 by 2 inches.

Place the fried catfish in the tomato mixture, cover, and simmer about 15 to 20 minutes. Test the fish for doneness. Taste for seasonings, adding some of the Cajun Catfish Seasoning if needed to spice the broth.

Serve in gumbo dishes or large shallow soup plates over hot buttered rice.

NOTE: Redfish, red snapper, drum, grouper, scrod, lingcod, or rockfish can also be used.

MENU: Deep-fried okra / Acadian catfish court bouillon with hot buttered rice / Red-tipped lettuce salad with cumin-flavored vinaigrette / Fresh strawberry pie

SUGGESTED BEVERAGES: Beer / Sauvignon Blanc

Cream of Scallop Soup with Saffron

SERVES 6

A simple but very satisfying dish for a winter night, or an elegant first course for a dinner party. The use of saffron makes this especially attractive in taste and appearance.

> 1 quart White Wine Court Bouillon (page 198)
> ½ teaspoon Spanish saffron threads
> 3 tablespoons unsalted sweet butter
> 3 leeks, white part, thinly sliced
> 4 tablespoons all-purpose flour
> 1½ cups hot whole milk or light cream
> 1 pound sea or bay scallops, well cleaned of sand, chopped
> ½ cup heavy cream
> 2 large egg yolks
> ¼ cup minced fresh parsley or chives, for garnish

Prepare the court bouillon, strain, return to pan, add the saffron, and keep warm.

Melt the butter in a large saucepan, add the leeks and cook until soft, stir in the flour, and cook over low heat, stirring constantly, 4 to 5 minutes. Add the hot court bouillon all at once, whisk vigorously, and cook at a simmer until smooth, about 4 to 5 minutes.

Slowly stir in the hot milk or cream. Simmer soup 10 minutes.

¶ The soup can be made a day ahead to this point and refrigerated. To use, reheat gently.

Add scallops and cook 2 minutes. (Please note: the scallops should cook no more than 4 to 5 minutes in the soup. Remember that as long as the soup is hot, the scallops continue to cook, and an over-cooked scallop is a rubbery scallop.)

While scallops cook, whisk the cream and egg yolks together in a bowl. Slowly add 1 cup of the hot soup to the egg mixture, whisking constantly. Add the egg mixture to the soup and keep warm over low heat.

Adjust seasonings, sprinkle with parsley, and serve immediately.

NOTE: One-third pound sliced mushrooms can be added along with the leeks.

MENU: Cream of scallop soup with saffron / *Mushrooms braised with garlic and herbs / Endive salad / Walnut cake with bitter chocolate icing

SUGGESTED WINES: Chardonnay / Muscadet / Soave

Deep-Fried Squid

SERVES 4 TO 6

From Italy, Greece, and Spain comes this wonderful hot appetizer.

2 pounds small fresh squid, cleaned (head cut off,
  insides removed and rinsed out), dark skin scraped
  or pulled off, sliced into ¼-inch rings
3 tablespoons fresh lemon juice
2 tablespoons extra-virgin olive oil
2 quarts safflower oil
2 cups all-purpose flour
½ teaspoon salt
¼ teaspoon freshly ground black pepper
½ teaspoon dried oregano
pinch of cayenne pepper
3 large eggs, beaten
lemon slices, for garnish

Marinate the squid in lemon juice and olive oil for 30 minutes. Drain and dry squid on paper towels, blotting all liquid.

Slowly heat the safflower oil until it almost reaches 375°. Dip the squid into the flour mixed with the seasonings, then into the egg, then back into the flour, and deep-fry until crisp and golden brown, about 2 to 3 minutes. Serve hot with lemon slices in a basket lined with napkins.

MENU: Deep-fried squid / Pasta primavera / Green salad with feta and tomatoes / Fresh figs and almonds

SUGGESTED WINES: Orvieto / Sauvignon Blanc

Warm Bistro Salad with Scallops, Bacon, Greens, and Mustard Dressing

SERVES 2 AS A WHOLE MEAL

This salad is really a whole meal in one dish, with a lot of hearty flavors. Especially good on a cold night.

5 slices thick bacon, cured without maple or sugar
½ pound sea or bay scallops, well cleaned of sand, rolled in 2 tablespoons freshly grated black pepper (see Note)
2 shallots, minced
1 red onion, very thinly sliced in rings
2 tablespoons champagne vinegar or tarragon vinegar
½ tablespoon grainy French mustard
4 large leaves kale, cut across the rib into 2-inch strips, washed and dried
1 bunch fresh spinach, stemmed, washed, and dried
4 medium slices French bread, rubbed lightly with garlic, brushed with virgin olive oil, and toasted in a 375° oven for 10 to 15 minutes until golden
½ cup crumbled goat cheese
freshly ground black pepper

Gently cook the bacon until crisp in a large skillet, remove, drain on paper towels, and break into 1-inch pieces. Add scallops to bacon drippings, cook 2 minutes, and remove.

In 3 tablespoons of the bacon drippings, cook the shallots and onion until soft. Add the vinegar to the onions in the skillet and boil 1 to 2 minutes to reduce to 1 tablespoon.

Add the mustard, mix in well, then add the kale and spinach and stir over high heat until just barely wilted. Quickly stir in the scallops and bacon.

Remove from the heat, toss well, and serve with toasted bread spread with goat cheese. Sprinkle with freshly ground black pepper.

NOTE: You can use oysters or shrimp in place of scallops.

MENU: Warm bistro salad with scallops, bacon, greens, and mustard dressing / Potato pancakes / Oranges poached in red wine

SUGGESTED WINE: Mâcon Blanc

Crab, Lettuce, and Tomato Sandwiches on Toasted Cornmeal Brioche

SERVES 4

A "CLT," and a refined sandwich to serve for a special lunch.

Lemon and Red Pepper Mayonnaise
1 whole egg, at room temperature
1 teaspoon grated lemon peel
1 tablespoon lemon juice
1 teaspoon Dijon mustard
½ teaspoon salt
grind of white pepper
1 cup safflower oil
½ red bell pepper, very finely minced
1 tablespoon chopped chives
1 tablespoon chopped parsley

12 ounces fresh crab meat, lump or back fin
8 slices Cornmeal Brioche (page 194) or fine home-
    made white bread, toasted
3 ripe tomatoes, sliced
freshly ground black pepper
red-leaf or Boston lettuce, washed and dried

To prepare mayonnaise, combine egg, lemon peel and juice, mustard, salt, and white pepper in a food processor or blender. Very slowly, add the oil while the machine is running. Blend until thick. Stir in the red pepper and herbs.

If the crab is fresh, sauté in butter about 4 minutes; if it is pasteurized or precooked, remove from container and use as is.

Spread four toasted brioche or bread slices generously with mayonnaise. Press the crab into each slice, then add tomatoes, a grind of black pepper, and finally the lettuce. Cut in half and serve open-face, or add another slice of toasted brioche or bread to top; slice and serve.

MENU: *Cold watercress soup / Crab, lettuce, and tomato sandwiches on toasted cornmeal brioche / Blackberry pie

SUGGESTED WINE: Sauvignon Blanc

Hot Crab Soufflé
in Scallop Shells

SERVES 8 AS A FIRST COURSE,
OR 4 TO 6 AS A MAIN COURSE

You can keep filled unbaked scallop shells in your freezer to have on hand for a wonderful impromptu supper. This is one of the few fish dishes that freezes successfully; its delicate, savory taste is not diminished by being frozen. This dish may also be baked in small ramekins or in a 1½-quart soufflé dish.

> 6 tablespoons unsalted sweet butter
> 12 tablespoons finely grated Italian Parmesan cheese
> 3 tablespoons all-purpose flour
> 1 cup whole milk
> 1 large egg yolk, whisked
> ¼ teaspoon dry mustard
> ¼ cup finely chopped scallions
> 3 tablespoons freshly squeezed lemon juice
> ⅛ teaspoon Tabasco sauce
> ½ pound fresh or pasteurized precooked crab meat, lump or back fin, flaked
> ½ teaspoon salt
> 6 large egg whites, at room temperature
> ⅛ teaspoon cream of tartar
> 4 stalks watercress or ½ red bell pepper, chopped, for garnish
> lime wedges dipped in finely chopped parsley

Generously butter eight 5-inch scallop shells with 3 tablespoons of the butter. Sprinkle 8 tablespoons of the Parmesan evenly over the shells.

Melt the remaining 3 tablespoons of butter in a heavy saucepan. Add the flour and cook 5 minutes on low heat, stirring. Add the milk all at once, whisk until thickened, and simmer 5 minutes.

Let sauce cool slightly before adding the egg yolk, 4 tablespoons of the Parmesan, and the mustard, scallions, lemon juice, Tabasco, crab meat, and salt.

¶ The recipe can be made ahead to this point and held refrigerated overnight. Let come to room temperature before using.

Beat the egg whites with the cream of tartar until stiff. Mix one quarter of the egg whites thoroughly into the crab mixture. Carefully fold in the remaining whites.

Spoon the mixture into the prepared shells, place on a baking sheet, and bake in a preheated 400° oven for 12 to 15 minutes.

Garnish with watercress or red pepper and serve with parsleyed lime wedges.

NOTE: This dish can be frozen immediately after spooning into shells. To bake, simply place frozen shells on a baking sheet, put directly in preheated oven, and bake about 18 to 20 minutes.

MENU: Hot crab soufflé in scallop shells / Beet, celery, and walnut salad with walnut oil vinaigrette / Gingerbread

SUGGESTED WINES: Chardonnay / Muscadet

Crab Cakes, Southwestern Style, with Lime and Chiles

SERVES 4

Without the chiles, you would recognize this as the traditional crab cakes of Maryland. The chiles highlight the sweetness of the crab but do not overpower it. I love to serve this as a breakfast or lunch dish with hot biscuits or cornbread, or as a supper (see the menu on page 159).

> 1 large egg
> 2 tablespoons mayonnaise, crème fraîche (page 227), or sour cream
> 2 teaspoons Dijon mustard or the hotter Louisiana Creole mustard
> pinch of cayenne pepper
> ½ teaspoon freshly ground white pepper
> pinch of salt
> ¼ teaspoon Worcestershire sauce
> 1 pound fresh or pasteurized precooked crab meat, lump or back fin (see Note), flaked
> ¼ cup chopped parsley
> ¼ cup chopped scallions
> 8 to 10 saltine crackers, crushed, or 1 cup soft white bread crumbs
> 1 to 2 2-inch fresh serrano chiles, seeded and minced
> 2 tablespoons unsalted sweet butter
> 2 tablespoons vegetable oil
> lime wedges, for garnish

Mix together the egg, mayonnaise, mustard, peppers, salt, and Worcestershire sauce. Add the crab meat, parsley, scallions, saltines, and chiles. Mix thoroughly.

Shape and press the mixture into ten or twelve round patties, place on foil, cover, and chill for at least ½ hour before cooking.

¶ The recipe can be prepared ahead and refrigerated for 5 to 6 hours. Bring to room temperature before using.

Heat the butter and oil in a skillet. Add crab cakes and sauté on both sides over medium-high heat a few minutes or until golden and lightly crispy. Drain on paper towels. Serve hot with lime wedges.

~

MENU: Crab cakes, Southwestern style, with lime and chiles / Creamed corn with grilled red bell peppers / *Pecan biscuits / Pineapple sorbet

SUGGESTED BEVERAGE: Beer

Oysters Wrapped in Spinach with Champagne Sabayon

SERVES 4 TO 6

A sophisticated first course for a fine meal.

> 1 pound fresh spinach with large leaves, stemmed, washed, and dried
> 2 10-ounce jars fresh oysters, reserve liquor, or 2 dozen fresh shucked oysters

> *Champagne Sabayon*
> 1 cup dry champagne or sparkling wine (the better the champagne, the better the sauce)
> 4 large egg yolks
> 2 to 3 tablespoons heavy cream or crème fraîche (page 227)

Blanch the spinach in boiling salted water 1 minute and drain well.

Make the sauce: Reduce the champagne to ¼ cup over high heat in a 1½-quart cast-iron enameled saucepan. Into this whisk the yolks, and continue whisking over low heat until the sauce thickens. Add the cream or crème fraîche and 1 to 2 tablespoons of the oyster liquor until you have a hollandaise consistency. Season if desired and pour into a heated thermos to hold until the oysters are cooked.

In a 1½-quart cast-iron enameled saucepan, poach the oysters gently in their liquor 1 to 2 minutes over low heat or until the edges begin to curl. Wrap each oyster in one or two spinach leaves and place on oyster shells or in a shallow gratin dish. Heat oven to 450° and bake wrapped oysters 1 to 2 minutes.

Serve hot with Champagne Sabayon on top.

MENU: Oysters wrapped in spinach with champagne sabayon / *Wild rice with scallions / Hazelnut Cake

SUGGESTED WINES: Sparkling wine / Champagne

Creamy Shellfish Gratin

SERVES 6 AS A MAIN COURSE,
OR 10 AS AN APPETIZER

A gratin (from the French word for a golden crust) makes a wonderfully elegant first course or a satisfying dish for a buffet or late-night supper. Serve it over angel hair pasta.

1 cup dry white wine
1 cup bottled clam juice
1 cup heavy cream or crème fraîche (page 227)
1 imported bay leaf
½ teaspoon dried thyme
few grinds of white pepper
1 leek, white only, well rinsed and finely chopped
3 shallots, finely chopped
¾ pound small shrimp, peeled (see Notes)
1 pound sea or bay scallops, rinsed and carefully cleaned
    of sand, cut in 1-inch pieces (see Notes)
3½ tablespoons unsalted sweet butter
3½ tablespoons all-purpose flour
¼ teaspoon salt, or to taste
⅛ teaspoon freshly ground white pepper
¾ cup grated imported cheese, Gruyère, Emmen-
    thaler, or Italian Parmesan

Combine the wine, clam juice, cream, bay leaf, thyme, white pepper, leek, and shallots in a saucepan. Bring to a boil and simmer until reduced to 2 cups of broth. Poach the shrimp and scallops 1 minute in the broth, remove, and keep warm. Discard the bay leaf.

Melt the butter in another saucepan. Add the flour and cook 5 minutes over low heat, stirring constantly. Add the hot broth all at once and whisk vigorously until the sauce is thickened and smooth.

Gently simmer the sauce about 15 minutes to develop flavor and to thicken. Season with salt and pepper.

¶ The sauce can be prepared a day ahead and refrigerated. Reheat to use.

Preheat the broiler. Add the shrimp and scallops to the sauce and spoon into large buttered scallop shells, individual 6-ounce ramekins, or a 10-to-12-inch gratin dish. Sprinkle evenly with the grated cheese.

Place under the heated broiler about 4 inches from the heat (or in a preheated 425° oven) until the cheese melts and forms a golden crust.

NOTES: Add oysters, mussels, lobster, or crayfish to the gratin or make an all-oyster, -lobster, or -crayfish gratin, using a total of 1¾ pounds of shellfish.

Use leftovers, if any, as a sauce for pasta, adding light cream to extend the sauce if needed.

The gratin mixture can also be used as a filling for individual savory tartlets if the sauce is slightly thickened. Use ½ tablespoon more flour.

For a luxurious addition, mix in with the shellfish one or two whole fresh or canned French or Italian truffles, thinly sliced.

MENU: Creamy shellfish gratin / Angel hair pasta / Sautéed snow peas and red peppers / Lemon tart

SUGGESTED WINES: Meursault / California Chardonnay

Fried Oyster Sandwiches
with Hot Sauce
and Pickled Okra

SERVES 2

The memory of unforgettably good fried oyster sandwiches—a perfect rainy-day lunch enjoyed in a café in a small coastal town in southern Oregon—inspired this Texas version.

> 1½ quarts vegetable oil for deep-frying
> 12-inch length of French bread, cut in two 6-inch pieces
>   and split in half
> 1 tablespoon unsalted sweet butter, melted
> ½ cup cornmeal or corn flour (cornmeal ground to a
>   powder in blender or grinder)
> ½ teaspoon cayenne pepper
> ¼ teaspoon freshly ground black pepper
> ½ teaspoon salt
> 10 ounces oysters in a jar, drained and patted dry, or
>   12 to 18 large freshly shucked oysters
> 2 tablespoons bottled Mexican hot sauce, or freshly
>   made salsa (page 229)
> 8 spears pickled okra

Slowly heat the oil to 375°—this should take 10 to 15 minutes. Preheat the oven to 375°. Brush the split bread with melted butter, place on a baking sheet, and let crisp in the oven about 10 to 15 minutes.

Combine the cornmeal and seasonings. When the oil reaches 375°, roll the drained oysters in the cornmeal mixture, carefully drop into the hot oil in small batches, deep-fry about 2 to 3 minutes, and remove when the oysters are lightly browned.

Spread the first batch of fried oysters on paper towels on a baking sheet and place in the oven to keep warm while frying the rest.

Remove the hot bread from the oven, press the oysters onto one half of the bread, spread the other half generously with hot sauce, place on top of the oysters, and firmly press together. Cut in half and serve while nice and hot with the pickled okra.

MENU: Fried oyster sandwiches with hot sauce and pickled okra / Cold rice salad with pecan and vegetables / Watermelon

SUGGESTED BEVERAGE: Cold beer

CHAPTER 7

Grains, Vegetables, and Other Accompaniments to Fish Dishes

Fish deserve more exciting accompaniments than the ubiquitous boiled potato. In this section I have included some of my favorite grain, potato, and vegetable accompaniments for fish dishes, as well as some savory salads, soups, and relishes that complement seafood meals.

A stylish vegetable or grain dish can turn a seafood dinner into something unusual and wonderful. I look for texture and color, avoiding the all-white meal, especially when planning a menu around fish. Of course, the sauce or vegetable the fish dish may include must also be taken into account. A good rule of thumb is to try to alternate simple and prepared dishes: a simple dish would be an unadorned broiled, grilled, or steamed fish; a prepared dish is one that has quite a few ingredients and often a soft texture, such as a soufflé or a ratatouille.

White Rice

SERVES 2 TO 3

The texture and delicate flavor of rice make it a perfect accompaniment for many fish dishes, especially those with a sauce. Cooking rice is very simple, as the following recipe demonstrates.

> 1 cup long-grain white rice
> 2 cups water or chicken or beef broth
> ½ tablespoon unsalted sweet butter
> ¼ teaspoon salt
> ⅛ teaspoon white pepper
> 1 bay leaf
> pinch of dried thyme

Place all the ingredients in a heavy-bottomed 1½-quart saucepan. Bring to a boil, cover, and cook at a gentle simmer 15 to 20 minutes or until all the liquid is absorbed and the rice is tender.

Rice Pilaf

Follow the basic recipe but add ⅓ cup of red, white, or yellow onions, leeks, scallions, or shallots, cooked in 2 tablespoons of unsalted sweet butter. When the onion is soft, add the rice and stir over medium heat until the rice is translucent. Then add the liquid, usually broth, and simmer, covered, until done, about 15 to 20 minutes.

NOTE: Pine nuts and currants or chopped, dried apricots are nice additions to a pilaf. Add them when you add the liquid.

Rice: Some Variations on a Theme

There are many different kinds of rice, each with a distinctive flavor and texture. *Long-grain white rice* produces dry, fluffy, separate grains and is cooked according to a standard formula of 1 cup of rice to 2 cups of liquid. *Basmati rice* comes from the Himalayas; it has a delicately perfumed, milky flavor and is better when aged. *Tex-mati rice,* a cross between long-grain white and basmati rice, has a nutty flavor. *Pecan rice* from Louisiana is another hybrid rice; it has a delightfully elusive, nutty taste and, despite its name, contains no pecans.

Short-grain white rice takes about 10 to 15 minutes longer to cook and absorbs more liquid because it contains more starch. In this country, South Carolina is the source of this rice. However, the best short-grain rice comes from Italy and is called *Arborio*; it is the perfect rice for creamy risotto dishes. *Pearl rice* is a short-grain white rice used primarily in Asia; because of its starch content, this rice sticks together when cooked.

Brown rice is pure unprocessed rice with its bran coating left intact. It is chewy, has a nutty taste, and takes longer to cook than long-grain white rice (about 40 minutes). California-grown *Wehani rice*, sold in health food stores, is a striking, dark brownish red rice that tastes nutty and somewhat like a combination of brown rice and wild rice. It also takes about 10 to 15 minutes longer to cook.

Wild rice isn't really rice at all but the dark seed of a wild grass that is grown in northern Minnesota. It is now being cultivated in California, too. Cooked wild rice has a full-flavored nutty taste and aroma.

The darker varieties of rice call for 2 to 3 times more liquid than the standard 1 cup of rice to 2 cups of water formula.

Wild Rice
with Scallions

SERVES 4 TO 6

The rich nutty flavor and chewy texture of wild rice make it a perfect match with fish. Although it is expensive, a little goes a long way: 1 cup of raw wild rice yields 6 servings. And additions of cooked white rice or bulgur, onions, mushrooms, or hazelnuts, pecans, or almonds stirred into the cooked wild rice make it go even farther.

> 3 cups water
> 1 cup wild rice
> ½ teaspoon salt
> 2 tablespoons butter
> 5 medium scallions, white only, thinly sliced
> 2 tablespoons unsalted sweet butter

In a sieve, rinse the rice under cold running water for 2 minutes and drain it thoroughly. In a large saucepan, bring the water to a boil. Add the wild rice and salt; cover and simmer gently 30 to 40 minutes, or until the rice has absorbed all the water and the dark grains are just tender and beginning to show the white interior.

While the rice is cooking, gently sauté the scallions in butter until soft. Stir into the hot rice and serve.

Champagne Risotto

SERVES 4 TO 6

The short-grained Italian rice called Arborio is used to make this special creamy rice dish. In a classic risotto the liquid is added a little bit at a time, allowing the rice to cook gently so that, when done, it is tender but still a little firm in the center. The champagne adds a subtle lemony flavor to this recipe. Risotto is especially good with poached or grilled fish.

> 3 tablespoons unsalted sweet butter
> 1 medium yellow onion, minced
> 1½ cups Arborio rice, or if unavailable, long-grain white rice
> ½ cup champagne, sparkling, or dry white wine
> 3 cups hot chicken or beef broth (homemade if possible)
> ½ teaspoon saffron threads, softened in ¼ cup of the hot broth
> ½ teaspoon salt
> ⅛ teaspoon freshly grated pepper
> 2 tablespoons heavy cream, at room temperature
> ¼ cup freshly grated Parmesan cheese

Melt the butter in a 1½-quart heavy-bottomed saucepan and gently cook the onion until soft, about 8 minutes. Add the rice, and, stirring, cook over medium heat about 5 minutes. Add the champagne and cook 2 to 3 minutes. Add ¼ cup of the broth and saffron mixture and the salt and pepper. Stir well and cook uncovered over low heat until all the broth has been absorbed by the rice. Add another ½ cup of broth, let the rice absorb it; continue adding broth, ½ cup at a time, until the broth is used up. This takes about 30 to 35 minutes.

When the rice is done—tender but slightly chewy—stir in the cream and the cheese. Serve immediately.

Variation: *Seafood Risotto*—To the cooked risotto add 1 to 2 cups of cooked shellfish: shrimp, squid, scallops, oysters, mussels, or crab meat, or a mixture, cut into small pieces. Heat until the shellfish is warm throughout and serve immediately as a main course.

Crusty Persian Rice

SERVES 4

This simple dish lends an added dimension to rice with its chunky texture and golden color. The crust is broken up and scattered over the rice before serving. (Traditionally it is offered first, as the choicest portion, to honored guests.)

> 4 tablespoons vegetable oil
> 4 cups warm cooked long-grain white rice

Gently heat the oil until quite hot in the bottom of an 8- to 10-inch sauté pan or saucepan. Spread about 1½ cups of rice in the hot oil, pressing down lightly. Pile the remaining rice on top and continue cooking the rice over low heat 20 to 30 minutes or until the bottom layer of rice is golden and thoroughly crusted.

Turn out onto a warmed platter. Break up the crust and serve hot.

Couscous

SERVES 4 TO 6

Couscous is a wonderful light and delicious grain made from coarsely ground durum wheat or semolina. Because it is precooked it is fantastically practical for a quick meal. It cooks in only the time it takes to absorb a hot liquid and seasonings—about 5 to 8 minutes. A traditional dish from North Africa, couscous can be combined with chopped, cooked vegetables such as carrots, tomatoes, or zucchini, or with fish or meat to make a whole meal. Serve couscous in place of rice or as a bed for steamed or sautéed vegetables.

> 1 cup couscous
> 1¼ cups boiling water, chicken broth, or tomato juice
>   or light tomato sauce
> 1½ tablespoons unsalted sweet butter
> ⅛ teaspoon salt

Add the couscous to the water with butter and salt. Stir. Cover and remove from the heat. Let stand until the couscous has absorbed all the liquid, about 5 to 8 minutes.

Couscous with Tomatoes and Cinnamon

SERVES 4 TO 6

This recipe is adapted from a recipe for couscous timbales that appeared in *Gourmet* magazine. Couscous makes a wonderful accompaniment to fish dishes. It has great texture and lightness of flavor and combines well with interesting additions of dried fruits, nuts, or spices. This dish is particularly good with grilled fatty fish like swordfish or salmon and also goes well with any delicately steamed or poached lean fish.

> 2 shallots or 4 scallions, finely chopped
> 1 tablespoon unsalted sweet butter or virgin olive oil
> 1/8 teaspoon cinnamon
> 1 teaspoon ground cumin seed
> 1/4 teaspoon turmeric
> pinch of ground pepper
> 2 1/2 cups canned imported plum tomatoes, drained
>   and pureed in food processor
> 1/4 cup finely chopped fresh parsley, mint, or cilantro
> 1/3 cup pine nuts
> 1/3 cup dried apricots or dried currants, very finely
>   chopped
> 1 1/4 cup boiling chicken stock
> 1 cup couscous
> sprigs of parsley, mint, or cilantro for garnish

In a 2 1/2-quart saucepan, gently cook the shallots or scallions in the butter until soft, 3 to 4 minutes. Add the spices, tomatoes, parsley, pine nuts, apricots, and stock and bring to a boil. Stir in the couscous, cover, remove from the heat, and let stand until the couscous has absorbed all the liquid, about 5 to 8 minutes.

Bulgur with Lemon and Pine Nuts

SERVES 4

Bulgur, which is cracked wheat that has been parboiled and dried, is most familiar to us in tabbouleh, the delicious Middle Eastern summer salad made with tomatoes and parsley. However, cooked bulgur also makes an excellent accompaniment to all fish, especially grilled fish.

1 small clove garlic, peeled and mashed with a fork
4 large scallions with green, thinly sliced
2 tablespoons unsalted sweet butter
1 cup bulgur
2 cups chicken broth
¼ teaspoon salt
¼ teaspoon freshly ground white pepper
1 tablespoon freshly grated lemon rind
⅓ cup pine nuts
⅓ cup chopped parsley
Juice of ½ lemon

Gently cook the garlic and scallions in butter in a 1½-quart saucepan until soft. Add the bulgur and cook, stirring, for 1 to 2 minutes. Add the broth, salt, and pepper, and bring to a boil. Add the lemon rind; cover, reduce the heat, and simmer about 10 to 12 minutes, or until the liquid is absorbed. Mix in the pine nuts, parsley, and lemon juice, and serve hot.

Scalloped Potatoes with Garlic and Cream

SERVES 4 TO 6

This wonderful creamy potato dish complements Baked Mackerel in Mustard-Scallion Sauce or Baked Monkfish with Walnut Pesto, or any of the trout recipes. Since it is a filling dish, use it to round out a light meal.

> 2 pounds firm, red, waxy boiling potatoes, peeled, thinly sliced, and patted dry
> 1½ cups whole milk
> 1½ cups heavy cream
> 2 large cloves garlic, mashed with a fork
> ½ to ¾ teaspoon salt
> ½ teaspoon freshly ground white pepper
> ½ teaspoon dried thyme
> 2 tablespoons unsalted sweet butter
> ½ cup finely grated imported Swiss, Emmenthaler, or Gruyère cheese

Place prepared potatoes in a large saucepan. Add all the rest of the ingredients except the butter and cheese. Bring to a simmer.

Butter a shallow gratin dish and pour in mixture. Dot with butter and sprinkle with cheese.

Bake uncovered at 375° about 1 hour or until nicely browned.

Pommes de Terre au Diable

SERVES 4

This interesting and easy Provençal technique produces the most exquisite tasting potatoes! A perfect accompaniment to grilled fish with Olive Butter or Sun-Dried Tomato Butter. The potatoes dry-steam in their own moisture so there is never the watery taste of boiled potatoes. In Provence, a "diable," a specially designed unglazed clay pot, was traditionally used for roasting potatoes and chestnuts in the fireplace. Any unglazed or glazed clay pot or Romertöpf will work well, too, but if you can get a diable you will see that the special clay it's made from does transmit a special flavor to the potatoes. Any vegetable cooked in earthenware tastes better. If you use it, add no water; do not wash the pot, and rub it with salt to remove cooked bits of potato.

> 12 small to medium unpeeled new potatoes, well scrubbed
> 3 large branches fresh rosemary, crushed
> 6 large cloves garlic, crushed

Layer all the ingredients in a diable or in an unglazed earthenware pot, such as a Romertöpf. Cover, place on a metal or asbestos heat diffuser, and cook over a medium-high flame for 30 to 40 minutes, or place in a 375° oven and bake about 45 to 50 minutes or until cooked through. (If you are using a diable, halfway through the cooking turn it over.)

Quick Oven Potatoes with Rosemary

ALLOW 1 MEDIUM POTATO PER PERSON

These crusty rosemary-flavored potatoes are especialy delicious with any kind of fish baked in a sauce or with any grilled fish.

> baking potatoes
> virgin olive oil
> dried or fresh rosemary, pulverized
> freshly ground black pepper

Scrub potatoes well. Cut each potato in half lengthwise or crosswise, then slice into ⅓-inch slices.

Pour a little bit of olive oil into a large bowl. Turn the potatoes slices in the oil so that all sides are covered, then place on a large baking sheet. Sprinkle with pepper and rosemary.

Bake until lightly browned on both sides at 400° to 425°. Takes about 15 to 20 minutes.

NOTE: A delicate garlic flavor can be added by crushing to a pulp 1 or 2 garlic cloves in the olive oil before tossing the potatoes in it.

Potato Soufflé

SERVES 4 TO 6

A potato soufflé is delicious with steamed fish or with fish flavored with tomato or mushroom sauces. Because potatoes are dense, this soufflé cannot fall. It will also hold 10 to 15 minutes in a warm oven.

3 medium to large baking potatoes, peeled and cut
    into cubes
1½ tablespoons grated onion or shallot
4 tablespoons Italian Parmesan cheese
3 large egg yolks
¾ cup heavy cream, crème fraîche (page 227), or light
    cream
1 teaspoon salt
¼ teaspoon freshly ground white pepper
pinch of nutmeg, mace, or cayenne pepper
4 to 5 large egg whites, at room temperature
2 to 3 tablespoons Italian Parmesan cheese (additional)
    to coat bottom and sides of soufflé dish

Cook the potatoes in boiling salted water, drain, place in a saucepan over medium heat, and toss 1 minute or so to remove excess moisture. In a mixer, mash or beat until smooth. Add onion and cheese. Mix the egg yolks with the cream. Add all the seasonings.

¶ The recipe can be made a day ahead to this point and refrigerated. Let the mixture come to room temperature before proceeding with the recipe.

Beat the egg whites until stiff. Mix a third of the whites into the potato mixture to lighten, then fold in the rest.

Sprinkle the cheese in a buttered 1½-quart soufflé or baking dish and toss to coat the insides. Carefully pour soufflé mixture into dish and bake at 350° to 375° about 35 to 40 minutes.

Spaetzle

SERVES 4 TO 6

Spaetzle (pronounced shpātzli) means "little sparrows"—the shape of the cooked dough. Easily and quickly made, they taste like a delicious cross between a noodle and a dumpling. Spaetzle, which originated in Germany, are also popular in Austria and Hungary as a homemade accompaniment to stews, grilled fish, and game. They are especially good with trout, smoked fish, and other fish in light sauces. Although an inexpensive, simple spaetzle maker is helpful, it is not strictly necessary since the dough can be pushed through a colander with a spatula.

3 large eggs
⅓ cup milk
⅓ cup water
2¼ cups unbleached white flour
½ teaspoon and 1 tablespoon salt
2 to 4 tablespoons unsalted sweet butter, melted
½ teaspoon freshly grated black pepper

Bring about 4 quarts of water to a boil. Combine the eggs and liquids and gently mix them together. Place the flour and ½ teaspoon of the salt in a mixer or food processor and mix or process as you add the liquid ingredients. The dough is ready when just combined. It should be neither too stiff nor too liquid.

Add the remaining salt to the boiling water and place a colander or spaetzle maker over the top of the pan. As quickly as you can, press the dough through the holes into the boiling water. Spaetzle rises to the top when it is cooked, after 2 to 4 minutes. Remove the cooked spaetzle with a slotted spoon, drain, and toss in a warmed bowl with melted butter and pepper.

Variation: Toss buttered spaetzle with one or more of the following: 2 tablespoons of minced fresh parsley or thyme, ⅓ cup of freshly grated Parmesan cheese, ⅓ cup of fresh toasted bread crumbs, or ½ cup of light homemade tomato sauce.

Orzo with Feta and Tomatoes

SERVES 2

Orzo is a tiny rice-shaped pasta made from semolina that is widely used in Greece. It's a handy substitute for rice, cooks in only a few minutes, and can be added to soups or combined with sauces to make a wonderful accompaniment to sautéed, baked, or broiled fish.

> 1 cup orzo
> ¼ cup red onion, minced
> 1 tablespoon extra-virgin olive oil
> 1 large tomato, peeled, seeded, and finely chopped
> ½ teaspoon oregano or basil
> ⅓ cup crumbled feta cheese
> ¼ teaspoon freshly ground black pepper

Add the orzo to a pot of boiling salted water. Cook until al dente, 3 to 5 minutes, and drain.

While the orzo is cooking, in a large skillet, gently sauté the onion in olive oil until soft. Add the tomatoes and oregano and cook only until heated through. Stir in the orzo, feta, and pepper. Serve hot.

Polenta

SERVES 4 TO 6

Polenta, the classic northern Italian cornmeal pudding, is a delicious substitute for rice or potatoes. Excellent with fish cooked in red wine or on the grill, polenta can conveniently be made ahead. Simply spread cooked polenta into a shallow buttered baking pan while it is still hot. Let cool or chill overnight. Then cut it into squares and reheat on the grill, in the oven, or under the broiler.

> 3½ cups water
> 1¼ cups polenta, or yellow cornmeal
> 1 teaspoon salt
> ⅓ cup freshly grated Italian Parmesan or Fontina cheese
>   (optional)

Bring the water to a rapid boil, add the polenta and salt. Reduce the heat and simmer, whisking vigorously from time to time to keep the polenta from lumping. Cook until the polenta pulls away from the side of the pan, about 20 to 30 minutes. Add cheese if desired.

Serve immediately or pour into a pan as described above and chill for use for next day.

Green Beans with Shallots

SERVES 6 TO 8

Try these delicious beans with grilled swordfish or salmon or any lean fish that is baked, steamed, or broiled. This dish is also good with Rice with Shrimp, Sausage, and Oysters.

> 1½ pounds green beans, string removed, cut into 3-
> inch pieces
> boiling salted water
> 4 tablespoons unsalted sweet butter
> 4 to 5 shallots minced
> salt, freshly ground black pepper
> ¼ cup minced, fresh Italian parsley, for garnish

Cook the beans uncovered in water until just barely done, about 3 to 6 minutes, depending on the type and size. Drain and rinse immediately in cold water to stop cooking.

¶ This recipe can be made a day ahead and held in the refrigerator until ready to serve. Remove from the refrigerator 15 minutes before proceeding with the recipe.

Melt the butter in a large skillet, add the shallots and the beans. Turn up the heat and toss until heated through, season, and garnish with parsley.

Braised Artichokes

SERVES 6 TO 8

Provençal cooks have a magical way with vegetables. I learned many wonderful dishes when I lived in the Vaucluse, an area northeast of Avignon whose hillsides are covered with vineyards, truffle oaks, lavender fields, and fragrant wild thyme. This dish is a Vaucluse specialty and a perfect example of a braised vegetable dish, the flavors of onions, carrots, garlic, tomatoes, herbs, broth, and wine all blending to make a delectable sauce for the artichokes. This goes well with baked, grilled, steamed, or broiled fish.

2 tablespoons salt
6 large artichokes, trimmed, quartered, and dechoked
2 small yellow onions, chopped
2 carrots, chopped finely
3 cloves garlic, mashed with a fork
2 tablespoons extra-virgin olive oil
2 tablespoons unsalted sweet butter
1 to 2 large tomatoes, seeded and chopped
1 to 2 teaspoons dried thyme
2 tablespoons chopped fresh Italian parsley
1 imported bay leaf
½ teaspoon salt (additional)
⅛ teaspoon freshly ground pepper
1 to 1½ cups chicken broth
1 to 1½ cups dry white wine

Bring a 6-quart pot of water to a boil. Add 2 tablespoons of salt and the quartered artichokes and blanch (partially cook) uncovered about 7 to 10 minutes. Remove the artichokes and drain in a colander.

In a large, heavy casserole, sauté the onions, carrots, and garlic in the oil and butter until they take on color.

Add the tomatoes and seasonings and mix well. Add the broth and wine. Add the artichokes, cover, and simmer 1 to 1¼ hours on top of the stove or in a 325° oven.

Serve hot from the baking dish or a heated tureen or deep vegetable dish.

Artichokes and Mushrooms in Madeira Cream

SERVES 6 TO 8

This rich flavorful dish perfectly accompanies a lean fish simply cooked with herbs en papillote.

> 1 pound medium mushrooms, quartered
> 4 tablespoons unsalted sweet butter
> 6 shallots or scallions, minced
> 1 clove garlic, mashed to a paste with a fork
> 2 tablespoons all-purpose flour (optional)
> 1 cup hot chicken broth
> 1 cup crème fraîche (page 227)
> 3 to 4 tablespoons dry or Sercial Madeira, dry sherry, or dry white wine
> 12 ounces cooked artichokes or canned artichoke bottoms or hearts, or 8 home-prepared artichoke bottoms, chopped
> lemon juice
> pinch of salt
> grind of black pepper
> 1 to 2 teaspoons fresh snipped chives or tarragon

Sauté the mushrooms gently in the butter, then add the shallots and garlic. Cook 2 to 3 minutes. Add flour, if desired.

Add the chicken broth, cook down by half, then add the crème fraîche and Madeira.

Stir in the cooked artichokes and season with a few drops of lemon juice, salt, pepper, and chives.

¶ Can be made a day ahead to this point, refrigerated, and gently reheated.

Glazed Carrots

SERVES 4 TO 6

This is an especially good complement to fine lean fish like sole, black bass, halibut, flounder, cod, and redfish.

> 1 pound carrots, peeled, cut in 1-inch pieces
> 1 cup chicken broth
> ¼ teaspoon salt
> ⅛ teaspoon freshly ground white pepper
> 2 tablespoons unsalted sweet butter
> 2 to 3 teaspoons sugar
> 2 tablespoons minced parsley, for garnish

Place all the ingredients except the parsley in a small heavy-bottomed saucepan, partially cover, and simmer until the liquid has evaporated and the carrots are tender and glazed, about 10 to 12 minutes.

If the carrots cook before the liquid cooks down, remove them and boil down until a glaze forms. Toss the carrots in the syrupy glaze.

Serve hot, garnished with parsley.

Zucchini Gratin

SERVES 8

This savory gratin is especially good with baked whole fish.

> 6 pounds zucchini, peeled, seeded, and diced
> ½ cup unsalted sweet butter
> ½ to 1 teaspoon salt
> ⅛ teaspoon freshly ground white pepper
> ⅓ cup minced parsley
> 1 to 1½ cups finely grated imported Gruyère cheese

Cook the zucchini about 20 to 30 minutes in a large skillet, partially covered, in 4 tablespoons of the butter over low heat. When zucchini are very soft, remove from the heat and add the salt and pepper. Mash the zucchini with a wooden spoon until pureed, or put it through a food mill. Stir in another 3 to 4 tablespoons of butter and the parsley. Taste and adjust the seasoning.

Spread the puree on the bottom of a shallow buttered 8-by-12-inch baking or gratin dish. Sprinkle with the cheese and dot with 2 to 3 tablespoons of butter. Bake in a preheated 375° to 400° oven until the cheese is lightly browned and bubbly, about 10 to 12 minutes.

Baked Ratatouille

SERVES 8

Because of the way the fresh red tomatoes and green zucchini are layered on top, this is a very attractive version of ratatouille. A great dish for entertaining, ratatouille can be made ahead and kept refrigerated. It tastes good cold too, and is great with grilled, steamed, and broiled fish.

⅓ to ½ cup extra-virgin olive oil
2 yellow onions, chopped
2 small eggplants, peeled and chopped
2 green peppers, thinly sliced
2 cloves garlic, mashed to a paste with a fork
1 teaspoon salt
½ teaspoon freshly ground white pepper
1½ teaspoons dried thyme
½ teaspoon dried basil
½ teaspoon dried oregano
2 to 3 large ripe tomatoes, sliced and halved
2 to 3 medium zucchini, scored and thinly sliced
Additional salt, pepper, thyme, and olive oil for final
    seasoning

Heat the oil in a large sauté pan or casserole. Add the onions and eggplant, toss thoroughly in oil, and cook 10 minutes; add all the other ingredients except the tomatoes and zucchini. Cover and simmer 45 minutes. Remove the cover and cook an additional 15 to 30 minutes, until excess moisture has evaporated. Adjust the seasoning. You should have a thick vegetable puree.

Place the puree in the bottom of an oiled 8-by-12-inch baking dish and arrange the tomatoes and zucchini in alternating layers on top of the puree. Sprinkle with additional salt, pepper, thyme, and olive oil. Bake 10 to 20 minutes in a 375° oven.

Mushrooms à la Grecque

SERVES 10 TO 12

This combines salad and vegetable in one dish. It goes well with rice and almost any kind of fish. It makes a wonderful picnic dish as well as an hors d'oeuvre. Try this dish as an appetizer or salad with Sole with Eggplant, or with Braised Scrod with Leeks, Potatoes, Thyme, and Cream.

1½ to 2 pounds mushrooms, washed, trimmed, and quartered if large
3 to 4 shallots, minced
3 scallions, finely chopped with green tops
3 to 4 tomatoes, peeled, seeded, and chopped
½ teaspoon dried thyme
¼ teaspoon dried oregano
2 teaspoons peppercorns, crushed
2 teaspoons salt
½ teaspoon coriander seeds, crushed
2 imported bay leaves
⅓ cup extra-virgin olive oil
1 cup dry white wine
juice of one large lemon or 1½ small
½ cup water
1 tablespoon finely chopped fresh thyme, tarragon, or oregano (optional)

3 tablespoons finely chopped fresh Italian parsley, for garnish

Place all the ingredients except the parsley in a heavy saucepan. Bring to a boil and simmer, covered, 10 minutes or until the vegetables are barely tender.

Transfer to an earthenware or glass crock or bowl and let cool to room temperature. Cover and chill until ready to serve.

May be kept about 10 days in the refrigerator. The flavor improves with standing. Garnish with parsley before serving.

NOTE: In place of mushrooms, use cauliflower, carrots, broccoli, green beans, leeks, zucchini, fennel, cucumber, beets, jerusalem artichokes, or celery.

For example, cauliflower, carrots, and broccoli combine nicely. Or try fennel, cucumber, and beets; or beets and celery; or green beans, leeks, and zucchini. Cut each vegetable into bite-sized pieces. It is best to cook each separately if you wish to present two or three kinds of vegetables mixed together.

Mushrooms Sautéed with Garlic

SERVES 4 TO 6

This is one way mushrooms are prepared in the Bordeaux region of France. An easy and quick recipe, cooked at the last minute before serving, it goes fabulously well with sautéed, broiled, grilled, baked, steamed, or poached fish. The garlic should be noticeable, but it can be reduced. Try this recipe with Whole Fish Baked in Salt or Brook Trout with Pancetta, Sage, and Champagne Wine Vinegar.

> 1 pound large mushrooms, stems trimmed but left on,
>   quartered
> 1½ tablespoons virgin olive oil
> 3 tablespoons unsalted sweet butter
> pinch of salt
> grind of black pepper
> 4 shallots, minced, or 1 small bunch scallions, minced
> 2 to 3 cloves garlic, finely minced
> ¼ cup fine white bread crumbs
> 3 to 4 tablespoons minced parsley
> Pinch of *fines herbes* or minced chives

Quickly sauté the mushrooms in the oil and butter over a medium-high to high heat about 2 to 3 minutes or until very lightly browned. Season with salt and pepper.

Add the shallots, garlic, and bread crumbs. Stir and toss until lightly cooked, about 3 to 5 minutes. Add the herbs and taste for seasoning.

Serve very hot.

NOTE: Don't cook the mushrooms longer than suggested or they will start to release their liquid and the dish will become soupy instead of dry.

Mushrooms Braised with Garlic and Herbs

SERVES 6 TO 8

This dish has a fabulous aroma and goes well with any simply prepared fish such as Steamed Halibut Wrapped in Swiss Chard or Quick Scallop Sauté with Herbed Crumbs and Orange Wedges.

> ½ cup unsalted sweet butter
> 4 large cloves garlic, mashed to a paste with a fork
> 1½ pounds large mushrooms, with stems, quartered
>   through the stem
> ½ teaspoon salt
> ¼ teaspoon freshly ground white pepper
> ⅓ cup finely chopped mixed fresh herbs: Italian pars-
>   ley, chives, tarragon, and thyme, or use all parsley
>   and chives

Melt the butter in a large skillet, add the garlic, and cook gently for 5 minutes, but do not let garlic brown.

Add mushrooms, and season with salt and pepper. Cook 3 minutes, stirring.

Place in a covered casserole in a 350° oven for 15 minutes. Just before serving, stir in the herbs.

Tomatoes à la Provençale

SERVES 6

This easy 15-minute dish from the south of France goes well with any grilled, baked, or broiled fish or any other simply prepared fish that could take a bit of garlic as an accompaniment.

6 large ripe tomatoes, firmest possible
2 large cloves garlic, minced
3 tablespoons minced shallots or scallions
3 to 4 tablespoons minced parsley
½ teaspoon dried thyme or 2 teaspoons chopped fresh thyme
⅛ teaspoon dried basil
¼ teaspoon salt
⅛ teaspoon freshly ground pepper
⅔ cup fine white bread crumbs
3 to 4 tablespoons extra-virgin olive oil

Cut the tomatoes in half, seed, and press out the juices but do not mash. Sprinkle the halves with salt, then turn upside down on a wire cooling rack and let them drain 10 minutes.

Combine the rest of the ingredients, except the olive oil, to make the stuffing.

Fill the tomato halves with stuffing, and sprinkle with olive oil. Place in an oiled baking or gratin dish.

Bake at 400° for about 8 minutes, or until the crumbs are a bit browned but tomatoes are not too soft. Better to underbake, as they will continue to cook for a few minutes in their own heat when removed from the oven.

Spinach Bresse Style

SERVES 2 TO 4

An excellent accompaniment to steamed or poached fish. Bresse is an area just to the west of Grenoble and the Alps and is known for its good simple country cooking.

> 1 pound fresh spinach, washed several times in a large
> amount of water, rinsed, and stemmed
> 3 quarts boiling salted water
> 3 tablespoons unsalted sweet butter
> ¼ cup heavy cream or crème fraîche (page 227)
> ¼ teaspoon salt
> ⅛ teaspoon freshly ground white pepper
> ⅛ teaspoon freshly grated nutmeg

Blanch the spinach uncovered 2 to 3 minutes in boiling salted water. Drain. Press out excess liquid. Chop.

¶ The recipe can be made a day ahead and refrigerated well covered.

Place spinach in a large saucepan, let dry out a few minutes over medium-high heat, stirring all the while.

Gradually stir in butter and cream in small amounts over low heat. When all the butter and cream has been absorbed by the spinach, season carefully with salt, pepper, and nutmeg.

NOTE: Do not use aluminum utensils or carbon steel knives when preparing spinach. The metal interacts with the spinach and creates an unpleasant metallic taste.

Spinach Timbales

SERVES 4 TO 6

A timbale, a delicate vegetable-flavored custard, can be made from many vegetables—broccoli, cauliflower, corn, carrots, lettuce, Swiss chard. Use 1 pound of leafy greens and ¾ pound of other vegetables. Cook the vegetables, and drain very well, chop finely or puree, and adjust seasonings. This is an excellent vegetable dish to go with steamed sole, halibut, or flounder.

> 16 ounces fresh spinach, Boston lettuce, Swiss chard,
>   or sorrel, well washed and stemmed (or white
>   centers cut out)
> 4 quarts boiling salted water
> 2 large eggs, beaten
> ½ cup hot heavy cream
> ¼ teaspoon nutmeg
> salt
> freshly ground pepper
> 2 hard-cooked eggs, finely chopped, for garnish
> 4 thin lemon wedges or slices, for garnish

Cook the spinach 4 to 5 minutes in boiling water. Drain the spinach, let it cool, and squeeze dry. Chop finely.

Add the eggs to the spinach, stir in the hot cream, and season.

Pour into well-buttered, small metal baba molds, or individual 3-to-4-ounce soufflé or custard cups.

Bake in a bain marie (a large baking dish filled with 1 inch of simmering hot water) at 375° for 40 to 45 minutes, or until puffed and golden on top. Timbales will hold for 10 to 20 minutes in a warm oven.

To serve, invert first over a baking dish to remove excess liquid, then turn onto a small serving dish. Garnish with egg and lemon.

NOTE: Do not use aluminum utensils or carbon steel knives when preparing spinach.

Warm Potato Salad
with Tarragon
and Shallot Vinaigrette

SERVES 4 TO 6

This is an excellent match with smoked fish or cold poached fish and shellfish.

> 2 pounds new potatoes, scrubbed
> ½ cup dry white wine
> 2 teaspoons white wine vinegar
> ⅓ cup extra-virgin olive oil
> 3 shallots, minced
> 2 tablespoons finely chopped fresh chives or scallion tops
> 2 tablespoons chopped fresh parsley
> 3 tablespoons chopped fresh tarragon or, if unavailable, ¼ teaspoon dried
> ½ teaspoon salt
> ¼ teaspoon freshly ground white pepper
> chopped romaine, Boston lettuce, or watercress for serving

Boil or steam the potatoes until done. Drain and, while still warm, peel and slice them.

Combine all the remaining ingredients to make the dressing. Mix well, adjust the seasonings, and gently mix with the warm potatoes. Serve at room temperature on a bed of chopped romaine, Boston lettuce, or watercress.

Roasted Red, Green, or Yellow Pepper Salad

SERVES 2

A healthful accompaniment to grilled or sautéed fish dishes that provides a splash of color as well. Use the peppers individually or try a mix.

Vinaigrette
1 tablespoon fresh lemon juice
4 tablespoons extra-virgin olive oil
1 to 2 tablespoons mashed garlic cloves
½ teaspoon salt
⅛ teaspoon freshly ground black pepper

2 large regularly shaped green, red, or yellow bell peppers, washed and dried

Combine all the vinaigrette ingredients and mix well.

To roast the peppers, stick a fork firmly into the stem end, char the skin directly over an open gas flame or close to broiler heat or place very close to or directly on a hot electric burner. Turn so the charring is even. When black all over, place the peppers on a small plate. Cover immediately with a damp, cold paper towel. Leave for a few minutes to allow the steam to loosen the charred skin.

Then remove the skin: Holding a pepper with both hands, push the paper towel down with both thumbs, turning the charred skin to the inside and rolling it up in the paper towel. One continuous movement is better than a dabbing one.

When the skin is off and all the black bits removed from the plate, cut out the stem and seeds. Reserve the juices from the partially cooked pepper and add to the vinaigrette. Cut the peppers lengthwise into ½-inch strips. Place in a medium bowl and toss to coat well with the vinaigrette. Hold in a cool place for several hours, but serve at room temperature.

Marinated Corn Salad

SERVES 12

This salad makes a wonderful fresh accompaniment to any grilled fish or outdoor meal. It is excellent with Grilled Swordfish with Sun-Dried Tomato Butter or Grilled Tuna with Salsa Verde.

 2 to 3 ears of sweet corn, broken into 2 to 3 pieces each (optional)
 1 pound frozen corn kernels or kernels cut off the cob (do not use canned corn)
 4 large shallots, minced
 3 scallions with green, finely chopped
 3 to 4 tomatoes, peeled, seeded, and chopped
 ½ teaspoon dried thyme
 ½ teaspoon dried oregano
 2 teaspoons black peppercorns, crushed
 2 teaspoons salt
 ½ teaspoon coriander seeds, crushed
 2 imported bay leaves
 ⅓ cup extra-virgin olive oil
 1 cup dry white wine
 juice of 1 large lemon
 ½ cup water
 ¼ cup finely chopped fresh Italian parsley, for garnish

Place the corn pieces in a 5-to-6-quart heavy saucepan. Add the corn kernels, shallots, scallions, tomatoes, seasonings, olive oil, wine, lemon juice, and water and bring to a boil, then simmer covered for about 10 minutes.

¶ This dish should be made a day before serving.

Cool, and chill until ready to serve. Keeps well 3 to 4 days in the refrigerator. The flavor improves with standing.

Just before serving, garnish with chopped parsley.

NOTE: Drained well, corn salad (made with corn kernels only) can also be served in hollowed-out tomato halves or fresh red or green pepper halves.

Olive Salad

SERVES 4 TO 6

A perfect salad to follow paella and substantial enough to be served as a vegetable with steamed, baked or grilled fish such as Moroccan Fish with Cumin or Roasted Monkfish with Five-Pepper Butter.

Dressing
½ teaspoon salt
1½ tablespoons Spanish sherry wine vinegar
6 tablespoons extra-virgin olive oil
1 clove garlic, mashed to a paste with a fork
½ teaspoon freshly ground black pepper
½ teaspoon dried oregano

1 orange, peeled and cut into slices, then into quarters,
    or cut into wedges
½ cup Spanish green olives, rinsed and drained
⅓ cup radishes, thinly sliced (optional)
⅓ cup walnuts
2 quarts mixed salad greens (any combination of ro-
    maine, escarole, Boston lettuce, radicchio, red-
    tipped, oakleaf, curly endive), washed, dried, and
    broken into large pieces

Make the dressing by dissolving the salt in the vinegar, then stirring in the olive oil, garlic, pepper, and oregano and mixing well.

All salad ingredients can be prepared in advance and held, then tossed with the dressing just before serving.

Cold Tomato Soup

SERVES 4 TO 6

A fine-flavored, filling soup that complements many seafood entrées, especially shellfish. Follow this soup with Crab-Filled Omelet, Oyster-Parmesan Popovers, or Fried Oyster Sandwiches.

> 2 tablespoons unsalted sweet butter
> 1 large yellow onion, minced
> 2 large garlic cloves, minced
> 5 to 6 large red ripe tomatoes (about 2 pounds), seeded and chopped
> 3 cups chicken broth
> 2½ tablespoons tomato paste
> 2 tablespoons cornstarch, dissolved in ¼ cup of the cold broth
> ½ to 1 teaspoon salt
> ⅛ to ¼ teaspoon freshly ground white pepper
> ½ cup heavy cream or crème fraîche (page 227)
> 2 tablespoons freshly chopped herbs: dill, basil, tarragon, parsley, or chives, for garnish

Melt the butter in a heavy-bottomed casserole, add the onion and garlic, and cook over low heat about 10 minutes, or until the onions are soft.

Add the tomatoes and 1 cup of the broth. Simmer, covered, 15 minutes.

Add the remaining 2 cups of broth, and the tomato paste, cornstarch, and seasonings. Cook 10 minutes.

Let cool down, then blend in a blender (which will give a finer texture than in a food processor) and chill thoroughly.

Stir in the cream just before serving, and sprinkle the herbs on top.

Watercress Soup

SERVES 6

The peppery flavor of watercress is always a good complement to fish. This makes a nice beginning for a steamed, baked, or poached fish dinner.

> 4 tablespoons unsalted sweet butter
> 2 small yellow onions, chopped
> 2 leeks, washed well and chopped
> 2 large Idaho potatoes, scrubbed, peeled, and chopped
> 5 to 6 cups chicken broth, heated
> 2 large bunches watercress, trimmed and well washed
>   (reserve a few sprigs for garnish)
> pinch of salt
> grind of black pepper
> ¼ to ⅓ cup crème fraîche (page 227) (optional)

Melt the butter in a large saucepan. Cook the onions and leeks 10 minutes over low to medium heat; add the potatoes and cook 5 minutes.

Add the hot stock and watercress and cook uncovered until the potatoes are soft, about 10 to 15 minutes. Let cool.

Puree the soup, preferably in a blender or food processor.

¶ The soup can be made a day ahead to this point and refrigerated well covered. To use, reheat.

Check the seasonings and add the crème fraîche if desired. Serve hot or cold, garnished with watercress sprigs.

Marinated
Black-Eyed Pea Relish

SERVES 4 TO 6

This is especially good as a side dish with sautéed catfish, Pecan-Cayenne Butter, and cornbread. Or serve it with Fried Oyster Sandwiches or Tuna in Orange-Ginger Marinade.

½ teaspoon salt
scant 3 tablespoons sugar
¼ cup red wine vinegar
a few grinds black pepper
dash or two of Tabasco sauce
¼ cup safflower oil
½ clove garlic, mashed with a fork
½ green pepper, chopped
2 15-ounce cans black-eyed peas with snaps, drained
½ cup chopped red onion

Dissolve the salt and sugar in the vinegar. Add the ground pepper, Tabasco, oil, garlic, green pepper, black-eyed peas, and red onion. Mix well, cover, and refrigerate 24 hours before serving so that flavors can blend.

NOTE: This dish keeps well in the refrigerator about one week.

VARIATION: For a salad, add ⅔ cup of cooked corn and ½ cup of chopped red pepper and serve in a whole red cabbage that has been hollowed out or in a nest of radicchio leaves.

Shallot Confit

SERVES 6

These glazed shallots make a fine slightly *agro-dolce*, or tart-sweet, accompaniment to any fish that's broiled or sautéed, but are particularly good with salmon, striped bass, swordfish, trout, pompano, and halibut.

> 1 pound shallots, peeled
> 2 tablespoons unsalted sweet butter
> 1 tablespoon sugar
> ¼ cup raspberry wine vinegar
> pinch of salt
> grind of black pepper

Blanch the whole shallots in boiling salted water 5 minutes. Drain.

In a heavy 1½-quart casserole, melt the butter and add the sugar, shallots, and raspberry wine vinegar. Cook over medium heat about 15 minutes or until a syrupy glaze forms and the shallots are soft. Add seasonings to taste.

Serve hot on the side as a condiment to the fish listed above or any others of your choice.

Cornmeal Brioche

MAKES 2 LOAVES

Cornmeal added to a brioche dough gives this rich, soft egg-and-butter bread a delightful crunchy texture that toasts beautifully and makes a perfect base for Crab, Lettuce, and Tomato Sandwiches. Also try this toasted for a Fried Oyster Sandwich or Lobster Sandwich with Tapenade, or for breakfast with Sautéed Trout.

> 1 tablespoon active dry yeast
> ¼ cup warm water
> 2 tablespoons sugar
> 5 large eggs, at room temperature
> 1 cup unsalted sweet butter, softened
> 3½ cups all-purpose flour
> 1 cup yellow cornmeal
> 1 teaspoon salt

Dissolve the yeast in the warm water in a large bowl. Add the sugar, eggs, butter, and 2 cups of the flour mixed with cornmeal and salt. Beat in a mixer or food processor until well blended, 3 to 4 minutes.

Add the remaining flour, and beat until smooth. Cover the bowl with a towel or plastic wrap, and set in a warm place to rise about 1½ to 2 hours, or until the dough is doubled. (Because of all the eggs and butter, the dough will be very soft.)

Punch down the dough in the bowl. Cover and refrigerate overnight to chill for easier handling and to develop the dough's flavor. (Or omit this step and proceed with second rise.)

Place the chilled dough in two 7-by-3-by-4-inch loaf pans, leaving at least 3 inches at the top for rise. Set in a warm place to rise about 1 to 1½ hours, or until the dough is at the top of the pan.

Bake in a preheated 400° oven for 50 minutes or until browned on top. Remove from pans and cool on wire cooling racks. Let cool and firm for 2 to 3 hours before slicing.

NOTE: Cornmeal Brioche can be made into rolls and baked until browned, about 15 to 20 minutes. The baked bread or rolls can be wrapped and frozen after they have cooled. Makes 12.

Quick Cream- or Buttermilk-Pecan Biscuits

MAKES 4 LARGE BISCUITS

These easy biscuits take only 5 to 10 minutes to make and taste wonderful served for breakfast with Trout Meunière. For an exceptional brunch dish cover the hot baked biscuits with Tomato Crab Cream.

        2 cups all-purpose flour
        1 scant teaspoon salt
        1 tablespoon baking powder
        pinch of sugar
        ⅓ cup coarsely chopped pecans (optional)
        1 cup heavy cream or buttermilk

Preheat the oven to 425°.

Combine the flour, salt, baking powder, sugar, and pecans in a bowl. Quickly stir in the cream or buttermilk, stirring only until the ingredients are lightly blended and hold together. (Overmixing makes biscuits tough.)

Place the dough on a lightly floured surface, and knead a few times until smooth. Quickly pat or roll to ½- to ¾-inch thickness. Cut four 4-inch rounds and place on a buttered baking sheet.

Bake about 15 minutes at 425° or until biscuits are lightly browned. Remove and serve hot.

NOTE: This recipe can easily be doubled or tripled for a larger number of servings.

CHAPTER 8

Fish Fumet, Court Bouillons, Marinades, Butters and Sauces, Coatings, and Shellfish Boils

Here are the magic touches that expand your repertoire of fish dishes in a hundred ways with little or no effort. Choose a cooking technique from the basic recipes in Chapter 2, add a sauce or flavored butter to your own taste, and *voilà*, a new dish of your own making. See the suggested combinations listed in Chapter 2 for ideas.

Fish Fumet

MAKES 1 TO 1½ QUARTS

Of the two basic kinds of fish stock—court bouillon and fumet, the fumet is the more flavorful because it is made with fish trimmings.

Use fumet to poach fish, for sauces, and as a soup base, or clarify it and use it for aspic. You can also reduce a fumet by three quarters and use it as a concentrated fish glaze to add in small amounts to enrich sauces. Fish heads are desirable to use in making fumet because they are gelatinous and give a fine body to the stock. But avoid oily fish (and heads) as their stronger flavor will affect the delicacy of the taste. Never use the gills, which give a bitter taste.

> 2 tablespoons unsalted, sweet butter
> 1 large carrot, chopped
> 1 large yellow onion, chopped
> 2 large leeks, chopped
> 1 large shallot, chopped
> 1 stalk celery with leaves, chopped
> ¼ to ½ pound mushrooms, chopped, or use stems, chopped
> 1 clove garlic, unpeeled
> 3½ pounds or more of lean fish and fish trimmings: heads with gills cut out, skeletons or pieces of fish, or 1 whole fish, all well rinsed and free of blood
> 1½ cups dry white wine
> 2 to 3 quarts cold water
> 2 teaspoons fresh lemon juice
> 1 teaspoon dried thyme
> 1 imported bay leaf
> ⅓ cup chopped parsley stems
> 1 teaspoon salt
> 1 teaspoon black peppercorns, cracked
> 2 teaspoons coriander grains, crushed

Melt the butter in a large casserole or stockpot. Add the vegetables and cook over medium high heat 4 to 5 minutes, stirring. Do not allow to brown.

Add the fish heads, bones, and pieces, stir, and cook 2 to 3 minutes.

Add the white wine, cold water, and lemon juice. When stock comes to a simmer, skim off the foam before adding the herbs and seasonings.

Simmer gently, uncovered, 35 to 45 minutes. Let cool and strain through a fine-mesh strainer before using.

Keep fumet only one day in the refrigerator or freeze in 1-cup plastic containers for future use in sauces, aspics, and soups. Thaw and simmer or boil to reduce and concentrate the flavors.

Keep frozen only 3 to 4 months. (All frozen food is best when used within a 3-month period.)

NOTE: For fumets based on court bouillons, see below.

COURT BOUILLONS

Court bouillon refers to a seasoned liquid quickly cooked and flavored without fish. Any fish or shellfish can be cooked in plain water, but easy-to-prepare court bouillons give extra flavor to enhance fish and shellfish dishes, sauces, and soups.

Court bouillon means short or brief boiling or cooking in French. Court bouillons are usually made up as needed since they only take a short time to cook and are not frozen, as are fumets. (A court bouillon becomes a fumet after a fish has been poached in it; it can then be frozen according to the directions on page 197.)

White Wine Court Bouillon

MAKES ABOUT 2 QUARTS

1½ quarts water
1 quart or less dry white wine
2 carrots, peeled and chopped in large chunks
2 stalks celery with leaves, chopped
2 yellow onions, chopped
1 to 2 leeks, white part only, chopped (optional)
⅓ cup chopped parsley stems
2 teaspoons salt
1 teaspoon whole black peppercorns
2 imported bay leaves
¼ teaspoon dried fennel seed (optional)
¼ teaspoon dried thyme
1 teaspoon coriander seeds, crushed

Combine all ingredients in a large saucepan or stockpot and bring to a boil. Simmer gently, uncovered, for 35 to 45 minutes.

Let cool and strain through a fine-mesh strainer before using.

To use a court bouillon for poaching a whole fish, fillets, or steaks, pour into a poacher or other appropriate receptacle and heat until steaming. Gently lower the fish on a rack or wrapped in dampened cheesecloth into the court bouillon and simmer with the lid slightly ajar for 10 minutes per inch of thickness.

Red Wine Court Bouillon

MAKES ABOUT 2 QUARTS

This is basically the same as White Wine Court Bouillon except that a dry red wine is used in place of the white wine, leeks are used instead of celery, and a pinch of dried tarragon or a sprig of fresh tarragon is added. More robust than its white wine cousin, this broth is used for fatty fishes such as salmon, trout, and mackerel.

> 1½ quarts water
> 1 quart or less dry red wine
> 2 carrots, peeled and chopped in large chunks
> 2 yellow onions, chopped
> 2 leeks, white part only, chopped
> ⅓ cup chopped parsley stems
> 2 teaspoons salt
> 1 teaspoon whole black peppercorns
> 2 imported bay leaves
> ¼ teaspoon dried fennel seed (optional)
> ½ teaspoon dried thyme
> 1 teaspoon coriander seeds, crushed
> pinch of dried tarragon, or a sprig of fresh

Combine all the ingredients in a large saucepan or stockpot and bring to a boil. Simmer gently, uncovered, for 35 to 45 minutes.

Let cool and strain through a fine-mesh strainer before using.

See directions for using court bouillon on page 198.

White Wine Court Bouillon for Soups and Chowders

MAKES ABOUT 2 QUARTS

This court bouillon is excellent as a base for fish and shellfish soups and chowders.

2½ cups cold water
4 cups dry white wine
3 cups bottled clam juice
3 carrots, peeled and cut in 1-inch chunks
1 cup roughly chopped parsley sprigs
1 yellow onion, quartered
2 shallots, finely chopped
2 leeks, well rinsed and roughly chopped
1 imported bay leaf
¼ teaspoon dried thyme
12 black peppercorns, crushed

Bring all the ingredients to a boil in a large saucepan or stockpot and simmer, uncovered, for 30 minutes.

Strain through a fine-mesh strainer before using.

NOTE: If desired, ¼ pound of minced mushrooms can be added for a richer flavor.

Vinegar Court Bouillon

MAKES 3 QUARTS

Use this court bouillon for poaching fresh trout, mackerel, or bluefish. The mild vinegar highlights moderately fatty and fatty fish and is a good way to cook fish that are going to be served cold in a salad or with a sauce.

2 quarts water
3¼ cups good-quality wine or cider vinegar (do not
  use distilled white vinegar)
1 teaspoon dill seed
1 teaspoon celery seed
1 teaspoon white peppercorns, cracked
1 teaspoon coriander seed
2 carrots, peeled and chopped
2 onions, chopped

Combine all the ingredients in a large saucepan or stockpot and simmer, uncovered, for 35 to 45 minutes. Strain through a fine-mesh strainer before using.

Milk Court Bouillon

MAKES ABOUT 6 CUPS

A milk court bouillon keeps white-fleshed fish such as cod, scrod, haddock, pollack, and halibut very white when cooked.

3 cups milk
1¾ cups water
2 thick slices lemon
½ teaspoon white peppercorns, cracked
2 teaspoons salt
¼ teaspoon dried or ½ teaspoon fresh thyme
1 imported bay leaf
½ yellow onion, cut in chunks
1 carrot, peeled and sliced

Combine all the ingredients and use for poaching. (This does not have to be simmered or strained before using.)

MARINADES

A marinade is a mixture of aromatic liquids—usually oil and an acidic liquid such as vinegar, wine, buttermilk, or lemon, orange, or lime juice—and herbs and seasonings. A good basic marinade can be made from a good vinaigrette or oil and vinegar dressing, but use a little more acid and less or no salt.

A marinade does not serve to tenderize fish, as it does with meat, because fish is naturally tender, but it does add extra flavor and moisture. Basting with a marinade keeps fish moist when cooking by dry-heat methods—baking, broiling, and grilling.

Because fish flesh is so tender it will absorb a marinade very quickly, so long marination is not necessary. A fish will take on more of the flavor of the marinade the longer it marinates. Depending on the strength of the marinade ingredients, anywhere from 15 minutes for stronger marinades to 1 hour for milder ones is sufficient time. Be careful with citrus marinades because a high proportion of lime or lemon juice will actually "cook" the flesh of a delicate fish (as the scallops in ceviche are "cooked" in lime juice).

Use about ⅓ to ½ cup of marinade for every pound of fish to be marinated. Always marinate fish in the refrigerator.

If marinating a whole fish to bake or grill, score both sides with a thin, sharp knife, cutting two large X's about ½ inch deep, turn fish in the marinade to get as much of the marinade as possible in the cuts. (See, for example, Baked Whole Fish à la Provençale, page 66.)

The easiest and neatest way to marinate is to place the marinade and fish (fillets, steaks, chunks, or whole fish) in a heavy-duty plastic bag. This facilitates turning and keeping the fish in continuous contact with the marinade.

Marinade	Fish
⅓ cup	¾ to 1 pound
½ cup	1 pound
⅔ cup	about 1½ pounds
¾ cup	1½ pounds
1 cup	2 pounds

Orange-Fennel Marinade

MAKES ABOUT ½ CUP

Wonderful with scallops, flounder, shrimp, swordfish, and bluefish.

>1 teaspoon grated orange rind
>¼ cup freshly squeezed orange juice
>2 teaspoons fennel seed
>3 tablespoons safflower oil or melted butter
>1 tablespoon dry white wine

Combine all the ingredients. Marinate the fish for 30 minutes, then bake, broil, or grill, basting with the marinade if desired.

Greek Oregano Marinade

MAKES ABOUT 1 CUP

These Mediterranean flavors go well with swordfish, tuna, mackerel, redfish, grouper, and orange roughy.

>¼ cup fresh lemon juice
>½ cup extra-virgin olive oil
>1 clove garlic, mashed to a paste with a fork
>1 teaspoon dried oregano, or 2 teaspoons chopped or
>   bruised fresh oregano
>½ red onion, halved and thinly sliced

Combine all the ingredients. Marinate the fish about 30 minutes, then grill, broil, or bake, basting with the marinade if desired.

Hot Pepper
and Lime Marinade

MAKES ABOUT ½ CUP

Good for all lean and fatty fish.

⅓ cup fresh lime juice
3 tablespoons safflower oil
1 fresh hot serrano or jalapeno pepper, seeded and
minced

Combine all the ingredients. Marinate the fish 15 minutes, then bake, grill, or broil, basting with the marinade if desired.

NOTE: If hot fresh green peppers are not available, use 1 teaspoon of dried red pepper flakes.

Mustard Seed Marinade

MAKES ABOUT ½ CUP

Try this with full-flavored bluefish, mackerel, salmon, swordfish, or tuna.

4 tablespoons extra-virgin olive oil
1 to 2 tablespoons white wine vinegar or lemon juice
¼ teaspoon salt
¼ teaspoon freshly ground white pepper
1 teaspoon prepared Dijon mustard
1 tablespoon mustard seeds, heated in ½ tablespoon
of the olive oil until they burst
1 tablespoon chopped Italian parsley

Combine all the ingredients. Marinate the fish 30 minutes and grill, broil, bake, basting with the marinade if desired.

Garlic-Anchovy Marinade

MAKES ABOUT ½ CUP

Try this with any lean, white-fleshed, firm fish fillets, such as red snapper, redfish, shark, monkfish, and scallops, or with salmon, bluefish, or tuna.

> 4 to 5 anchovies, rinsed, patted dry, and mashed
> 2 cloves garlic, mashed with a fork
> ⅓ cup extra-virgin olive oil
> ½ teaspoon fresh rosemary, crushed, or ¼ teaspoon
>   dried, pulverized rosemary
> 1 to 2 teaspoons good red wine vinegar
> ⅛ teaspoon freshly ground black pepper

Combine all the ingredients. Marinate the fish for 30 minutes, then grill, bake, or broil, basting with marinade if desired.

French Mushroom Marinade

MAKES ABOUT 1 CUP

Wonderful for flounder, sole, cod, halibut, red snapper, striped bass, orange roughy, or any lean fish. (See Basic Baked Fish, page 34.)

> 4 ounces mushrooms, thinly sliced or chopped
> 2 shallots, finely chopped
> 1 tablespoon chopped fresh parsley
> 1 teaspoon fresh thyme, or ¼ teaspoon dried thyme
> 1 teaspoon fresh marjoram, or ¼ teaspoon dried mar-
>   joram
> 2 to 3 tablespoons dry white wine
> 3 to 4 tablespoons melted unsalted sweet butter
> pinch of salt
> grind of white pepper

Combine all the ingredients. Marinate the fish fillets 30 minutes to 1 hour, and then bake, basting with the marinade if desired.

NOTE: You can add ¼ to ½ cup of heavy cream to the pan during baking to make a sauce.

Orange and Saffron Marinade

MAKES ABOUT ⅔ CUP

Especially good with shrimp, but can also be used with lean fish or as a base to steam clams and mussels.

½ teaspoon pure saffron threads
¼ cup dry white wine
2 cloves garlic, mashed to a paste with a fork
¼ cup extra-virgin olive oil
1 teaspoon grated fresh orange peel
2 tablespoons fresh orange juice

Pound the saffron with a little heated white wine to extract the flavor. Mix all the ingredients together and let sit 15 minutes before using. Marinate shrimp or fish 30 minutes, then grill or broil.

Lime and Mint Marinade

MAKES ABOUT ½ CUP

Especially good with scallops, swordfish, shark, and red snapper.

¼ cup fresh lime juice
3 tablespoons safflower oil or melted unsalted sweet
    butter
⅓ cup chopped fresh mint leaves

Combine all the ingredients. Marinate the fish ½ hour, then grill, broil, or bake, basting with marinade if desired.

Mediterranean Marinade

MAKES ABOUT ⅔ CUP

This is good with shrimp, swordfish, trout, pompano, tuna, and all firm, lean fish.

⅓ cup extra-virgin olive oil
2 tablespoons white or red wine vinegar
2 tablespoons dry white or red wine
2 imported bay leaves, broken in pieces
2 cloves garlic, mashed to a paste with a fork
1 tablespoon fresh rosemary, or 1 teaspoon dried and
    crushed rosemary

Mix all ingredients and let stand 15 minutes to blend flavors before using. Marinate fish ½ hour, then bake, broil, or grill, basting with the marinade if desired.

Hot Thai Marinade

MAKES ABOUT ⅓ CUP

Try this with shrimp or lean fillets like red snapper and redfish, as well as with fatty fish like bluefish and salmon. The lemon grass and fish sauce are what makes this marinade "Thai" and distinctive. (See Chapter 1 for a discussion of these ingredients.)

3 hot serrano peppers, seeded and finely chopped
1 6-inch stalk lemon grass, cut into ½ inch pieces
3 tablespoons fresh lime juice
1 tablespoon Thai fish sauce (Squid brand is best)
1 tablespoon water
2 tablespoons chopped fresh cilantro

Combine all ingredients. Marinate fish 15 minutes, then grill or broil, basting with the marinade if desired.

Sesame-Sake Marinade

MAKES ABOUT ½ CUP

Good for all kinds of fish as well as for shrimp and scallops. Especially good with salmon or tuna.

> ¼ cup white sesame seeds, toasted in a dry skillet until
>   golden
> ¼ cup sake or dry sherry
> 2 tablespoons soy sauce
> 1½ tablespoons finely grated fresh ginger root

Combine all the ingredients. Marinate the fish 1 to 2 hours, then sauté, grill, broil, or bake, basting with the marinade if desired.

Ginger-Soy Marinade

MAKES ABOUT ¾ CUP

Great with shrimp and scallops, or cod, grouper, lingcod, orange roughy, bluefish, and swordfish.

> ⅓ cup soy sauce
> ⅓ cup peanut or other vegetable oil
> 3 scallions, minced
> 2 cloves garlic, mashed to a paste with a fork
> 2 tablespoons freshly grated fresh ginger
> 1½ tablespoons rice wine vinegar
> 1 teaspoon seeded and minced hot serrano or jalapeno
>   pepper
> 1 teaspoon dark sesame oil

Combine all the ingredients. Marinate the fish about 15 minutes, then bake, broil, or grill, basting with the marinade if desired.

Juniper Berry
and Gin Marinade

MAKES ABOUT ½ CUP

Great for trout or salmon, halibut, bluefish, or mackerel.

1 tablespoon juniper berries, crushed
½ tablespoon gin
2 shallots, minced
1 imported bay leaf
½ teaspoon dried or fresh thyme
2 tablespoons dry vermouth
2 tablespoons fish fumet, court bouillon, or clam juice
3 tablespoons melted butter

Combine all the ingredients. Marinate the fish for 30 minutes, then broil, bake, or grill.

Buttermilk and
Black Pepper Marinade

MAKES ABOUT 1 CUP

A wonderful marinade for all fish, but especially good with flounder, sea trout, catfish, and other freshwater fish such as lake trout, lake whitefish, and lake perch. Fish can then be sautéed, broiled, grilled, or baked.

1 cup fresh buttermilk
½ teaspoon freshly ground black pepper
pinch of cayenne
pinch of salt

Combine all the ingredients. Marinate the fish for 4 to 24 hours.

Basic French Vinaigrette

One of the best marinades for fish is just a classic vinaigrette dressing. The secret of this wonderful basic sauce, useful in so many ways, for marinating fish and seasoning cold fish salads is in the proportions and the quality of the ingredients. For a discussion of the various types of oils and vinegars, see Chapter 1.

Vinaigrettes work equally well as marinades and salad dressings for fish and shellfish dishes but are especially good with shrimp or lobster. Although a vinaigrette can be made ahead in any quantity and stored in the refrigerator, I normally make it up just before using.

> 1 tablespoon red wine vinegar or fresh lemon juice
> ½ teaspoon salt
> ¼ teaspoon freshly ground black or white pepper
> 1 teaspoon prepared Dijon mustard (*never* dry mustard)
> 4 to 5 tablespoons French or Italian virgin or extra-virgin olive oil
> ½ to 1 tablespoon chopped fresh herbs (parsley, chives, thyme, basil, mint, tarragon, or oregano)

As a marinade: Combine all the ingredients and marinate the fish in the refrigerator about 30 minutes to 1 hour before cooking.

As a dressing: Combine all the ingredients and pour over warm, plainly cooked (steamed, poached, or grilled) fish. Let cool for 1 hour; refrigerate and serve as a salad with greens and chopped mushrooms, red peppers, or herbs.

Other Good Flavor Combinations (follow the general proportions in the recipe above):

Champagne wine vinegar, virgin olive oil, shallots, tarragon

½ red wine and ½ raspberry vinegar, 1 part walnut oil to 3 parts virgin olive oil, whole walnuts, pinch dried basil

Sherry wine vinegar, extra-virgin olive oil, mashed garlic

Balsamic vinegar, extra-virgin olive oil, Italian Parmesan cheese

Rice wine vinegar, safflower oil, ginger, sesame oil, coriander, chives

Tarragon Vinaigrette

MAKES ABOUT ½ CUP

An excellent dressing for cooked lobster, monkfish, crab meat, or shrimp. Tarragon complements the flavor of lobster especially well.

> 2 tablespoons champagne or white wine vinegar
> 6 tablespoons virgin olive oil
> 2 tablespoons chopped fresh tarragon leaves, or ½
>   teaspoon dried tarragon, crumbled
> ¼ teaspoon freshly ground white pepper
> 1 shallot, finely chopped
> pinch of salt

Combine all the ingredients and use as dressing for cooked seafood.

Spicy Yogurt Marinade

MAKES 1 CUP

Excellent with all lean fish, especially cod, grouper, flounder, lingcod, rockfish, orange roughy, and catfish.

2 teaspoons ground coriander seeds
1 teaspoon ground cumin
½ teaspoon cayenne pepper
½ teaspoon ground turmeric
¼ teaspoon ground ginger
¼ teaspoon freshly ground white peppercorns
1 cup plain yogurt

Heat the ground spices in a small skillet just 1 minute to bring out the flavors. Stir into the yogurt.

Marinate the fish fillets 30 minutes to 1 hour and bake, basting with the marinade.

Balsamic Vinegar and Basil Marinade

MAKES ABOUT ¾ CUP

Marinate fresh shucked oysters in this, thread them on skewers, then grill them *en brochette*; use the sauce for dipping. This is also good as a basting sauce for fresh grilled lobster. Use it to marinate and baste grilled shrimp, salmon, and trout.

2 tablespoons Italian balsamic vinegar
5 to 6 tablespoons extra-virgin olive oil
1 tablespoon chopped fresh Italian parsley
2 tablespoons finely chopped fresh basil or 1 teaspoon
    dried leaf basil, finely crumbled
⅛ teaspoon freshly ground white pepper
pinch of salt
1 large shallot, minced

Mix all the ingredients and combine with fish or shellfish to marinate 20 to 30 minutes.

FLAVORED BUTTERS

Flavored butters offer a wonderfully easy way to flavor simply-cooked fish—poached, steam-baked en papillote, baked, steamed, or grilled. Ingredients can be pounded together in a mortar, chopped and combined in a food processor, or mixed in an electric mixer. Always use unsalted sweet butter for finest flavor. Combine all the ingredients for a flavored butter, season, roll into a log shape, wrap in plastic wrap, then in foil, label and date, and store in the freezer. Keep four or five different flavors on hand.

To use, remove from the freezer 15 to 20 minutes ahead of time, slice off the amount you need, and refreeze the rest. These butters will keep 1 to 2 weeks in the refrigerator if wrapped well, but some butters retain their flavors better if stored in the freezer.

Flavored butters are not usually used in the cooking, but rather for adding flavor immediately after the fish is cooked. Some, however, are good cooked with fish either en papillote, steamed, or baked. To flavor cooked fish, place thin slices of softened butter, usually ½ to 1 tablespoon per serving, on top of steaming fish to melt or warm the butter in a small pan on top of stove and pour over the hot fish. If the butter is ice-cold when it is put on the fish, it will cool down the surface of the fish.

NOTE: ½ cup flavored butter = 8 tablespoons
⅔ cup = 11 tablespoons
¾ cup = 12 tablespoons

Herb Butters

MAKES ½ CUP

In butters, herbs that go well with fish are chives, dill, tarragon, watercress, parsley, basil, sorrel, cilantro, and thyme.

> ½ cup unsalted sweet cold butter
> **plus**
> 2 tablespoons chopped fresh chives, dill, or tarragon
> **or**
> ⅓ cup chopped watercress or minced parsley, or sorrel
> **or**
> ¼ cup chopped fresh basil
> **or**
> 2 tablespoons fresh thyme leaves or cilantro
> pinch of salt
> grind of black pepper
> ¼ to ½ teaspoon lemon juice

Cream the butter and mix the herb of choice and other ingredients until well blended. Roll into a log shape, wrap well, and refrigerate or freeze.

NOTE: A little salt does not make the butters salty but helps to bring out the flavors.

Lemon, Orange, or Lime Butter

MAKES ½ CUP

With its clear, clean, sharp citrus flavor, this is an excellent butter for all poached, steamed, baked, broiled, baked, or grilled fish.

> ½ cup unsalted sweet cold butter
> 1 tablespoon fresh lemon, orange, or lime juice
> 1 teaspoon freshly grated lemon, orange, or lime peel
> ⅛ teaspoon salt
> ⅛ teaspoon freshly ground pepper

Cream the butter, and mix all the ingredients together until well blended. Roll into a log shape, wrap well, and refrigerate or freeze.

Garlic, Shallot, and Parsley Butter

MAKES ½ CUP

Put on oysters to be grilled, baked, or broiled on the half shell. Allow 1 to 2 teaspoon per oyster.

½ cup unsalted sweet cold butter
2 cloves garlic, mashed to a paste with a fork
1 shallot, minced
a few drops lemon juice
1 tablespoon fresh chopped parsley

Cream the butter and mix all the ingredients together until well blended. Roll into a log shape, wrap well, and refrigerate or freeze.

Anchovy Butter

MAKES ½ CUP

Excellent over grilled or broiled salmon or swordfish steaks, halibut, mullet, red snapper, rockfish, tuna, and amberjack.

½ cup unsalted sweet cold butter
2 tablespoons anchovy paste, or more to taste
⅛ teaspoon freshly ground black pepper
1½ teaspoons finely chopped parsley

Cream the butter and mix all the ingredients together until well blended. Roll into a log shape, wrap well, and refrigerate or freeze.

Grainy Mustard Butter

MAKES ½ CUP

Use over broiled or grilled mackerel, bluefish, tilefish, salmon, or trout.

>½ cup unsalted sweet cold butter
>3 tablespoons grainy French mustard or Creole mustard
>¼ teaspoon salt
>⅛ teaspoon freshly ground black pepper
>a few drops lemon juice

Cream the butter and mix all the ingredients together until well blended. Roll into a log shape, wrap well, and refrigerate or freeze.
>NOTE: For a sharper taste, add 1 tablespoon of chopped scallions.

Shrimp Butter

MAKES ⅔ CUP

One or two tablespoons enriches soups, sauces, and stuffings. This butter is also good over hot poached fish or used as a spread on hot toast.

>½ cup unsalted sweet cold butter
>4 ounces shrimp, cooked and peeled, pureed or pounded to a paste with 1 tablespoon heavy cream
>¼ teaspoon salt
>⅛ teaspoon freshly ground white pepper

Cream the butter and mix all the ingredients together until well blended. Roll into a log shape, wrap well, and refrigerate or freeze.

Tomato Butter

MAKES ABOUT ¾ CUP

Good tossed with hot cooked pasta and shrimp.

> ½ cup unsalted sweet cold butter
> 3 small tomatoes, peeled, seeded, minced, and patted
>   dry, or 1 tablespoon tomato paste
> 3 cloves garlic, mashed to a paste with a fork
> ¼ cup chopped parsley
> 2 tablespoons finely chopped fresh basil or 1 teaspoon
>   dried basil
> 1 tablespoon lemon juice

Cream the butter and mix all the ingredients together until well blended, roll into a log shape, wrap well, and refrigerate or freeze.

Red Wine Butter

MAKES ½ CUP

Excellent with poached, grilled, or broiled trout, salmon, and oysters.

> ½ cup good-quality red wine
> 3 shallots, finely chopped
> 1 teaspoon red wine vinegar
> ⅛ teaspoon salt
> ⅛ teaspoon freshly ground black pepper
> ½ cup unsalted sweet cold butter

In a small saucepan, boil down the wine, shallots, and vinegar until only 2 tablespoons remain. Season with salt and pepper and cool.

Cream the butter and blend in the wine mixture. Roll into a log shape, wrap well, and refrigerate or freeze.

Green Peppercorn Butter

MAKES ½ CUP

Use on any grilled fish, poached salmon steaks, steamed sole, or on shrimp or scallops steam-baked en papillote.

½ cup unsalted sweet cold butter
1 tablespoon green peppercorns in brine, drained, rinsed, and pounded to a paste in a mortar
1 small clove garlic, mashed to a paste in a mortar
1 shallot, finely chopped

Cream the butter and mix all the ingredients together until well blended. Roll into a log shape, wrap well, and refrigerate or freeze.

Orange-Chive Butter

MAKES ½ CUP

Use with steamed or grilled shellfish: shrimp, mussels, scallops, or lobsters. Perfect for scallops en papillote.

½ cup unsalted sweet cold butter
1 to 2 teaspoons grated orange zest
2 tablespoons fresh orange juice
2 tablespoons fresh chopped chives

Cream the butter and mix all the ingredients together until well blended. Roll into a log shape, wrap well, and refrigerate or freeze.

Cilantro-Lime Butter

MAKES ½ CUP

Great over grilled, broiled, or baked redfish, halibut, tilefish, bluefish, mackerel, and amberjack.

> ½ cup unsalted sweet cold butter
> ⅓ cup chopped cilantro
> 2 teaspoons fresh lime juice
> ⅛ teaspoon salt
> ⅛ teaspoon freshly ground pepper

Cream the butter and mix all the ingredients together until well blended. Roll into a log shape, and wrap well, and refrigerate or freeze.

Caviar Butter

MAKES ABOUT ½ CUP

This is an elegant butter sauce that brings a special flavor to poached or steamed fine-flavored fish such as sole, flounder, red snapper, striped bass, salmon, or sea trout. The butter can also be served as a special sauce for steamed potatoes.

> ½ cup unsalted sweet cold butter
> 1½ tablespoons finely chopped fresh chives
> 1 teaspoon freshly grated lemon rind
> ¼ teaspoon freshly ground white pepper
> 2 tablespoons black caviar, lumpfish, or whitefish or
>   red salmon caviar
> ⅓ cup sour cream

Cream the butter and combine all the ingredients. Beat until well-mixed. Serve softened with additional caviar and chives to garnish.
NOTE: This butter does not freeze well.

Ancho Chile Butter

MAKES ABOUT ¾ CUP

Ancho chile butter goes best with full-flavored fish such as bluefish and swordfish.

> 6 ounces unsalted sweet cold butter
> 1½ to 2 tablespoons ancho chile powder, or about 4
> large dried ancho chiles, ground to a fine powder
> in a spice grinder
> ½ teaspoon salt

Cream the butter, add the chile powder and salt, and blend. Roll into a log shape, wrap well, and refrigerate or freeze. Soften or melt to use.

Jalapeno-Cumin Butter

MAKES ABOUT ½ CUP

Try this with fried catfish or sautéed, baked, or grilled redfish, snapper, swordfish, or scallops.

> ½ cup unsalted sweet cold butter
> 1 tablespoon fresh jalapeno, seeded and minced
> 2 teaspoons ground cumin, heated in a dry skillet
> ¼ teaspoon salt

Cream the butter, mix in the jalapeno, salt, and cumin, and blend. Roll into a log shape, wrap well, and refrigerate or freeze.

NOTE: Be careful in handling hot chile peppers. Do not rub skin, eyes, or nose while working with fresh hot chiles.

Mango-Mint Butter

MAKES ABOUT ¾ CUP

This is especially good over grilled, broiled, or baked red snapper, redfish, and mahimahi, and on pompano steam-baked en papillote.

> ½ cup plus 2 tablespoons unsalted sweet cold butter
> 8 ounces fresh or canned mango, pureed
> 2 teaspoons fresh lime juice
> 2 tablespoons fresh, finely chopped mint
> pinch of salt

Cream the butter, and mix in all ingredients together until well blended. Wrap well and chill (see Note). Serve softened but not melted over hot fish.

NOTE: This butter should not be frozen.

Pecan-Cayenne Butter

MAKES ABOUT ½ CUP

Perfect for sautéed or baked catfish or broiled snapper or mullet.

> ½ cup unsalted sweet cold butter
> ½ cup toasted, but not browned, pecans, ground
> ¼ heaping teaspoon cayenne pepper
> ¼ teaspoon salt

Cream the butter, and beat in the pecans, cayenne, and salt. Roll into a log shape, wrap well, and refrigerate or freeze. Serve melted or very soft on steaming fish.

Poblano Butter

MAKES ABOUT ⅔ CUP

This rich and smoky but not burning chile flavor goes well with grilled fish, especially tuna, swordfish, and amberjack.

> ½ cup unsalted sweet cold butter
> 1 or 2 large fresh poblano chiles, roasted and skinned
>   (see page 187) and finely chopped
> ¼ teaspoon salt

Cream the butter, and mix in the poblanos and salt. Roll into a log shape, wrap well, and refrigerate or freeze.

Sun-Dried Tomato Butter

MAKES ¾ CUP

This warm, intense tomato flavor goes well with grilled, steamed, or poached fish and polenta or pasta. Commercial sun-dried tomatoes vary a lot in flavor. Try different brands until you find one you like, or make your own (see page 20).

> ⅓ cup chopped sun-dried tomatoes (see Note)
> ½ cup unsalted sweet cold butter
> ½ teaspoon dried basil or 1 tablespoon fresh chopped
>   basil
> pinch of salt
> ¼ teaspoon freshly grated black pepper

Cream the butter and mix all the ingredients until well blended. Roll into a log shape, wrap well, and refrigerate or freeze.

NOTE: If sun-dried tomatoes are stored in oil, drain them; if dried, soften them in hot water.

SAUCES

Every cook needs a few special sauces in his/her repertoire to add a touch of luxury, of delight to a dish. I can't think of a fish that wouldn't welcome a little judicious saucing. The sauces that follow can be used in many different ways with fish and shellfish.

Ivory Shallot Butter Sauce (Beurre Blanc Sauce)

MAKES ABOUT 1 CUP (SERVES 6 TO 8)

I first tasted this superb sauce with poached salmon trout at the three-star restaurant Chez Barrier in Tours, France, many years ago. This wonderful creation from the Loire Valley is my favorite sauce for poached, steamed, or plain baked fish or steam-baked fish en papillote. It is perfect with poached salmon, grilled scallops and oysters, baked sea bass, grilled redfish, and red snapper en papillote. This sauce takes only 10 minutes to make, and while it is usually made just before serving, it holds perfectly for several hours in a warmed thermos. The sauce is served very warm, but cannot be steaming hot or it would melt. This sauce does not taste or look the same reheated, because only whisked air holds it together, but if any is left over, it can be used as a flavored butter on hot vegetables—especially asparagus— as well as on grilled salmon, scallops, steak, veal chops, or poached eggs. Many beurre blanc recipes leave out the vinegar, which is odd because it is the vinegar that gives the sauce its distinctive flavor. Various herbs and seasonings can be added to beurre blanc for interesting variations.

> 1/3 cup French champagne vinegar, French tarragon
> vinegar or white wine vinegar
> 1/3 cup good dry white wine (Muscadet, Mâcon Blanc)
> 2 tablespoons finely chopped shallots
> 1/2 teaspoon salt
> 1/8 teaspoon freshly ground white pepper
> 1/2 pound unsalted sweet butter, cut into 1-tablespoon
> pieces, chilled

Bring the vinegar, wine, shallots, salt, and pepper to a boil in a heavy 1½-quart saucepan. (A Le Creuset enameled cast-iron saucepan is perfect for this sauce.) Boil until the liquid and shallots are reduced to 1 tablespoon, about 2 to 3 minutes.

Remove the pan from the heat and, using a small wire whisk and whisking constantly, add 3 tablespoons of butter. They will melt from the heat of the pan. This forms the base of the sauce.

Whisk in the remaining pieces of butter, blending in a tablespoon at a time, moving the pan off and on a low flame only as needed to melt the butter. Too much heat and the sauce liquefies. Never leave the pan on the fire without whisking for more than 6 to 8 seconds. Whisk the last pieces of butter vigorously into the sauce until you have a light ivory-colored sauce.

If you have measured the salt and pepper carefully, the sauce will not need any additional seasonings. Pour immediately into a heated thermos, or keep on a warm stove a few minutes until serving.

Pour into a warmed sauce boat and serve immediately.

NOTES: If unexpected guests arrive, 2 to 3 tablespoons of warmed heavy cream can be whisked into the finished sauce to stretch it a little further.

Additions of tomato, leek, and red pepper will increase the yield on the basic recipe to about 1⅓ or 1½ cups (enough for 8 to 10 servings).

Variations:

Herb Beurre Blanc: Add to the finished sauce 1 to 2 tablespoons of one of the following minced fresh herbs: basil, dill, tarragon, thyme, chervil, or mint.

Tomato Beurre Blanc: Add to the finished sauce 1 medium tomato, peeled, seeded, drained, and finely chopped.

Tomato-Basil Beurre Blanc: Add 1 to 2 tablespoons of fresh chopped basil to Tomato Beurre Blanc.

Leek Beurre Blanc: Add to the finished sauce 1 medium leek, well rinsed of dirt, thinly sliced, and cooked until soft in 2 tablespoons of water and seasoned with salt and pepper. Drain and pat dry before adding.

Caviar Beurre Blanc: Add to the finished sauce 1 tablespoon of good caviar. This is excellent with sole.

Mustard Beurre Blanc: Add to the finished sauce 2 teaspoons of prepared Dijon mustard.

Garlic Beurre Blanc: Add to the finished sauce, 2 to 3 large cloves of garlic, peeled, blanched 5 minutes, then simmered in a second batch of boiling water until the garlic is soft. Puree and add.

Roasted Red Pepper Beurre Blanc: Add to the finished sauce, 1 large red bell pepper, roasted, skinned, stemmed, and seeded (see page 187) and finely minced.

Aioli
(Provençal Garlic Mayonnaise)

MAKES ABOUT 1½ CUPS

In Provence, this sauce is made with more garlic and only with green extra-virgin Provençal olive oil, which may be a little strong for American tastes. Aioli makes an excellent sauce for any deep-fried shellfish; for example, try the Chipotle Aioli with deep-fried shrimp or oysters. This sauce keeps up to three days refrigerated.

   4 to 6 large cloves garlic
   4 large egg yolks
   1 tablespoon boiling water
   1 tablespoon fresh lemon juice
   ½ teaspoon salt
   pinch of cayenne pepper
   1⅓ cups oil (⅔ cup safflower and ⅔ cup extra-virgin
      olive oil)

Puree the garlic with the egg yolks in a blender or food processor, or pound them together in a large mortar. Add water and lemon juice.

   Add oil to the mixture in the processor or mortar a teaspoon at a time, processing on high speed or whisking, until half the oil is incorporated. The aioli will be very thick. Add the rest of the oil in larger amounts, 2 to 3 tablespoons at a time, processing or mixing well after each addition.

Variations:

   Chipotle Aioli: Add 2 to 3 tablespoons of canned Mexican chipotle chiles, drained and chopped.

   Sun-Dried Tomato Aioli: Add ¼ cup of drained and finely chopped sun-dried tomatoes.

   Basil Aioli: Add ¼ cup of finely chopped fresh basil.

   Horseradish Aioli: Add 1 to 2 tablespoons of drained and squeezed prepared horseradish.

Pesto
(Fresh Basil Sauce)

MAKES ABOUT 1½ CUPS

The sharp clean taste of basil Pesto brightens the flavor of any food it touches. Make it in large quantities during basil season and freeze for use all year long.

2 cups fresh basil leaves, washed and dried
5 medium garlic cloves, mashed with a fork
⅓ to ½ cup pine nuts
½ cup extra-virgin olive oil
¾ to 1 cup Italian Parmesan cheese, finely grated
pinch of salt
grind of black pepper

Pound in a mortar or chop in a food processor the basil, garlic, and nuts. Add the oil in a slow stream until well blended. Mix in the cheese and seasonings.

Refrigerate only a short time before using, or prepare without cheese and freeze in 1-cup containers.

NOTE: Pesto is traditionally served with linguine or fettuccine but try these variations: Use over grilled salmon steaks, monkfish, or as a seasoning for preparations en papillote. Pesto is also excellent tossed with cold shrimp and mussels. Add to a vinaigrette; add 2 to 3 tablespoons to fish stews, bean soups, or mixed vegetable soups; add to mayonnaise, scrambled eggs, tomato sauces, hot rice. Stuff pesto under the skin of roasting chicken; use as a sauce for cold chicken or fish, on hot zucchini or green beans or steamed new potatoes. Use in tomato and mozzarella sandwiches, in potato salad, in bacon, lettuce, and tomato sandwiches.

Variations:
Use walnuts or pistachios in place of pine nuts. Use spinach and parsley in place of some of the basil: 1 cup basil, ½ cup parsley, ½ cup spinach.

Crème Fraîche
(French Sour Cream)

OVER 1 CUP

Pour 1 cup of heavy whipping cream into a jar with 1 to 2 tablespoons of buttermilk. Cover and shake vigorously to mix. Cover the jar with a paper towel and leave in a warm place—75° to 85°—for 24 to 36 hours or until the cream is as thick as sour cream. Refrigerate (keeps up to 3 weeks). Use in place of heavy cream in any recipe. The sharp clean taste of crème fraîche goes well with many different herbs and seasonings for cold sauces for fish. Use crème fraîche in place of mayonnaise for any fish salad.

Crème Fraîche Sauces:
   Lemon-Thyme Sauce: Add 1 tablespoon of lemon juice and 1 teaspoon of fresh thyme to 1 cup of crème fraîche for a wonderful cold dressing for a potato and mussel salad.
   Cucumber-Dill Sauce: Add a handful of fresh chopped dill, 1 cucumber that has been peeled, seeded, and finely chopped, white pepper, and a little lemon juice to 1 to 2 cups of crème fraîche for a refreshing sauce for cold poached salmon.

Roasted Red Pepper Sauce

MAKES ABOUT 2 CUPS

Serve this sauce with baked halibut or broiled flounder.

>   8 large red bell peppers, skinned, stemmed, seeds removed, and roasted (see page 187), juices reserved
>   ¼ teaspoon salt
>   1 to 2 tablespoons extra-virgin olive oil or heavy cream

Puree the peppers with their juices in a food processor or blender, season with salt, and add the oil or cream to make a saucelike consistency. Hold the sauce in the refrigerator until needed. (It keeps 1 day.) Reheat the sauce before serving or serve at room temperature.

Tomato Sauce

MAKES ABOUT 2½ CUPS

Use this for braising or baking fish steaks or fillets, or on pasta.

> 2 large yellow onions, chopped
> 2 tablespoons unsalted sweet butter
> 2 tablespoons virgin olive oil
> 2 cloves garlic, mashed to a paste with a fork
> 1 teaspoon dried thyme
> 1 teaspoon dried basil
> 1 imported bay leaf
> 2 pounds canned Italian plum tomatoes, drained
> 2 tablespoons tomato paste
> ½ teaspoon sugar
> ½ teaspoon salt
> ¼ teaspoon freshly ground black pepper or to taste

Cook the onions gently in butter and olive oil in a large saucepan until soft. Add the garlic, herbs, tomatoes, and tomato paste. Simmer 10 minutes or until the sauce thickens. Add the sugar, salt, and pepper and cook another 5 minutes. This sauce freezes well.

Chipotle Sauce

MAKES ABOUT 1¼ CUPS

A chipotle chile is really a smoked jalapeno that has been pickled (*en vinagre*) or sauced (adobo). Its unusual smoky taste goes very nicely with deep-fried shellfish or grilled fatty fish. Use as a dipping sauce for fried clams and oysters.

> 1 cup sour cream
> pinch of salt
> ¼ cup drained, minced canned chipotles in adobo
>   sauce or *en vinagre*

Mix all the ingredients together, and taste for seasoning. Serve chilled on the side as a dipping sauce.

NOTE: The sauce cannot be frozen.

French Salsa

MAKES 1 CUP

1 large ripe tomato, peeled, seeded, and finely chopped
1 large shallot, minced
5 leaves arugula, basil, spinach, washed, dried, and
    finely chopped
1 to 2 teaspoons Spanish sherry wine vinegar
pinch of salt
grind of black pepper

Combine all the ingredients just before serving.

Tomatillo Salsa

MAKES 1½ CUPS

1 serrano chili, seeded and minced
½ pound fresh or canned tomatillos, peeled, blanched
    3 minutes, and rinsed in cold water
½ clove garlic, mashed to a paste with a fork
3 scallions, chopped
¼ cup minced fresh Italian parsley
1½ tablespoons fresh lime juice
⅛ teaspoon salt
⅛ teaspoon freshly ground white pepper
1½ tablespoons virgin olive oil

Puree all the ingredients in a food processor or blender until smooth.
   NOTE: This sauce can be prepared the morning of the day it is to
be used.

Horseradish Sauce

MAKES ABOUT 1 CUP

Serve this tart creamy sauce with smoked fish or with cold poached fish or shrimp.

> 1 cup crème fraîche (page 227) or sour cream
> 2 tablespoons drained bottled horseradish
> 1 to 2 tablespoons freshly chopped parsley
> ¼ teaspoon salt
> ⅛ teaspoon freshly ground black pepper
> a few drops of fresh lemon juice

Combine all the ingredients and adjust the seasonings to taste. Refrigerate before serving. Keeps about 3 to 4 days.

Ginger Dipping Sauce for Crab

MAKES ABOUT ⅔ CUP

This is the perfect sauce to serve with fresh boiled or steamed crabs or crab claws.

> ½ cup rice wine vinegar
> 1 tablespoon water
> 1 tablespoon peeled and grated fresh ginger
> 3 tablespoons mirin (see Note)
> pinch of salt
> 2 tablespoons chopped scallions

Combine all the ingredients. Keeps well refrigerated 3 to 4 days.

NOTE: This sweet syrupy inexpensive Japanese rice wine can be found in health food stores and Oriental markets. If you cannot find it, you can substitute 3 tablespoons of dry sherry and 2 teaspoons of sugar.

Tapenade (Provençal Olive and Caper Sauce)

MAKES ABOUT 1 ¼ CUPS

This pungent, dense olive spread nicely complements firm-textured fish and shellfish, lobster, monkfish, and shrimp. You can add 2 to 3 tablespoons of mayonnaise or aioli to thin the sauce a little. (Do not try to make this with American canned olives.) For a tasty hors d'oeuvre, spread Tapenade on warm toasted sourdough bread and top with cooked shrimp.

½ pound imported black olives (Kalamata, Moroccan, or Niçoise, in brine or oil-cured), pitted
8 anchovy fillets, drained and rinsed
2 tablespoons small or nonpareil capers, drained and rinsed
⅓ cup canned tuna, drained
⅛ teaspoon red wine vinegar
¼ teaspoon brandy
¼ teaspoon freshly ground black pepper
1½ teaspoons Dijon mustard
1 small clove garlic, mashed to a paste with a fork
¼ teaspoon dried sage
¼ teaspoon dried oregano
¼ teaspoon dried basil
3 to 4 tablespoons extra-virgin olive oil

With a pestle, pound the olives, anchovies, capers, and tuna to a paste in a large mortar. Stir in all the seasonings and slowly add the oil, mixing well so the sauce gradually absorbs it all. You can blend all the ingredients in a food processor, but the texture will be much thinner and not as authentic.

Let Tapenade sit an hour or so before using. It is best used the day it is made.

Minced Mushrooms and Shallots (Duxelles)

MAKES ABOUT 1¾ CUPS

An elegant stuffing for fish, particularly whole sole or flounder. Use as is, or combime with fresh herbs, fine bread crumbs, rice, vegetables, scallions, crab meat, or green peppercorns to vary the flavor. Duxelles cook twice, so squeezing the liquid out of the mushrooms before cooking, rather than evaporating it during cooking, keeps cooking time short and the mushrooms fresher and firmer. Duxelles can also be added to a béchamel or mornay sauce. French restaurant kitchens keep duxelles on hand at all times. Store in a jar in the refrigerator with a little melted butter to seal (keeps up to a week) or in the freezer.

> 1 pound mushrooms, washed and minced by hand
> (do not use food processor)
> 4 to 5 tablespoons unsalted sweet butter
> 4 shallots, minced
> pinch of salt
> grind of black pepper or to taste
> a few gratings of whole nutmeg
> 3 tablespoons minced fresh parsley

Place a third of the raw minced mushrooms in the center of a double thickness of clean cheesecloth (24 inches by 24 inches) wrap tightly, and press the ball with one hand to squeeze out as much liquid from the mushrooms as possible. Repeat with the remaining mushrooms.

Melt the butter in a large skillet. Add the shallots, cook gently until softened, then add the mushrooms and cook until they absorb the butter, only about 4 to 5 minutes. Season with salt, pepper, and nutmeg, and add the parsley.

NOTE: Use as a stuffing for potatoes, tomatoes, zucchini, and other vegetables, and all kinds of fish, poultry, and meats, or on toast as an hors d'oeuvre or mixed with herbs and tomatoes as a sauce for pasta.

Creole Okra Relish

MAKES ABOUT 2 CUPS

Serve this sprightly sauce with fried oysters, sautéed shrimp, or crab cakes. Use it on Fried Oyster Sandwiches with Hot Sauce (page 162) in place of pickled okra.

> 1 cup thick, hot, and full-flavored Mexican-style hot
>   sauce
> 6 to 8 pods pickled okra, drained and sliced
> 1/3 cup finely chopped red onion
> 1/3 cup fresh or frozen corn, blanched in boiling water
>   1 minute and drained
> 1/2 red bell pepper, finely chopped
> 2 tablespoons chopped cilantro

Prepare the relish by combining all the ingredients. Refrigerate before serving. Keeps about 2 to 3 days in the refrigerator.

Papaya Corn Relish

MAKES ABOUT 2 1/4 CUPS

This flavorful fruit-and-vegetable combination pairs nicely with simply grilled redfish, salmon, or amberjack.

> 1/2 fresh papaya, peeled, seeded, and finely cubed
> 1/4 cup seeded and finely chopped red bell pepper
> 1/4 cup finely chopped red onion
> 1/3 cup cooked fresh or frozen corn
> 3 tablespoons fresh lime juice
> 1/4 teaspoon salt
> 1/2 ripe avocado, chopped
> 1 to 2 tablespoons fresh chopped cilantro
> 2 tablespoons finely minced jicama (optional)

Combine all the ingredients and season to taste. Refrigerate covered. Keeps 2 to 3 days.

COATINGS FOR FRYING, DEEP-FRYING, AND BROILING FISH FILLETS OR SHELLFISH

Coatings keep the surface of broiled, deep-fried, or pan-fried fish from drying out and give them a flavorful crispness. Be sure fish is completely dry before coating, and coat just before cooking to prevent sogginess.

Seasoned Flour

½ cup all-purpose flour
½ teaspoon salt
¼ teaspoon freshly ground black pepper
¼ teaspoon cayenne pepper
½ teaspoon dried thyme

Mix together and use to dust fillets to be fried, deep-fried, or sautéed.

Cornmeal Mixed with Seasoned Flour

¾ cup yellow or white cornmeal
¼ cup Seasoned Flour (above)

Use for catfish fillets to be pan-fried or deep-fried.

Fine Dry Bread Crumbs or Cracker Crumbs

Rub fish with melted butter or oil, or dip fish in a mixture of 2 beaten eggs and 2 tablespoons of milk, or in buttermilk or thinned yogurt, and then coat with crumbs.

Cornstarch: Produces a very light and crisp coating which the Japanese and Chinese use for fish to be deep-fried.
Cornflour: Cornmeal ground finely in a blender is especially good for coating oysters to be deep-fried.
Ground Pecans, Almonds, Hazelnuts, Pine Nuts, or Macadamia Nuts: Nuts are especially good on catfish, mahimahi, flounder, and redfish. Use as crumbs, above.

BATTERS FOR FRYING AND DEEP-FRYING FISH

Batters coat lean fish and shellfish and keep them from absorbing oil while they cook. The coating crisps and browns and adds a nice taste.

Beer Batter

MAKES ABOUT 2½ CUPS OR ENOUGH TO COAT 2 POUNDS OF FISH

1 cup all-purpose flour
pinch of cayenne pepper
½ teaspoon salt
⅛ teaspoon freshly ground white pepper
1 tablespoon safflower oil
¾ cup beer
2 large eggs, separated

Mix the flour and seasonings. Stir in the oil, beer, and egg yolks and mix very well. Let stand 1 to 6 hours in the refrigerator. Beat the whites until stiff and fold into batter when ready to use.

Dip fish or shellfish into the batter and lower immediately into hot (375°) oil and cook until the batter is lightly browned.

Tempura Batter

MAKES ABOUT 1½ CUPS OR ENOUGH TO COAT 2 POUNDS OF FISH

This is a very thin, light batter which gives a very delicate crisp crust. It is especially good with shrimp, scallops, or squid.

1 large cold egg
¾ cup ice water
1 cup all-purpose flour or rice flour, or ½ cup corn-
    starch and ½ cup flour
½ teaspoon salt
1 teaspoon baking powder

Beat the egg and water together until well blended. Add flour mixed with salt and baking powder and stir until the batter is mixed. (Don't worry if it is a bit lumpy.) Dip seafood in batter and deep-fry.

SHELLFISH BOILS

A "boil" is a mixture of herbs and spices used to flavor water in which shrimp, crab, or crayfish are cooked. There are a number of good commercial crab "boils" available, but it's more interesting to concoct your own mixture with herbs and spices that appeal to your own taste.

NOTE: You may prefer to put spice mixture in a cheesecloth bag so the seasonings do not cling to the cooked shellfish.

Dark Beer Shrimp Boil

SERVES 2 TO 4

There is no reason why flavorful dark beer cannot be used as a cooking medium. It's delicious and imparts its excellent flavor to the shrimp.

> 1 cup dark beer
> 1 cup water
> 2 teaspoons dill seed
> 2 teaspoons fennel seed
> ½ teaspoon salt
> ½ pound small shrimp, in or out of shell

Simmer the beer, water, and seasonings together for a few minutes.

Add the shrimp to the beer and cook at a simmer for 2 minutes. Remove the shrimp and drain. Peel and chill.

Serve shrimp with Horseradish-Dill Sauce (page 227) on pumpernickel or chop the shrimp for Belgian Shrimp and Endive Sandwiches (page 124).

NOTE: This recipe can easily be doubled or tripled.

Spiced Shrimp, Crab, and Crayfish Boil

MAKES ABOUT 1 CUP OR ENOUGH
TO COOK 4 POUNDS OF SHELLFISH

The addition of cloves, allspice, and hot pepper gives this mixture an unusually hotter and deeper spice flavor.

Spice Boil
1 tablespoon black peppercorns, cracked
1 teaspoon red pepper flakes
1 teaspoon cayenne pepper
1 tablespoon coriander seed, cracked
¼ teaspoon mustard seed or dry mustard
8 whole allspice, cracked
8 whole cloves, cracked
4 imported bay leaves, broken up
2 teaspoons celery seeds
1 teaspoon dried thyme

3 quarts cold water
4 tablespoons salt
2 cloves garlic, crushed
1 yellow onion, sliced
1 lemon, washed and sliced
⅓ cup chopped parsley stalks

Combine the herbs and spices.

To cook 2 pounds of fresh shrimp, crabs, or crayfish in the shell, bring the water to a boil in a 6-to-8-quart stockpot, and add 3 tablespoons of the spice boil and the salt, garlic, onion, lemon, and parsley stalks. Simmer this mixture about 15 minutes to blend the flavors. Bring water back to a boil and add the shellfish. Cook about 2 to 3 minutes for shrimp, and 7 to 10 minutes for crabs or crayfish.

Herb and Seed Boil
for Shrimp, Crabs, and Crayfish

MAKES ABOUT ½ CUP
OR ENOUGH FOR 2 POUNDS OF SHELLFISH

This seasoned spice mix is excellent for cooking crabs, crayfish, and shrimp.

Herb and Seed Boil
4 imported bay leaves, broken up
½ teaspoon dried thyme
½ teaspoon dried basil
1 teaspoon celery seed
1½ teaspoons fennel seed
1½ teaspoons dill seed
1 tablespoon mustard seed
1 tablespoon coriander seed
¼ cup black peppercorns

3 quarts cold water
4 tablespoons salt
1 onion, thinly sliced
1 lemon, thinly sliced
2 cloves garlic, unpeeled
⅓ cup fresh chopped parsley stalks

Place all the herbs and spices in a mortar and gently pound to crack the peppercorns and bruise the spices.

To cook 2 pounds of fresh shrimp, crabs, or crayfish in the shell, bring the water to a boil in a 6-to-8-quart stockpot, and add 3 tablespoons of the herb and seed boil and the salt, onion, lemon, garlic, and parsley stalks. Simmer this mixture about 15 minutes to blend the flavors. Bring to a boil again and add the shellfish. Cook about 2 to 3 minutes for shrimp, and 7 to 10 minutes for crabs or crayfish.

Lexicon of
Fish and Shellfish

The following list is not intended to be comprehensive. It includes the fish and shellfish commonly available in the United States and covers all the seafood called for in the recipes in this book.

SALTWATER FISH

AMBERJACK
A 3- to 20-pound loose-textured, soft-fleshed, moderately fatty fish with flavorful dark meat, fished in South Atlantic and Gulf Coast waters. Available year round. Sold mostly in steak form. Excellent grilled, broiled, or baked.

BASS, BLACK SEA
A 1- to 5-pound firm-fleshed lean fish with a delicate mild flavor, found year round in Atlantic waters. Sold whole and in fillets.

BASS, STRIPED
A 2- to 10-pound firm-fleshed, fine-textured moderately fatty fish of excellent flavor, available year round in Atlantic and Pacific waters. Sold whole and in steaks and fillets. Makes a superb presentation poached and served whole. Because of PCB contamination this East Coast favorite is currently off the market. Check its status with local health authorities.

BASS, WHITE SEA
A 10- to 50-pound firm-fleshed, mild-flavored moderately fatty fish, found year round in southern Pacific coast waters. Sold in fillets.

All sea bass can be baked, poached, steamed, broiled, stuffed, or sautéed.

BLUEFISH

A 3- to 9-pound fine-textured, soft-fleshed fatty fish with a distinctive flavor, available in spring, summer, and fall on the Atlantic coast. It is generally available in fillets, dressed, and whole. Bluefish is best when very fresh. It does not freeze well. Be sure to remove the strong-flavored dark strip that runs down the center of the fillets. Because of its oiliness, bluefish is excellent with all manner of acidic (wine, citrus fruit) marinades and is good grilled, baked, and broiled.

BONITO

A 1- to 5-pound firm-fleshed, moderately fatty fish with a hearty flavor, available year round on the Pacific coast and marketed whole, dressed, and in steak and fillet form. Good marinated and baked, broiled or grilled.

BUTTERFISH

This small, bony, fatty fish, averaging 3 to 4 pounds, has a fine texture, soft flesh, and a delicate, buttery flavor. Available spring, summer, and fall on the Atlantic and Pacific coasts. On the Pacific coast it is called Pacific pompano. Usually cooked whole, it is best baked, pan-fried, broiled, or smoked.

COD

An 8- to 12-pound white, firm-fleshed, loose-textured lean fish with a very mild flavor, fished year round on the Atlantic and Pacific coasts. It is marketed in smoked, salted, and dried forms as well as fresh in steaks, fillets, dressed, and whole forms. It is excellent baked, steamed, fried, poached, or used in stews and chowders, but remember it flakes very easily. Poaching cod in a milk court bouillon (see recipe page 201) keeps its flesh very white. Cod is a perfect fish for pan-frying or deep-frying.

CROAKER/DRUM

(Redfish, Red Drum, Black Drum, Channel Bass, Kingfish)

A ½- to 10-pound white, firm-fleshed lean fish with an excellent sweet flavor, available year round on the South Atlantic and Gulf coasts. Marketed whole and in fillet, steak, and dressed form, these fish are excellent cooked all kinds of ways—poached, sautéed, baked, steamed, broiled, grilled, and steam-baked en papillote as well as in soups and stews. Gulf redfish is one of the finest, most versatile fish found in United States waters today. Its fine, full but delicate flavor makes it a star no matter how it is prepared or seasoned. In recent years Gulf redfish have been overfished both by commercial and sport fishermen. A two-year state ban on harvesting redfish has prompted the development of commercially grown redfish on freshwater farms in South Texas. By current estimates, the first crop of 2- to 3-pound redfish will be marketed in October, 1987.

FLOUNDER/SOLE

A ½- to 3-pound fine-textured, lean flatfish of very mild to delicate flavor, available year round on the Atlantic, Pacific, and Gulf coasts. It is marketed whole, dressed, and in fillets. Common Atlantic varieties include American plaice, lemon sole, gray sole, winter or summer flounder, and yellowtail flounder. The Pacific varieties include three small and very fine-flavored fish: the petrale sole, the rex sole, and the sand dab, all of which are usually served whole or in fillets. All varieties of flounder/sole are good sautéed, baked, steamed, broiled, steam-baked en papillote, or poached; they are also excellent fish to bone, stuff, and bake whole. The true European sole, the Dover sole, is not found in American waters. Because of the demand and cost, Dover sole is not commonly found in fish markets, but is imported in season by some of the finest restaurants. To be really tasty, flounder must be pristine fresh, as it loses flavor very quickly out of the water.

GROUPER

(Black Grouper, Red Grouper, Nassau, Yellowfish Grouper, Jewfish)
A 3- to 20-pound firm-fleshed, loose-textured lean fish with a good mild flavor; available winter to summer on the South Atlantic coast. Similar to and sometimes marketed as sea bass, grouper is sold whole, dressed, and in fillets and steaks. Its tough skin should be removed before cooking. All forms of grouper are excellent deep-fried, pan-fried, poached, steamed, baked, grilled, or used in soups and chowders.

HADDOCK

Smaller but similar to cod. Smoked haddock is known as finnan haddie.

HAKE

Similar to cod.

HALIBUT

A 5- to 100-pound white, firm-fleshed, fine-textured lean flatfish of mild flavor, available year round on the Atlantic and Pacific coasts. Marketed whole and in fillets and steaks, halibut is excellent poached in a milk court bouillon to preserve its whiteness (see recipe, page 201). It can also be steamed, baked, broiled, sautéed, or used in soups and stews.

LINGCOD

A 3- to 20-pound firm-fleshed, loose-textured lean fish of excellent flavor, available year round on the Pacific coast. Usually sold whole, dressed, and in fillets or steaks, it is excellent poached, baked, steamed, sautéed, or used in soups and stews. Not a true cod, this flavorful and versatile West Coast fish is an excellent all-purpose fish that adapts to a variety of seasonings.

MACKEREL

A ½- to 25-pound firm-fleshed, fine-textured fatty fish with a rich, assertive flavor, available in spring and summer on the Atlantic coast and year round on the Pacific coast. Generally marketed whole or in fillets, this beautifully sleek and shimmering blue-gray-black fish varies widely in size and flavor. The large (5- to 25-pound) king mackerel or kingfish is the strongest-flavored. The Pacific jack also has an assertive flavor. The small (½- to 2-pound) Atlantic mackerel has an excellent flavor, and the Spanish mackerel is the most delicate and fine-flavored of all. Because of its fattiness, mackerel is best poached in a wine- or vinegar-flavored court bouillon and served cold with a tart sauce, such as a horseradish sauce. It can also be scored, marinated, and grilled, or smoked, baked, or broiled. Mackerel is generally inexpensive.

MAHIMAHI
(Dolphin fish)

A 2- to 50-pound firm-fleshed, moderately fatty fish found in Pacific and Atlantic waters in spring and summer. This flavorful fish, marketed in steaks and fillets, can be baked, grilled, sautéed, or poached.

MONKFISH
(Anglerfish, Goosefish, Lotte)

A 2- to 20-pound very firm-fleshed, dense-textured lean fish with a sweet, rich, lobster-like flavor, available year round in Atlantic waters. Only the boneless V-shaped tail portion is edible. Monkfish can be successfully poached, steamed, baked, braised, or grilled. It is perfect in stews and soups because it holds its shape and doesn't fall apart.

MULLET

A ½- to 6-pound firm-fleshed, loose-textured moderately fatty fish with a mild, nutty flavor found in the South Atlantic waters in late fall and early winter. Sold whole or head dressed, mullet is good baked, broiled, grilled, fried, or sautéed.

OCEAN PERCH
(Sea Perch, Redfish, Rock Fish)

A 1- to 2-pound medium firm-fleshed, loose textured lean fish with a distinctive flavor, available in April and in June through October in North Atlantic and Pacific waters. Not a true perch, this species provides most of the frozen fish in the U.S. market, and is excellent baked or poached whole.

ORANGE ROUGHY
A 2- to 3-pound loose-textured, firm-fleshed lean fish with a very bland flavor found year round in New Zealand waters. Generally marketed frozen in fillets and steaks, it can be cooked any way, but because it is so mild in flavor, it needs robust or assertive sauces. Though highly touted as the perfect all-purpose fish when it first appeared on the market, its complete lack of taste makes it much overrated.

POLLOCK
Similar to cod but a little more distinctive in flavor.

POMPANO
A ½- to 4-pound firm-fleshed, fine-textured moderately fatty fish with a rich, distinctively delicate buttery flavor. Found year round in the South Atlantic and Gulf Coast waters, it is sold whole or in fillets and is excellent when steam-baked en papillote, stuffed and baked, grilled, broiled, or steamed. This beautiful silvery fish provides the very best eating fish in the South, from New Orleans to Florida. Cooking pompano en papillote, a New Orleans specialty, perfectly highlights its fine flavor.

PORGY
A 1- to 5-pound firm-fleshed, loose-textured lean bony fish with a mild sweet flavor, available year round except summer in Atlantic waters. Sold whole or dressed, the best preparations for porgy are baking, broiling, grilling, or sautéeing.

REDFISH
See Croaker/Drum.

RED SNAPPER
A 1- to 6-pound firm-fleshed, fine-textured lean fish with an excellent flavor, available year round in South Atlantic and Gulf waters. Sold whole and in fillets, red snapper is excellent baked, stuffed, poached, steamed, sautéed, steam-baked en papillote, broiled, grilled, and cooked in soups and stews. Because of its color, beauty, and size, red snapper is a perfect fish to bake and present whole. True Gulf snapper is a superb eating fish, but beware of the false claims that Pacific snapper is just as good.

ROCKFISH
(Rock Cod, Pacific Snapper, Pacific Ocean Perch)
A 2- to 5-pound firm-fleshed, loose-textured, mild but good-flavored lean fish found all year on the Pacific coast. It can be nicely steamed, deep-fried, baked, grilled, broiled, poached, and sautéed, as well as used in soups and stews. Rockfish is much appreciated by Oriental cooks.

SABLEFISH
(Black Cod, Alaska Cod)
A 1- to 12-pound soft-fleshed, fine-textured fatty fish with a mild buttery flavor, available year round on the Pacific coast. Sold whole, dressed, and in fillets and steaks, this fatty fish is excellent smoked, baked, broiled, or grilled.

SALMON, ATLANTIC
A 5- to 10-pound firm and dense-textured fatty fish with a light pink color and excellent mild flavor found in North Atlantic waters in spring and summer. Salmon combines well with all kinds of seasonings and is excellent poached, steamed, baked, steam-baked en papillote, broiled, grilled, and braised. Much of the Atlantic salmon catch is smoked.

SALMON, PACIFIC
Season varies.
    King (Chinook)—5 to 30 pounds, red.
    Sockeye (Red)—3 to 7 pounds, red-orange.
    Coho (Silver)—3 to 12 pounds, bright orange, excellent for smoking.
    Pink (Humpback)—2 to 8 pounds, pink, canned.
    Chum (Keta)—7 to 10 pounds, pale pink, less fatty.
Pacific salmon can be cooked in the same ways as Atlantic salmon. Whole small King and Coho salmon are the right size for poaching or baking whole. A small variety (about ¾ pound) of Coho salmon is commercially raised and sold in dressed form. It is good sautéed or baked.

Salmon, like shad, is an anadromous fish which returns every spring to spawn in fresh water streams and rivers.

SCROD
A 1- to 3-pound baby cod with the finest flavor of all the cod family (see Cod). Best poached, steamed, or baked.

SEA TROUT
(Weakfish, Speckled Trout)
A 1- to 6-pound soft-fleshed, fine-textured lean to moderately fatty fish with a sweet, delicate, mild flavor, available year round in the Gulf and Atlantic coasts. Sold whole, dressed, and in fillets, sea trout is excellent poached, steamed, steam-baked en papillote, stuffed, baked, or pan-fried. Best eaten only when very fresh.

SHAD
(Buck, White, and Roe Shad, Alose)
A 3- to 4-pound fatty fish with an excellent flavor and a soft flesh,

fine texture, and a lot of small bones. Caught in rivers in the spring along the Atlantic and North Pacific coasts, shad is normally sold whole, boned, and in fillets. The unfertilized eggs of the shad, the roe, are excellent sautéed or broiled and served with a tart creamy sauce of pureed sorrel or watercress. Shad can be baked, broiled, grilled, sautéed, or planked.

SHARK

A 12- to 30-pound firm-fleshed, dense-textured lean fish with a mild, meat-like flavor found all year on the Atlantic, Pacific, and Gulf coasts. Mako and blue shark have the finest, mildest flavor and texture and are sometimes sold as the more expensive swordfish. Leopard, soup-fin, and dogfish sharks are quite common. The least appealing variety of shark is the thresher shark which is coarse in texture and strong in flavor. Sold in steaks, chunks, or fillets, shark can be grilled, sautéed, baked, or broiled. It combines well with assertive seasonings. Marinate in milk for 20 minutes to remove the natural ammonia smell.

SHEEPSHEAD

See freshwater Sheepshead.

SOLE

See Flounder.

SWORDFISH

A large, moderately fatty fish weighing between 200 and 600 pounds with firm flesh, dense texture, and a rich meaty flavor, available in summer on the Pacific and Atlantic coasts. Sold in steak form, swordfish can take distinctive seasoning; like tuna, swordfish is wonderful grilled, and is also excellent broiled or baked.

TILEFISH

A 2- to 25-pound firm-textured lean fish with a sweet, rich flavor similar to scallops or lobster, found in Pacific and Atlantic waters year round. Marketed whole, dressed, and in fillets and steaks, tilefish can be poached, steamed, steam-baked en papillote, baked, broiled, grilled, fried, sautéed, and used in stews and soups.

TUNA

(Albacore, Bluefin, Bonito, Yellowfin)

A 10- to 200-pound dense-textured fatty fish with a full flavor, available in spring, summer, and fall on the Pacific and Atlantic coasts. Albacore, the mild, lighter-colored tuna, is generally considered finest in flavor. Sold in steak or chunk form, tuna can take assertive flavorings and is best grilled, baked, broiled, or braised.

WHITING

Similar to Hake.

FRESHWATER FISH

BASS
(Largemouth, Smallmouth, Rock, Spotted)
A 2- to 6-pound medium firm-fleshed lean fish with an excellent flavor, found throughout the United States. Cooked whole or in fillets, bass is very good baked, stuffed, pan-fried, grilled, and broiled.

CARP
A 2- to 7-pound firm-fleshed, dense-textured, bony, moderately fatty fish of mild flavor, caught all over the United States and best eaten in winter. Cooked whole or in fillets, carp is good baked, stuffed, poached, or braised. Carp are widely used by the Chinese and can be found in Oriental fish markets.

CATFISH
(Channel, Bullhead)
A ½- to 3-pound (if aquacultured), 2- to 8-pound (if wild) medium firm-fleshed, fine-textured lean fish with a delicious sweet flavor, available all year from catfish farms and inland lakes and rivers. Aquacultured catfish is probably the *freshest* fish regularly available in large quantities throughout the Midwest and across the South. Catfish is very versatile; it can be used in any recipe calling for lean fish, and it is excellent smoked. Sold whole, dressed, and in fillets with the tough skin removed. Catfish is wonderful poached, baked, braised, broiled, grilled, stuffed, steam-baked en papillote, steamed, pan-fried, deep-fried, sautéed, smoked, and used in soups and stews. Although throughout the South it is typically served dipped in a cornmeal batter and deep-fried, catfish does not deserve to be relegated to just one basic preparation.

PERCH
(White, Yellow)
A ½- to 4-pound firm-fleshed, fine-textured lean fish with a delicate sweet flavor, fished mostly in the northeast United States. Cooked whole, dressed, and in fillets, perch is best pan-fried, baked, broiled, and grilled.

PIKE
(Northern, Walleye)
A 1- to 10-pound white, firm-fleshed, fine-textured lean fish with a very fine, delicate flavor, caught in the northeastern and north central

United States. It can be baked, poached, steamed, stuffed, smoked, braised, or grilled, and it makes an especially delicate stuffing when pureed.

SHEEPSHEAD
(Freshwater Drum)

A 1- to 5-pound white, firm-fleshed lean fish of good mild flavor, fished mostly in southern and midwestern lakes and rivers all year round. Cooked whole, dressed, or in fillets, sheepshead is good baked, poached, steamed, broiled, grilled, sautéed, or used in soups and stews. Sheepshead makes an excellent addition to a bouillabaisse or stew.

SMELT
(Whitebait)

A 1- to 4-ounce soft-fleshed, fine-textured moderately fatty fish with a rich flavor, harvested in Lake Superior in great numbers in the spring. The smallest smelt are best deep-fried and eaten whole. Larger smelt need to be gutted and headed. The two best methods of cooking are frying or sautéeing.

STURGEON

A 7- to 700-pound firm-fleshed, dense-textured fatty fish with a rich strong meat-like flavor, fished in Atlantic and Pacific coastal waters. While good smoked, sturgeon is mainly harvested for its roe to make caviar. Sold in steaks or chunks, sturgeon is best marinated and then grilled, broiled, or baked.

SUNFISH
(Crappies, Bluegill)

A ¼- to 2-pound lean, sweet-tasting small fish, found mostly in the Midwest and the length of the Mississippi Valley. Cooked whole, it is best pan-fried or broiled.

TROUT
(Rainbow, Brook, Lake)

A ½- to 8-pound firm-fleshed, fine-textured moderately fatty to fatty fish that has no scales. All rainbow trout are farm-raised and are available year round whole, dressed, boned, and butterflied. Trout can be poached, steamed, steam-baked en papillote, broiled, grilled, pan-fried, braised, or smoked.

WHITEFISH
(Cisco)

A 1- to 6-pound firm-fleshed fatty fish of excellent flavor, fished in the Northeast and Great Lakes areas. Cooked whole, dressed, or in fillets or steaks, whitefish can be baked, stuffed, broiled, pan-fried, steamed, poached, or smoked. The roe of whitefish is considered a delicacy.

SHELLFISH

Shellfish can be divided into two basic categories:
   Mollusks, which include abalone, clams, conch, mussels, oysters, and scallops;
   Crustaceans, which include crabs, crayfish, lobster, and shrimp.
   Squid, an acephalopod, is in neither category.
   As with fish, the smaller sizes and varieties of shellfish have more delicate flavor and texture.

ABALONE
Harvested by divers on the Pacific coast for its edible 6-inch-long foot-like muscle; this is cut across the grain into thin steaks, approximately 6 by 3 inches, that are pounded to tenderize. Abalone is best when dredged in seasoned flour and sautéed 1 minute only in a mixture of hot butter and oil or clarified butter. Very large, tough abalone are best minced for chowder, fritters, or salads.

CLAMS
Clams are generally sold by the pound.

ATLANTIC HARD-SHELLED CLAMS
(Littlenecks, Cherrystone, Atlantic Razors, Quahogs or Chowder Clams)
   The smallest of these varieties are best eaten raw. Cherrystones are excellent clams for stuffing and baking. Quahogs, the largest ones (over 3 inches long), are good for chowder.

ATLANTIC SOFT-SHELLED CLAMS
(Steamers, Ipswich)
   This clam, with a neck (or siphon) protruding from its shell, is generally cut up and steamed, fried, or used in chowder.

Atlantic clams are at their best between September and May.

PACIFIC HARD-SHELLED CLAMS
(Pismo, Butter, Manila, Littlenecks)
   All are best served raw.

PACIFIC SOFT-SHELLED CLAMS
(Razor)

These long slender shells contain clams that are similar to the Atlantic steamers. Razor clams are better fried than raw or steamed.

GOEDUCK CLAMS

Huge Pacific clams weighing about 3 pounds each. Mince before steaming.

Pacific clams are at their best between November and April.

CONCH

Shelled conch meat from the West Indies and the Gulf, and Florida coasts is available year round. Tenderize conch meat by parboiling or pounding it; use in chowders and soups, pasta sauces, or fritters.

CRABS

Sold live in the shell (hard or soft) or in containers of fresh-cooked or pasteurized crab meat. The biggest pieces and best quality are lump meat and back fin; claw meat and flake are less expensive. Live whole crab is best steamed or boiled, or sautéed if soft-shelled.

BLUE CRAB
—Atlantic and Gulf

These fine-flavored hard- or soft-shell crabs weigh between 1/5 and 1 pound. Blue crabs are marketed all year round. In June the blue crab moults and becomes a soft-shell crab. The season usually lasts until September.

DUNGENESS CRAB
—Pacific

A 1½- to 2½-pound crab with deliciously sweet meat. Available year round on the northwest Pacific coast and from November to August in California.

ALASKA KING CRAB
—Pacific

From 6 to 20 pounds; only the red-coated white leg meat is edible. Normally sold frozen. Thaw and use in salads, sauces, or gratins.

STONE CRAB
—Florida only

A delicious variety of crab with very large claws, which provide all of the meat. Steam or boil and serve claws cold with a sauce.

CRAYFISH
(Crawfish, Crawdad)

Small estuary crustaceans, crayfish are sold either whole in the shell, to be boiled or steamed live, or in containers of tail meat which has been removed from the shells and precooked. Crayfish are between 3 and 7 inches long; the larger ones are from western rivers, the smaller ones from Mississippi and Louisiana rivers. Best season is from mid to late summer. Crayfish have a sweet, rich flavor.

LOBSTER
A large-clawed crustacean with a superb full, rich, sweet, and subtle flavor. Available year round, lobsters are best when bought and cooked live. The famous Maine lobster is most flavorful when under 2 pounds. The rock or spiny lobster from the Gulf and southern waters of both coasts provides a broad meaty tail section. Steam or boil whole lobsters; broil, grill, or bake lobster tails.

MUSSELS
Sold by the dozen fresh in the shell or by the pound, the blue 2-to-3-inch-long mussel is available year round on the Atlantic coast and from November through April on the Pacific coast. Mussels are excellent steamed and served hot by themselves or added to soup and rice dishes or served cold in salads.

OYSTERS
Oysters are sold live in the shell or shucked and, although available and good to eat all year around, they are at their peak of flavor in fall and winter. Atlantic oysters include the Malpeque (Canada), Wellfleet (Massachusetts), blue point (New York), Chincoteague (Maryland, Virginia), and Apalachicola (Florida). The two main oysters from the Gulf are the Mobile Bay and the New Orleans (Louisiana). The two best oysters from the Pacific coast are the tiny Olympia (Washington) and the much larger Japanese oyster, found up and down the coast under local names. The best way to eat fresh oysters is raw on the half shell. Oysters are also excellent in soups and fried, steamed, poached, broiled, and in sauces.

SCALLOPS
All scallops sold in the United States come without their shell and coral roe, which is very perishable. Markets carry two basic types of scallops, bay and sea, available September through April. Bay scallops, about ½ inch in diameter, are sweet and succulent. Larger sea scallops, 1½ inch in diameter, are not quite as delicate in flavor and texture as the bay scallop. Scallops can be steamed, sautéed, steam-baked en papillote, deep-fried, broiled, baked, and used in soups or stews.

SHRIMP
Really fresh, never-been-frozen shrimp in the shell are harder and harder to find. There are many different sizes and varieties of shrimp found in the United States coastal waters. Most are fished year round, but the peak season for shrimp is summer. Shrimp are good steamed, boiled, baked, broiled, sautéed, grilled, steam-baked en papillote, braised, and in soups and stews, but take care not to overcook them or they will be rubbery and have more texture than flavor.

ROCK SHRIMP
These medium-large rich-tasting shrimp, found in the Gulf and off the coast of Virginia, are distinguished by a very tough shell.

BROWN SHRIMP
Found in the Gulf and sold by size, these provide the bulk of shrimp harvested in U.S. waters.

MONTEREY PRAWNS
These beautiful large shrimp from the California coast around Monterey are wonderful when simply grilled.

SQUID
Squid, a tentacled mollusk without a shell, is found in both Pacific and Atlantic coastal waters all year round. Marketed whole, cleaned, and frozen, squid requires careful cooking to keep it from becoming rubbery. Its firm, sweet, and mild-tasting flesh should be quickly cooked, only 2 to 3 minutes if deep-fried, sautéed or grilled, or 20 minutes to an hour if braised. Squid are good deep-fried, sautéed, grilled, and braised.

Index

Abalone, 248
Acadian catfish court bouillon, 150
Aioli (Provençal garlic mayonnaise), 225
  bluefish with chipotle, broiled, 83
  variations on, 225
Alaska cod. *See* Sablefish
Albacore. *See* Tuna
Almond coating, ground, 234
Amberjack, 239
  baked, 34–35
  with capers and lemon, piccata of, 88
  with sun-dried tomato butter, grilled, 77
Ancho chile butter, 220
Anchovy(ies):
  butter, 215
  garlic-, marinade, 205
  salsa verde, 94
  tapenade (Provençal olive and caper sauce), 231
  tart, Provençal onion and (Pissaladière), 142–43
Anglerfish. *See* Monkfish
Arborio rice, 165
  champagne risotto, 166
Artichokes:
  braised, 176
  and mushrooms in Madeira cream, 177
Asparagus:
  crab, and potato salad, 136

  pasta primavera with mussels, 112
Avocado:
  gazpacho with roasted tomatoes, basil, and, bay scallop, 122–23
  scallop ceviche with orange and, 132–33

Bacon:
  salad with scallops, greens, and mustard dressing, warm bistro, 154
  See also Pancetta
Baker's (cooking) parchment, 23–24
Baking, 33–35
  basic baked fish, 34–35
  stuffed baked fish, 35
Baking dishes, 21, 22
Balsamic vinegar and basil marinade, 212
Basil, 8–9
  aioli (Provençal garlic mayonnaise), 225
  beurre blanc, tomato-, 224
  butter, 214
  gazpacho with roasted tomatoes, and avocado, bay scallop, 122–23
  marinade, balsamic vinegar and, 212
  pesto (fresh basil sauce), 226

walnut, baked monkfish with, 64
Basmati rice, 164
Bass, 246
   in red wine, braised, 70–71
   with wild mushrooms, fresh
      herbs, and crème fraîche,
      74–75
   See also Black sea bass; Striped
      bass; White sea bass
Batters for frying and deep-frying
      fish, 235
   beer, 235
   tempura, 235
Bay leaf, 9
Beer:
   batter, 235
   shrimp boil, dark, 236
Belgian shrimp and endive sand-
      wiches, 124
Beurre blanc sauce (ivory shallot
      butter sauce), 223–24
   variations on, 224
Biscuits, pecan:
   quick cream- or buttermilk-, 195
   tomato crab cream over, 145
Black bass:
   baked, 34–35
Black cod. *See* Sablefish
Black-eyed pea:
   relish, marinated, 192
   salad, marinated, 192
Black sea bass, 239
   with chipotle aioli, broiled, 38
   See also Bass; Sea bass; White
      sea bass
Bluefin. *See* Tuna
Bluefish, 240
   à la Provençale, baked, 66–67
   baked, 34–35
   with capers and lemon, piccata
      of, 88
   with chipotle aioli, broiled, 83
   grilled, 37
   meunière, fresh, 73
   in mustard-scallion sauce, baked,
      91
   with orange, red onion, and fen-
      nel, 85

poached, 47, 48
   with sun-dried tomato butter,
      grilled, 77
Bluegill. *See* Sunfish
Boiling:
   boiled live crayfish, 45
   shellfish boils, 236
   dark beer shrimp boil, 236
   herb and seed boil for shrimp,
      crabs, and crayfish, 238
   spiced shrimp, crab, and crayfish
      boil, 237
   steamed or boiled live hardshell
      crabs, 46
   steamed or boiled live lobster, 44
Boils. *See* Boiling, shellfish boils
Bonito, 240
Bonito tuna. *See* tuna
Braising, 39–40
   basic braised fish, 40
Brazilian sautéed shrimp with coco-
      nut milk, peanuts, and
      chiles, 98–99
Bread:
   crumbs, 234
      herbed, quick scallop sauté
         with, and orange wedges, 99
Bresse style spinach, 184
Brioches:
   cornmeal, 194
      crab, lettuce, and tomato sand-
         wiches on toasted, 155
Broiling, 38–39
   basic broiled fish, 39
   coatings for, 234
   foolproof broiled fish, 39
Brook trout, 247
   with pancetta, sage, and cham-
      pagne wine vinegar, 72
   in red wine, braised, 70–71
   with wild mushrooms, fresh
      herbs, and crème fraîche,
      74–75
   See also Rainbow trout; Sea
      trout; Trout
Brown rice, 165
Bulgur with lemon and pine nuts,
      169

Butter, clarifying, 17
Butterfish, 240
  with chipotle aioli, broiled, 83
  meunière, fresh, 73
Butterflied pan-dressed fish, 5, 29–30
Buttermilk:
  marinade, black pepper and, 209
  -pecan biscuits, 195
Butters, 17
  clarified, 17
  flavored, 213–22
    ancho chile, 220
    anchovy, 215
    caviar, 219
    cilantro-lime, 219
    cooking with, tips for, 213
    five-pepper, 63
    garlic, shallot, and parsley, 215
    green peppercorn, 218
    herb, 214
    jalapeno-cumin, 92, 220
    lemon, 214
    lime, 214
    lime-cilantro, 219
    lime-ginger, 96
    mango-mint, 221
    mustard, grainy, 216
    olive, 59
    orange, 214
    orange-chive, 218
    pecan-cayenne, 92, 221
    poblano, 222
    red wine, 217
    shrimp, 216
    sun-dried tomato, 222
    tomato, 217
Buying tips, 1–5
  for fish:
    amount to buy, 5
    the basic cuts, 4–5
    fresh fillets and steaks, 3
    fresh versus frozen, 6
    fresh whole, 1–3
  shellfish, 3–4, 31–32
    amount to buy, 5

Cabbage, monkfish braised with leeks and savoy, with tomato

beurre blanc, 62–63
Cajun catfish seasoning, 150
Capers, 16
  shark with lemon and, piccata of mako, 88
  tapenade (Provençal olive and caper sauce), 231
Carp, 246
Carrots:
  fish en papillote with julienned leeks, cucumber, zucchini, and, 80–81
  glazed, 178
  scallops en papillote with, and lime ginger butter, 96
Catfish, 246
  baked, 34–35
  with capers and lemon, piccata of, 88
  cold, wrapped in lettuce, 120
  cold fish fillets Marseilles style, 126–27
  court bouillon, Acadian, 150
  with ginger and scallions, steamed, 65
  grilled, 37, 38
  with leeks, potatoes, thyme, and cream, braised, 89
  meunière, fresh, 73
  Mexican style with sautéed garlic and lime, 84
  rigatoni with eggplant, tomatoes, and, 82–83
  sautéed/stir-fried, 49–50
  steamed, 44
  with two Texas butters, sautéed, 92–93
Caviar:
  beurre blanc, 224
  butter, 219
Cayenne, 12
  butter, pecan-, 92, 221
Champagne:
  oysters wrapped in spinach with, sabayon, 159
  risotto, 166
Champagne wine vinegar, 20
  brook trout with pancetta, sage, and, 72

Channel bass. *See* Drum
Charcoal, 24–25
Cheese. *See individual types of
        cheese* e.g., Feta cheese;
        Parmesan cheese
Chervil, 9
Chile peppers, 16
  butter:
    ancho, 220
    jalapeno-cumin, 220
    poblano, 222
  chipotle aioli, 225
  chipotle sauce, 228
  crab cakes, Southwestern style
        with lime and, 158–59
  and lime marinade, 204
  shrimp with coconut milk, pea-
        nuts, and, Brazilian sautéed,
        98–99
  squid salad with hot green, and
        mint, Thai, 129
  Thai marinade, hot, 207
  tomatillo salsa, 229
Chinese parsley. *See* Cilantro
Chipotle aioli, 225
Chipotle sauce, 228
Chives, 13–14, 15
  butter, 214
    orange-, 218
Chunks of fish, 30
  cooking methods for, 30
Cider vinegar, mussel salad with
        mint, and crème fraîche,
        cold Normandy, 128
Cilantro, 9
  butter, 214
  -lime, 219
Cinnamon:
  couscous with, and tomatoes,
        168
Cisco. *See* Whitefish
Citrus fruits, 16–17. *See also indi-
        vidual citrus fruits*
Clam juice, 17
Clams, 248–49
  buying, 3–4, 32
  cooking time for, 32
  linguine with garlic, and cream à
        la Watkins, 109

portion size, 5
refrigerator storage of, 6
steamed, in the shell, 45
Coatings for frying, deep-frying,
        and broiling fish fillets and
        shellfish, 234
  bread crumbs or cracker crumbs,
        fine dry, 234
  cornflour, 234
  cornmeal mixed with seasoned
        flour, 234
  cornstarch, 234
  ground pecans, almonds, hazel-
        nuts, pine nuts, or macada-
        mia nuts, 234
  seasoned flour, 234
Coconut milk, shrimp with, pea-
        nuts, and chiles, Brazilian
        sautéed, 98–99
Cod, 240
  cold fish fillets Marseilles style,
        126
  with cumin, Moroccan, 76
  with eggplant, 86–87
  fish salad chiffonade with walnut
        oil dressing and dill,
        poached, 130–31
  with leeks, potatoes, thyme, and
        cream, braised, 89
  milk-poached, with parsley but-
        ter, 93
  poached, 47, 48
  rigatoni with eggplant, tomatoes,
        and, 82–83
  in tomato-mushroom sauce, 90
Conch, 249
Cooking methods and seasoning,
        factors in determining, 26–
        32
  size and cut, 29–30
  texture and firmness, 28–29
  type of fish, 26–28
  fatty, 26, 27, 28
  lean, 26–27, 28
  moderately fatty, 27–28
Cooking time:
  for shellfish, 32
  testing for doneness, 31
  thickness of fish and, xiii, 29, 31

Cooking time (*cont'd.*)
  *See also individual techniques for
    cooking fish and shellfish*
    e.g., Baking; Broiling;
    Steaming
Coriander, fresh. *See* Cilantro
Coriander seed, 12
Corn:
  Creole okra relish, 233
  fish soup with, and zucchini,
    146–47
  relish, papaya, 233
  salad, marinated, 188
Cornmeal:
  brioches, 194
    crab, lettuce, and tomato sand-
      wiches on toasted, 155
  cornflour, 234
  mixed with seasoned flour, 234
  polenta, 174–75
Corn oil, 18
Cornstarch coating, 234
Court bouillons, 198–201
  milk, 201
  poaching fish in, 199
  red wine, 200
  vinegar, 201
  white wine, 198–99
    for soups and chowders, 200
Couscous, 167
  with tomatoes and cinnamon,
    168
Crab, 249
  boil:
    herb and seed, 238
    spiced, 237
  boiled live hardshell, 46
  buying, 3–4, 32
  cakes, Southwestern style with
    lime and chiles, 158–59
  cold, wrapped in lettuce, 120
  cream over pecan biscuits, to-
    mato, 145
  feast, pasta and, 117
  fish soup with corn and zucchini,
    146–47
  with fried noodles, ginger, and ses-
    ame oil, stir-fried, 108–109

with ginger, sautéed soft-shelled,
    114–15
  ginger dipping sauce for, 230
  herb and seed boil for, 238
  kiwi, and orange salad with to-
    mato vinaigrette, 134
  lettuce, and tomato sandwiches,
    on toasted cornmeal
    brioches, 155
  pasta with, 116–17
  portion size, 5
  preparing soft-shelled, technique
    for, 114–15
  refrigerator storage of, 6
  salad, asparagus, potato, and,
    136–37
  seafood risotto, 166
  soufflé in scallop shells, hot, 156–
    57
  steamed live hardshell, 46
Cracker crumbs, fine dry, 234
Crappies. *See* Sunfish
Crayfish, 250
  à la Provençale with persillade,
    100–101
  bisque, 148–49
  boil, spiced, 237
  boiled live, 45
  buying, 3–4
  cooking time for, 32
  creamy shellfish gratin, 160–61
  kiwi, and orange salad with to-
    mato vinaigrette, 134
  omelette, 144
  pasta with, 116–17
  red pepper, grilled, 118
  refrigerator storage of, 6
  rice with, sausage, and oysters,
    110–11
Cream:
  creamy mustard shrimp with
    pasta, 103
  crème fraîche (French sour
    cream), 17, 227
  linguine with garlic, clams, and, à
    la Watkins, 109
  -pecan biscuits, Quick, 195
  potatoes with garlic and, scal-

loped, 170
scallop mousse with roasted red
pepper beurre blanc, hot,
104–105
of scallop soup with saffron,
152–53
scrod with leeks, potatoes,
thyme, and braised, 89
shellfish gratin, 160–61
spinach Bresse style, 184
tomato crab, over pecan biscuits,
145
Crème fraîche (French sour cream),
17, 227
artichokes and mushrooms in Madeira cream, 177
brook trout with wild mushrooms, fresh herbs, and, 74–
75
cucumber-dill sauce, 227
horseradish sauce, 230
lemon-thyme sauce, 227
mussel salad with mint, cider vinegar and, cold Normandy,
128
Creole okra relish, 233
Croaker. See Drum
Cucumber(s), 15
fish en papillote with julienned
leeks, carrots, zucchini, and,
80
removing seeds from, 15
sauce, dill-, 227
Cumin:
butter, jalapeno-, 92, 220
Moroccan fish with, 76
Cumin seed, 12
Cuts of fish, 5, 29–30
cooking methods for different,
29, 30

Deep-frying, 50–52
basic deep-fried fish or shellfish,
51–52
batters for, 235
coatings for, 234
See also Oven-frying; Pan-frying

Dill, 9
butter, 214
fish salad chiffonade with walnut
oil dressing and, poached,
130–31
sauce, cucumber-, 227
Dolphin fish. See Mahimahi
Dressings:
basic French vinaigrette, 210
tarragon vinaigrette, 211
Drum, 240
à la Provençale, baked, 66–67
baked in salt, 69
court bouillon, Acadian, 150–51
with cumin, Moroccan, 76
en papillote with carrots and
lime-ginger butter, 96–97
fish salad chiffonade with walnut
oil dressing and dill,
poached, 130–31
Mexican style with sautéed garlic
and lime, 84
with orange, red onion, and fennel, 85
See also Redfish
Duxelles (minced mushrooms and
shallots), 232

Eel for smoked fish for Sunday
brunch or supper, 138
Eggplant:
ratatouille, baked, 179
sole with, 86–87
rigatoni, and tomatoes, 82
Eggs:
aioli (Provençal garlic mayonnaise), 225
omelette, crab-filled, 144
potato soufflé, 172
salade Niçoise, 121
spaetzle, 173
Endive and shrimp sandwiches,
Belgian, 124
Equipment, 21–25
for indoor grilling, 25
other supplies, 23–24
for outdoor cooking and grilling,
24–25

Equipment (*cont'd.*)
  pots and pans, 21, 22–23
  tools and utensils, 21–22

Fatty fish, xiii, 26, 27
  cooking methods for, 27
  cooking time for, 31
  freezer storage of, 6
  list of, 28
  seasonings for, 27
Fennel, 9–10
  fish fillets with orange, red onion,
    and, 85
  orange-, marinade, 203
Fennel seed, 12
Feta cheese, orzo with, and toma-
    toes, 174
Filleted fish, 5, 25
  cooking methods for, 29, 30
  cooking time for, 31
    testing for doneness, 31
  refrigerator storage of, 6
Firmness and texture of fish, xiii,
    28–29
Fish fumet, 197–98
Fish oils, xii
Fish stocks, 19–20
  court bouillons, 198–201
    milk, 201
    red wine, 199
    vinegar, 201
    white wine, 198–99, 200
  fish fumet, 197–98
Flavored butters. *See* Butters, fla-
    vored
Flavor base, 19–20
Flounder, 241
  baked, 34–35
  with capers and lemon, piccata
    of, 88
  cold, wrapped in lettuce, 120
  with cumin, Moroccan, 76
  en papillote with carrots and
    lime-ginger butter, 96–97
  en papillote with julienned leeks,
    carrots, cucumber, and zuc-
    chini, 80–81
  with ginger and scallions,

    steamed, 65
  grilled, 37
  rigatoni with eggplant, tomatoes,
    and, 82–83
  steamed, 83
  in tomato-mushroom sauce, 90–
    91
  with walnuts, red onions, and po-
    megranate seeds, 68–69
  See also Sole
Freezing:
  fish. *See* Frozen fish and shellfish
  herbs, 7–8
  tomatoes, 15–16
French mushroom marinade, 205
French salsa, 229
French vinaigrette, basic, 210
Fresh fish and shellfish:
  buying:
    amount to buy, 5
    the basic cuts, 4–5
    fillets and steaks, 3
    storage of, 5–7
    whole, 1–3
  frozen versus, 1
  improving fish not pristine fresh,
    30
Freshwater drum. *See* Sheepshead
Frozen fish and shellfish:
  freezer storage of, 6
  fresh versus, 1
  thawing instructions, 4, 6–7
    in the microwave, 53
Frying. *See* Deep-frying; Oven-
    frying; Pan-frying
Fumet, fish, 197–98

Garlic, 14
  aioli (Provençal garlic mayon-
    naise), 225
  -anchovy marinade, 205
  beurre blanc, 224
  bread, 14
  butter, shallot, parsley, and, 215
  linguine with, clams, and cream à
    la Watkins, 109
  mushrooms braised with herbs
    and, 182

mushrooms sautéed with, 181
pesto (fresh basil sauce), 226
potatoes with, and cream, scalloped, 170
red snapper Mexican style with sautéed, and lime, 84
shrimp à la Provençale with persillade, 100–101
Gazpacho with roasted tomatoes, basil, and avocado, bay scallops, 122–23
Gin and juniper berry marinade, 209
Ginger:
  crab with:
    fried noodles, and sesame oil, stir-fried, 108–109
    sautéed soft-shelled, 114–15
  dipping sauce for crab, 230
  -glazed grilled salmon, 79
  lime-, butter, 96
  orange-, marinade, tuna in, 78
  -soy marinade, 208
  whole fish with scallions and, steamed, 65
Grape leaves, 17
Grapeseed oil, 19
Greek oregano marinade, 203
Green beans:
  salade Niçoise, 121
  with shallots, 175
Green peppers:
  ratatouille, baked, 179
  salad, roasted, 187
Grilling, 37–38
  basic grilled fish, 37–38
  grilled shrimp, 37–38
  of shellfish, 32
Grills:
  indoor, 25
  outdoor, 24
Grouper, 241
  cold fish fillets Marseilles style, 126–27
  court bouillon, Acadian, 150–51
  with cumin, Moroccan, 76
  Mexican style with sautéed garlic and lime, 84

with orange, red onion, and fennel, 85
in red wine, braised, 70
rigatoni with eggplant, tomatoes, and, 82–83
with salsa verde, grilled, 94

Haddock, 241
  with cumin, Moroccan, 76
  with leeks, potatoes, thyme, and cream, braised, 89
  milk-poached, with parsley butter, 93
Hake, 241
  with leeks, potatoes, thyme, and cream, braised, 89
  milk-poached, with parsley butter, 93
Halibut, 241
  baked, 34–35
  ceviche with orange and avocado, 132–33
  cold fish fillets Marseilles style, 127
  with cumin, Moroccan, 76
  en papillote with carrots and lime-ginger butter, 96–97
  en papillote with julienned leeks, carrots, cucumber, and zucchini, 80–81
  fish salad chiffonade with walnut oil dressing and dill, poached, 130–31
  with ginger and scallions, steamed, 65
  with leeks, potatoes, thyme, and cream, braised, 89
  Mexican style with sautéed garlic and lime, 84
  milk-poached, with parsley butter, 93
  with orange, red onion, and fennel, 85
  in orange-ginger marinade, 78
  poached, 47, 48
  in red wine, braised, 71
  with salsa verde, grilled, 94
  steam-baked, 41–42

Halibut (*cont'd.*)
steamed, 44
in tomato-mushroom sauce, 90
wrapped in Swiss chard, 87
Hazelnut oil, 19
Hazelnuts:
ground, coating, 234
Head-dressed fish, 5
Herb(s), 7–11
basil, 8
bay leaf, 9
beurre blanc, 224
boil for shrimp and crabs, seed
and, 238
brook trout with wild mushrooms, fresh, and crème
fraîche, 74–75
butters, 214
chervil, 9
cilantro (fresh coriander or
Chinese parsley), 9
dill, 9
dried, 8
fresh herb equivalents, 8
fennel, 9
freezing, 7–8
herbed bread crumbs, quick scallop sauté with, and orange
wedges, 99
infusion of, 8
lemon grass, 10
mint, 10
mushrooms braised with garlic
and, 182
oregano, 10
parsley, 10
rosemary, 10
sorrel, 11
storage of, 7–8
tarragon, 11
thyme, 11
watercress, 11
See also Spices
Herring for smoked fish for Sunday
brunch or supper, 138
Hibatchi, 24
Hickory charcoal, 25
Horseradish:
aioli, 225

sauce, 230
Hot sauce, oyster sandwich with,
and pickled okra, fried, 162

Indonesian shrimp, 113
Ivory shallot butter sauce (beurre
blanc sauce), 223–24

Jalapeno peppers, 16
-cumin butter, 92, 220
Juniper berries and gin marinade,
209

Kingfish. *See* Drum
Kiwi, lobster, and orange salad with
tomato vinaigrette, 134
Knives, 21, 22

Lake trout, 247. *See also* Trout
Lean fish, xiii
cooking methods for, 26–27
freezer storage of, 6
list of, 28
seasonings for, 27
Leeks, 13–14, 15
beurre blanc, 224
fish en papillote with julienned,
carrots, cucumber, and zucchini, 80–81
monkfish braised with, and Savoy cabbage with tomato
beurre blanc, 62–63
scrod with, potatoes, thyme, and
cream, braised, 89
Lemon grass, 10
hot Thai marinade, 207
Lemon(s), 16–17
bulgur with, and pine nuts, 169
butter, 214
mayonnaise, red pepper and,
155
sauce, thyme-, 227
shark with capers and, piccata of
mako, 88
Lettuce:
crab:
cold, wrapped in, 120
and tomato sandwiches on

toasted cornmeal brioches,
    155
olive salad, 189
Lime(s), 16–17
    butter, 214
        cilantro-, 219
        ginger, 96
    crab cakes, Southwestern style
        with, and chiles, 158
    and hot pepper marinade, 204
    mint and, marinade, 206
    red snapper Mexican style with
        sautéed garlic and, 84
Lingcod, 241–42
    baked, 34–35
    cold, wrapped in lettuce, 120
    cold fish fillets Marseilles style,
        126–27
    court bouillon, Acadian, 150–51
    with cumin, Moroccan, 76
    fillet baked with paprika and wal-
        nut sauce, 60
    fish salad chiffonade with walnut
        oil dressing and dill,
        poached, 130–31
    grilled, 37–38
    with orange, red onion, and fen-
        nel, 85
    poached, 47, 48
Lobster, 250
    baked, 34
    bisque, 148–49
    boiled live, 44
    buying, 3, 32
    cold, wrapped in lettuce, 120
    cream over pecan biscuits, to-
        mato, 145
    creamy shellfish gratin, 160–61
    in five-pepper butter, roasted, 63
    with fried noodles, ginger, and ses-
        ame oil, stir-fried, 108–109
    kiwi, and orange salad with to-
        mato vinaigrette, 134
    omelette, 144–45
    poached, 47–48
    refrigerator storage of, 6
    sandwiches with tapenade, 137
    steam-baked, 42–43
    steamed live, 44

    with walnut pesto, baked, 64
Lotte. See Monkfish

Macadamia nut coating, ground,
    234
Mackerel, 242
    with chipotle aioli, broiled, 83
    grilled, 37–38
    in mustard-scallion sauce, baked,
        91
    poached, 47, 48
    for smoked fish for Sunday
        brunch or supper, 138
Mahimahi, 242
    baked, 34–35
    with capers and lemon, piccata
        of, 88
    with chipotle aioli, broiled, 83
    in mustard-scallion sauce, baked,
        91
    steam-baked, 42–43
    with sun-dried tomato butter,
        grilled, 77
Mango-mint butter, 221
Marinades, 202–211
    balsamic vinegar and basil, 212
    basic French vinaigrette, 210
    buttermilk and black pepper, 209
    French mushroom, 205
    garlic-anchovy, 205
    ginger-soy, 208
    Greek oregano, 203
    hot pepper and lime, 204
    hot Thai, 207
    Indonesian, 113
    instructions for marinating, 202
    juniper berry and gin, 209
    lime and mint, 206
    Mediterranean, 207
    for Moroccan fish with cumin, 76
    mustard seed, 204
    orange-fennel, 203
    orange and saffron, 206
    orange-ginger, 78
    pepper, 61
    red pepper, 118
    sesame-sake, 208
    spicy yogurt, 212
    tarragon vinaigrette, 211

Mayonnaise:
  aioli (Provençal garlic mayon-
    naise), 225
  lemon and red pepper, 155
Mediterranean marinade, 207
Mesquite charcoal, 25
Mexican style snapper with sautéed
    garlic and lime, 84
Microwaving, 53
  basic microwaved fish, 53
  to thaw fish, 53
Milk, 17
  court bouillon, 201
Mint, 10
  butter, mango-, 221
  marinade, lime and, 206
  mussel salad with, cider vinegar,
    and crème fraîche, cold Nor-
    mandy, 128
  squid salad with hot green chiles
    and, Thai, 129
Moderately fatty fish, xiii, 27–28
  cooking methods for, 27–28
  cooking time for, 31
  list of, 28
  seasonings for, 27–28
Monkfish, 242
  en papillote with julienned leeks,
    carrots, cucumber, and zuc-
    chini, 80–81
  in five-pepper butter, roasted, 63
  with leeks and savoy cabbage
    with tomato beurre blanc,
    braised, 62
  with orange, red onion, and fen-
    nel, 85
  poached, 47, 48
  steamed, 43–44
  with walnut pesto, baked, 64
Moroccan fish with cumin, 76
Mullet, 242
  baked, 34–35
  with chipotle aioli, broiled, 83
  grilled, 37–38
  in mustard-scallion sauce, baked,
    91
  in orange-ginger marinade, 78
  with sun-dried tomato butter,
    grilled, 77

  with two Texas butters, sautéed,
    92–93
Mushrooms, 17–18
  à la Grecque, 180
  artichokes and, in Madeira
    cream, 177
  braised with garlic and herbs,
    182
  brook trout with wild, fresh
    herbs, and crème fraîche,
    74–75
  marinade, French, 205
  pasta primavera with mussels,
    112
  sauce, flounder in tomato, 90–91
  sautéed with garlic, 181
  and shallots, minced (duxelles),
    232
  shrimp à la Provençale with per-
    sillade, 100–101
  types of, 17–18
Mussels, 250
  buying, 3–4
  cooking time for, 31–32
  creamy shellfish gratin, 160–61
  fish soup with corn and zucchini,
    146–47
  with orange, steamed, 97
  pasta primavera with, 112
  portion size, 5
  refrigerator storage of, 6
  salad with mint, cider vinegar and
    crème fraîche, cold Nor-
    mandy, 128
  seafood risotto, 166
  steamed in the shell, 45
Mustard:
  beurre blanc, 224
  butter, grainy, 216
  creamy, shrimp with pasta, 103
  dressing, warm bistro salad with
    scallops, bacon, greens, and,
    154
  -scallion sauce, baked mackerel
    in, 91
  seed marinade, 204

New Orleans barbecued shrimp,
    107

Nutritional qualities of fish and
     shellfish, xii
Nuts:
  coatings, 234
  oils, 19
  See also individual types of nuts

Oak charcoal, 25
Ocean perch, 243
  with capers and lemon, piccata
     of, 88
  See also Perch
Oils, 18–19
  aioli (Provençal garlic mayon-
     naise), 421
  for deep-frying, 51
  grilling or basting, 19
  for marinades. *See* Marinades
Okra:
  oyster sandwich with hot sauce
     and pickled, fried, 162
  relish, Creole, 233
Olive oil, 18
Olives:
  onion and anchovy tart, Proven-
     çal (Pissaladière), 142–43
  salad, 189
  salmon grilled with, butter, 59
  tapenade (Provençal, and caper
     sauce), 231
Omega-3 fatty acids, xii
Omelet, crab-filled, 144
Onion(s):
  family, 13–15
  rice pilaf, 164
  tart, Provençal anchovy and (Pis-
     saladière), 142
  types of, 13–15
Orange roughy, 243
  with capers and lemon, piccata
     of, 88
  grilled, 37–38
  poached, 47, 48
Orange(s), 16–17
  butter, 214
     -chive, 218
  -fennel marinade, 203
  fish fillets with, red onion, and
     fennel, 85

-ginger marinade, tuna in, 78
lobster salad with tomato vinai-
     grette, kiwi, and, 134
marinade, saffron and, 206
mussels with, steamed, 97
scallop ceviche with, and avo-
     cado, 132
scallop sauté with herbed crumbs
     and, quick, 99
walnut salad, 189
Oregano, 10
  marinade, Greek, 203
Orzo:
  with feta and tomatoes, 174
Oven-frying, 52
  basic oven-fried fish, 52
  batters for, 235
  coatings for, 234
  See also Deep-frying; Pan-frying
Oyster(s), 250
  buying, 3, 32
  cooking time for, 32
  creamy shellfish gratin, 160–61
  fish soup with corn and zucchini,
     146–47
  on the half shell with five spicy
     sauces, 139
  -Parmesan popovers, 141
  portion size, 5
  refrigerator storage of, 6
  rice with shrimp, sausage, and,
     110–11
  salad with bacon, greens, and
     mustard dressing, warm bis-
     tro, 154
  sandwiches with hot sauce and
     pickled okra, fried, 162
  sautéed/stir-fried, 49
  seafood risotto, 166
  steam-baked, 42
  in tomato-mushroom sauce, 90–
     91
  wrapped in spinach with cham-
     pagne sabayon, 159

Pacific ocean perch. *See* Rockfish
Pacific snapper. *See* Rockfish
Pan bagnat (Provençal summer
     sandwich), 125

Pancetta, 19
  brook trout with, sage, and
      champagne wine vinegar, 72
  See also Bacon
Pan-dressed fish, 5, 29
Pan-frying, 50
  basic pan-fried fish, 50
  batters for, 235
  coatings for, 234
  See also Deep-frying; Oven-
      frying
Papaya corn relish, 233
Paprika, salmon fillet baked with,
    and walnut sauce, 60
Parmesan cheese:
  champagne risotto, 166
  crab soufflé in scallop shells, hot,
      156–57
  oyster-, popovers, 141
  pesto (fresh basil sauce), 226
  shellfish gratin, creamy, 160
Parsley, 10
  butter, 214
    garlic, shallot, and, 215
    halibut with, milk-poached, 93
  salsa verde, 94
  shrimp à la Provençale with per-
      sillade, 100–101
Pasta:
  crab:
    fried noodles with, ginger, and
        sesame oil stir-fried, 108
    meat feast, 117
    with crayfish, 116
  fettuccini and crab meat feast,
      117
  linguine:
    with garlic, clams, and cream à
        la Watkins, 109
    primavera with mussels, 112
  primavera with mussels, 112
  rigatoni with eggplant, tomatoes,
      and sole, 82
  shrimp with, creamy mustard,
      103
Peanut oil, 18
Peanuts and shrimp:
  with coconut milk and chiles,

  Brazilian sautéed, 98
  in spicy Malaysian coconut sauce,
      grilled, 106
Pearl rice, 165
Peas:
  black-eyed, relish, marinated,
      192
  pasta primavera with mussels,
      112
Pecan biscuits:
  quick cream- or buttermilk-, 195
  tomato crab cream over, 145
Pecan rice, 164
Pecans:
  butter, cayenne-, 92, 221
  ground, coating, 234
Pepper, 13
  butter:
    five-, monkfish in, roasted, 63
    green peppercorn, 218
  marinade, 61
    buttermilk and black, 209
  red. See Red pepper (flakes)
Peppers. See Chile peppers; Green
      peppers; Red peppers; Yel-
      low peppers
Perch, 246
  with ginger and scallions,
      steamed, 65
  grilled, 37–38
  sautéed/stir-fried, 49
  See also Ocean perch
Persian rice, crusty, 167
Pesto (fresh basil sauce), 226
  walnut, baked monkfish with, 64
Pike, 246–47
  fillet baked with paprika and wal-
      nut sauce, 60
  poached, 47, 48
  steam-baked, 41–42
Pine nuts:
  bulgur with lemon and, 109
  ground, coating, 234
  pesto (fresh basil sauce), 226
Pissaladière (Provençal onion and
      anchovy tart), 142–43
Poachers, 23
Poaching, 47–48

basic poached fish, 47, 48
in court bouillons, 199
poached scallops, 47–48
Poblano butter, 222
Poblano peppers, 16
Polenta, 74–75
Pollock, 243
with leeks, potatoes, thyme, and
cream, braised, 89
Pomegranate seeds, fish with walnuts, red onions, and, 68–69
Pompano, 243
à la Provençale, baked, 66–67
baked, 34–35
grilled, 37, 38
Popovers, oyster-Parmesan, 141
Porgy, 243
à la Provençale, baked, 66–67
baked in salt, 69
with capers and lemon, piccata
of, 88
cold fish fillets Marseilles style,
126–27
with cumin, Moroccan, 76
en papillote with carrots and
lime-ginger butter, 96–97
fillet baked with paprika and walnut sauce, 60
with ginger and scallions,
steamed, 65
Mexican style with sautéed garlic
and lime, 84
with orange, red onion, and fennel, 85
with salsa verde, grilled, 94
sautéed/stir-fried, 49
in tomato-mushroom sauce, 90–
91
with walnuts, red onions, and pomegranate seeds, 68
with wild mushrooms, fresh
herbs, and crème fraîche,
74–75
Portion sizes, 5
Potato(es):
pommes de terre au diable, 170–
71
with rosemary, quick oven, 171

salad:
asparagus, crab, and 136
with tarragon and shallot vinaigrette sauce, warm, 186
salade Niçoise, 121
scrod with leeks, thyme, and
cream, braised, 89
soufflé, 172
watercress soup, 191
Pots and pans, 21, 22–23
Prawns, Monterey, 251
Preparation and cooking tips:
for fish, 31, 32–33
testing for doneness, 31
for shellfish, 31–33

Radishes for olive salad, 189
Rainbow trout, 247
in red wine, braised, 70–71
See also Brook trout; Sea trout;
Trout
Raspberry wine vinegar, salmon
with, 58
Ratatouille, baked, 179
Redfish, 240–41
à la Provençale, baked, 66–67
baked, 34–35
in salt, 69
with chipotle aioli, broiled, 83
cold:
fish fillets Marseilles style, 126–
27
wrapped in lettuce, 120
court bouillon, Acadian, 150–51
with cumin, Moroccan, 76
with eggplant, 86–87
en papillote with carrots and
lime-ginger butter, 96–97
en papillote with julienned leeks,
carrots, cucumber, and zucchini, 80–81
fillet baked with paprika and walnut sauce, 60–61
fish salad chiffonade with walnut
oil dressing and dill,
poached, 130–31
with ginger and scallions,
steamed, 65

Redfish (cont'd.)
  grilled, 37–38
  Mexican style with sautéed garlic
    and lime, 84
  with orange, red onion, and fen-
    nel, 85
  poached, 47, 48
  with raspberry wine vinegar, 58
  in red wine, braised, 70–71
  with salsa verde, grilled, 94
  steam-baked, 41–42
  steamed, 43–44
  in tomato-mushroom sauce, 90–
    91
  with walnuts, red onions, and po-
    megranate seeds, 68–69
  with wild mushrooms, fresh
    herbs, and crème fraîche,
    74–75
  wrapped in Swiss chard, 87
  See also Drum
Red onions, 13–14, 15
  fish with walnuts, and pomegran-
    ate seeds, 68–69
  salade Niçoise, 121
Red pepper (flakes) for grilled
    shrimp, 118
Red peppers:
  beurre blanc, roasted, 224
  mayonnaise, lemon and, 155
  salad, roasted, 187
  sauce, roasted, 227
Red snapper, 243
  à la Provençale, baked, 66–67
  baked, 34–35
    in salt, 69
  with capers and lemon, piccata
    of, 88
  ceviche with orange and avo-
    cado, 132–33
  with chipotle aioli, broiled, 83
  cold fish fillets Marseilles style,
    126–27
  court bouillon, Acadian, 150–51
  with cumin, Moroccan, 76–77
  with eggplant, 86–87
  en papillote with carrots and

    lime-ginger butter, 96–97
  en papillote with julienned leeks,
    carrots, cucumber, and zuc-
    chini, 80–81
  fillet baked with paprika and wal-
    nut sauce, 60
  fish salad chiffonade with walnut
    oil dressing and dill,
    poached, 130–31
  with ginger and scallions,
    steamed, 65
  grilled, 37, 38
  Mexican style with sautéed garlic
    and lime, 84
  with orange, red onion, and fen-
    nel, 85
  poached, 47, 48
  with raspberry wine vinegar, 58
  in red wine, braised, 70–71
  with salsa verde, grilled, 94
  steam-baked, 41–42
  in tomato-mushroom sauce, 90–
    91
  with walnuts, red onions, and po-
    megranate seeds, 68–69
  with wild mushrooms, fresh
    herbs, and crème fraîche,
    74–75
  wrapped in Swiss chard, 87
Refrigerator storage, 6
Relish:
  Creole okra, 233
  marinated black-eye pea, 192
  papaya corn, 233
Rice:
  crusty Persian, 167
  pilaf, 164
  saffron, and shrimp salad, 135
  with shrimp, sausage, and oys-
    ters, 110–11
  white, 164–65
  wild, 165
    with scallions, 165
  See also Risotto
Rice wine vinegar, 20
Rigatoni with eggplant, tomatoes,
    and sole, 82–83

Risotto, champagne, 166
  seafood, 166
Rock cod. *See* Rockfish
Rockfish, 243
  à la Provençale, baked, 66–67
  baked, 34–35
    in salt, 69
  with capers and lemon, piccata
    of, 88
  cold fish fillets Marseilles style,
    126–27
  court bouillon, Acadian, 150–51
  with cumin, Moroccan, 76
  en papillote with julienned leeks,
    carrots, cucumber, and zuc-
    chini, 80–81
  fish salad chiffonade with walnut
    oil dressing and dill,
    poached, 130–31
  with ginger and scallions,
    steamed, 65
  Mexican style with sautéed garlic
    and lime, 84
  with orange, red onion, and fen-
    nel, 85
  poached, 47, 48
  in red wine, braised, 70–71
  with salsa verde, grilled, 94
  sautéed/stir-fried, 49
  in tomato-mushroom sauce, 90–
    91
  with walnuts, red onions, and po-
    megranate seeds, 68–69
  wrapped in Swiss chard, 87
Rosemary, 10–11
  in pommes de terre au diable,
    170–71
  potatoes with, quick oven, 171

Sablefish, 244
  with chipotle aioli, broiled, 83
  for smoked fish for Sunday
    brunch or supper, 138
Safflower oil, 18
Saffron, 13
  marinade, orange and, 206
  rice and shrimp salad, 135

  scallop soup with, cream of, 152
Sage, brook trout with pancetta,
    and champagne wine vine-
    gar, 72
Sake marinade, sesame-, 208
Salad(s):
  asparagus, crab, and potato,
    136–37
  bistro, with scallops, bacon,
    greens, and mustard dress-
    ing, warm, 154
  black-eyed pea relish, marinated,
    192
  corn, marinated, 188
  lobster, kiwi, and orange, with to-
    mato vinaigrette, 134
  mussel, with mint, cider vinegar
    and crème fraîche, cold Nor-
    mandy, 128
  Niçoise, 121
  pepper, roasted red, green, or
    yellow, 187
  poached fish, chiffonade with
    walnut oil dressing and dill,
    130–31
  potato:
    asparagus, crab, and, 136–37
    with tarragon and shallot vinai-
    grette, warm, 186
  saffron rice and shrimp, 135
  squid, with hot green chiles and
    mint, Thai, 129
Salmon, 244
  with capers and lemon, piccata
    of, 88
  coho:
    in mustard-scallion sauce,
    baked, 91
    in red wine, braised, 70–71
  en papillote with julienned leeks,
    carrots, cucumber, and zuc-
    chini, 80–81
  feast, roasted, 61
  fillet-baked with paprika and wal-
    nut sauce, 60
  ginger-glazed grilled, 79
  grilled, 37, 38

Salmon (*cont'd.*)
    with olive butter, 59
    in orange-ginger marinade, 78
    poached, 47, 48
    with raspberry wine vinegar, 58
    with salsa verde, grilled, 94
    sautéed/stir-fried, 49
    for smoked fish for Sunday
        brunch or supper, 138
    steam-baked, 41–42
    steamed, 43–44
    in tomato-mushroom sauce, 90
Salsa verde, grilled tuna with, 94
Salt, 19
    whole fish baked in, 69
Sandwich(es):
    crab, lettuce, and tomato, on
        toasted cornmeal brioches,
        155
    lobster, with tapenade, 137
    oyster, with hot sauce and pic-
        kled okra, fried, 162
    Provençal summer (pan bagnat),
        125
    shrimp and endive, Belgian, 124
Saucepans, 21, 23
Sauce(s):
    aioli (Provençal garlic mayon-
        naise), 225
        variations on, 225
    chipotle, 228
    coconut, spicy Malaysian, 106
    crème fraîche (French sour
        cream), 227
    Creole okra, relish, 233
    cucumber-dill, 227
    French salsa, 229
    ginger dipping, for crab, 230
    horseradish, 230
    ivory shallot butter (beurre blanc
        sauce), 223–24
        variations on, 224
    lemon-thyme, 227
    mushrooms and shallots, minced
        (duxelles), 232
    mustard-scallion, 91
    papaya corn relish, 233

    paprika and walnut, 60
    pesto (fresh basil sauce), 226
    red pepper, roasted, 227
    salsa verde, 94
    tapenade (Provençal olive and
        caper sauce), 231
    tomatillo salsa, 229
    tomato, 228
        -mushroom, 90
    walnut pesto, 64
Sausage, rice with shrimp, and oys-
    ters, 110
Sautéeing and stir-frying, 49
    basic sautéed/stir-fried fish or
        shellfish, 49
Scallions, 14, 15
    mustard-, sauce, baked mackerel
        in, 91
    whole fish with ginger and,
        steamed, 65
    wild rice with, 165
Scallops, 250
    baked, 34
    buying, 3, 4, 32
    ceviche with orange and avo-
        cado, 132–33
    cold, wrapped in lettuce, 120
    cooking time for, 32
    cream over pecan biscuits, to-
        mato, 145
    creamy shellfish gratin, 160–61
    en papillote with carrots and lime
        ginger butter, 96–97
    en papillote with julienned leeks,
        carrots, cucumber, and zuc-
        chini, 80–81
    fish soup with corn and zucchini,
        146–47
    in five-pepper butter, roasted, 63
    with fried noodles, ginger, and ses-
        ame oil, stir-fried, 108–109
    gazpacho with roasted tomatoes,
        basil, and avocado, 122–23
    grilling, 32
    kiwi, and orange salad with to-
        mato vinaigrette, 134
    mousse with roasted red pepper

beurre blanc, hot, 104–105
pasta with, 116
poached, 47, 48
portion size, 5
red pepper, grilled, 118
salad with bacon, greens, and
  mustard dressing, warm bistro, 154
sauté, with herbed crumbs and
  orange wedges, quick, 99
sautéed/stir-fried, 49
seafood risotto, 166
shells, hot crab soufflé in, 156
soup with saffron, cream of, 152
in tomato-mushroom sauce, 90
with walnut pesto, baked, 64
Scrod, 244
baked, 34–35
cold:
  fish fillets Marseilles style, 126–
    27
  wrapped in lettuce, 120
court bouillon, Acadian, 150–51
with leeks, potatoes, thyme, and
  cream, braised, 89
milk-poached, with parsley butter, 93
steamed, 44
Sea bass:
à la Provençale, baked, 66–67
en papillote with julienned leeks,
  carrots, cucumber, and zucchini, 80–81
See also Black sea bass
Seasonings, 7–21
aromatic or flavoring vegetables,
  13–16
herbs, 7–11
other flavorings and ingredients,
  16–21
spices, 12–13
type of fish and appropriate, 27–
  28
Sea trout, 244
baked, 34–35
with eggplant, 86–87
fish salad chiffonade with walnut

oil dressing and dill,
  poached, 130–31
with ginger and scallions,
  steamed, 65
grilled, 37, 38
Mexican style with sautéed garlic
  and lime, 84
poached, 47, 48
rigatoni with eggplant, tomatoes,
  and, 82–83
steamed, 43–44
with two Texas butters, sautéed,
  92–93
with walnuts, red onions, and pomegranate seeds, 68–69
See also Brook trout; Rainbow
  trout; Trout
Sesame oil, 19
crab with fried noodles, ginger,
  and, stir-fried, 108–109
Sesame-sake marinade, 208
Shad, 244–45
Shallot(s), 13–14
butter, garlic, parsley, and, 215
confit, 193
green beans with, 175
ivory, butter sauce (beurre blanc
  sauce), 223–24
mushrooms and, minced (duxelles), 232
shrimp à la Provençale with persillade, 100–101
and tarragon vinaigrette, warm
  potato salad with, 186
Shark, 245
in five-pepper butter, roasted, 63
grilled, 37, 38
piccata of mako, with capers and
  lemon, 88
with salsa verde, grilled, 94
smell of fresh, 2
Sheepshead, 247
à la Provençale, baked, 66–67
baked in salt, 69
with chipotle aioli, broiled, 83
Mexican style with sautéed garlic
  and lime, 84

Shrimp, 251
  à la Provençale with persillade,
    100–101
  baked, 34–35
  barbecued, New Orleans, 107
  bisque, 148–49
  boil:
    dark beer, 236
    herb and seed, 238
    spiced, 237
  Brazilian sautéed, with coconut
    milk, peanuts, and chiles,
    98–99
  butter, 216
  butterflying, technique for, 107
  buying, 4
  cold, wrapped in lettuce, 120
  cooking time for, 32
  creamy mustard, with pasta, 103
  and endive sandwiches, 124
  fish soup with corn and zucchini,
    146–47
  freezer storage of, 6
  with fried noodles, ginger, and ses-
    ame oil, stir-fried, 108–109
  grilled, 32, 37–38
  hot and crunchy, 102
  Indonesian, 113
  kiwi, and orange salad with to-
    mato vinaigrette, 134
  pasta with, 116–17
  poached, 47, 48
  portion size, 5
  red pepper, grilled, 118
  salad:
    with bacon, greens, and mus-
      tard dressing, warm bistro,
      154
    with hot green chiles and mint,
      Thai, 129
    saffron rice and, 135
  seafood risotto, 166
  in spicy Malaysian coconut sauce,
    grilled, 106
  steam-baked, 42
  steamed, 45
  in tomato-mushroom sauce, 90–
    91

  with walnut pesto, baked, 64
Skewers, 23
Skillets, 21, 22–23
Smelt, 247
  rigatoni with eggplant, tomatoes,
    and, 82–83
  sautéed/stir-fried, 49
Smoked fish for Sunday brunch or
    supper, 138
Snapper. See Red snapper
Sole, 241
  with capers and lemon, piccata
    of, 88
  with eggplant, 86
  en papillote with carrots and
    lime-ginger butter, 96–97
  en papillote with julienned leeks,
    carrots, cucumber, and zuc-
    chini, 80–81
  meunière, fresh, 73
  poached, 47, 48
  rigatoni with eggplant, tomatoes,
    and, 82–83
  steam-baked, 41–42
  steamed, 43–44
  in tomato-mushroom sauce, 90–
    91
  See also Flounder
Sorrel, 11
  butter, 214
Soufflés:
  crab, in scallop shells, hot, 156–
    57
  potato, 172
Soup(s):
  fish, with corn and zucchini, 146–
    47
  Scallop:
    bay, gazpacho with tomatoes,
      basil, and avocado, 122–23
    with saffron, cream of, 152–53
  shrimp bisque, 148–49
  tomato, cold, 190
  watercress, 191
Sour cream. See Crème fraîche
Soy sauce, 19
  marinade, ginger-, 208
Spaetzle, 173

Spices, 12–13
    cayenne, 12
    coriander seed, 12
    cumin seed, 12
    fennel seed, 12
    pepper, 13
    saffron, 13
    storage of, 12
    See also Herbs
Spinach:
    Bresse style, 184
    oysters wrapped in, with cham-
        pagne sabayon, 159
    timbales, 185
Squid, 251
    blanched, for salads, 54
    braised, 54
    cooking time for, 32
    deep-fried, 54, 153
    preparing, 53–54
    salad with hot green chiles and
        mint, Thai, 129
    seafood risotto, 166
Steaked fish, 5, 30
    cooking methods for, 30
    refrigerator storage of, 6
Steam-baking, 40–41
    basic steam-baked fish, 41–42
    basic steam-baked shellfish, 42
Steamers, 21, 22
Steaming, 43–46
    basic steamed fish, 43–44
    boiled live crayfish, 45
    steamed or boiled live hardshell
        crabs, 46
    steamed or boiled live lobster, 44
    steamed shrimp, 45
Stir-frying. *See* Sautéeing and stir-
        frying
Storage:
    of fish and shellfish, 5–7
        refrigerator, 6
    freezer, 6
        thawing instructions, 4, 6–7
    of herbs, 7–8
    of oils, 18–19
    of spices, 12
Striped bass, 239

baked, 34–35
    in salt, 69
ceviche with orange and avo-
    cado, 132–33
cold fish fillets Marseilles style,
    126–27
with cumin, Moroccan, 76
with eggplant, 86–87
en papillote with carrots and
    lime-ginger butter, 96–97
fish salad chiffonade with walnut
    oil dressing and dill,
    poached, 130–31
with ginger and scallions,
    steamed, 65
grilled, 37, 38
with orange, red onion, and fen-
    nel, 85
in orange-ginger marinade, 78
poached, 47, 48
with raspberry wine vinegar, 58
steam-baked, 41–42
in tomato-mushroom sauce, 90–
    91
with walnuts, red onions, and
    pomegranate seeds, 68–69
Sturgeon, 247
    for smoked fish for Sunday
        brunch or supper, 138
Sun-dried tomatoes, 20
    aioli, 225
    butter, 222
        grilled swordfish with, 77
Sunfish, 247
    meunière, fresh, 73
Swiss chard, halibut wrapped in,
    steamed, 87
Swordfish, 245
    à la Provençale, baked, 66–67
    baked, 34–35
    ceviche with orange and avo-
        cado, 132–33
    grilled, 37–38
        with olive butter, 59
    in orange-ginger marinade, 78
    with salsa verde, grilled, 94
    with sun-dried tomato butter,
        grilled, 77

Tamari sauce, 19
Tapenade (Provençal olive and ca-
    per sauce), 231
  lobster sandwiches with, 137
Tarragon, 11
  butter, 214
  potato salad with, and shallot vi-
    naigrette, 186
  vinaigrette, 211
  wine vinegar, 20
Techniques for cooking fish and
    shellfish, 32–54
  baking, 33–35
  braising, 40–41
  broiling, 38–39
  to cook squid, 53–54
  deep-frying, 50–52
  grilling, 35–38
  microwaving, 53
  oven-frying, 52
  pan-frying, 50–51
  poaching, 46–48
  sautéeing and stir-frying, 49
  steam-baking, 40–42
  steaming, 43–46
Tempura batter, 235
Testing for doneness, 31
Tex-mati rice, 164
Texture and firmness of fish, xiii,
    28–29
Thai marinade, hot, 207
Thai squid salad with hot green
    chiles and mint, 129
Thawing:
  of fish, 6–7
  of shellfish, 4
Thermometers, 21
Thickness of fish, cooking time and,
    xiii, 29, 31
Thyme, 11
  butter, 214
  sauce, lemon, 227
  scrod with leeks, potatoes, and
    cream, braised, 89
Tilefish, 245
  baked, 34–35
  with capers and lemon, piccata
    of, 88

cold:
  fish fillets Marseilles style, 126–
    27
  wrapped in lettuce, 120
Timbales, spinach, 185
Tomatillo salsa, 229
Tomato(es):
  à la Provençale, 183
  beurre blanc, 224
  -basil, 224
    monkfish braised with leeks
      and Savoy cabbage with, 62
  butter, 217
  catfish court bouillon, Acadian,
    150–51
  cold fish fillets Marseilles style,
    126–27
  corn salad, marinated, 188
  crab:
    cream over pecan biscuits, 145
    lettuce, and, sandwiches, on
      toasted cornmeal brioches,
      155
  fish soup with corn and zucchini,
    146–47
  freezing, 15
  French salsa, 229
  gazpacho with roasted, basil, and
    avocado, bay scallop, 122–
    23
  mushrooms à la Grecque, 180
  mushroom sauce, flounder in,
    90–91
  orzo with feta and, 174
  ratatouille, baked, 179
  removing seeds from, 15
  rigatoni with eggplant, and sole,
    82–83
  sauce, 228
  shrimp à la Provençale with per-
    sillade, 100–101
  soup, cold, 190
  sun-dried, 20
    aioli, 225
    butter, 222
    grilled swordfish with, 77
  vinaigrette, lobster, kiwi, and or-
    ange salad with, 134

Tools and utensils, 21–22
Trout, 247
    with capers and lemon, piccata
        of, 88
    with chipotle aioli, broiled, 83
    meunière, fresh, 73
    in mustard-scallion sauce, baked,
        91
    for smoked fish for Sunday
        brunch or supper, 138
    in tomato-mushroom sauce, 90
    See also Brook trout; Rainbow
        trout; Sea trout
Tuna, 245
    à la Provençale, baked, 66–67
    baked, 34–35
    with capers and lemon, piccata
        of, 88
    ceviche with orange and avo-
        cado, 132–33
    grilled, 37, 38
    in orange-ginger marinade, 78
    Provençal summer sandwich (pan
        bagnat), 125
    salade Niçoise, 121
    with salsa verde, grilled, 94
    with sun-dried tomato butter,
        grilled, 77
    tapenade (Provençal olive and
        caper sauce), 231

Utensils and tools, 21–22

Vegetable oils, 18–19
Vegetables:
    with seeds, 15–16
    See also individual vegetables
Vinegar(s), 20
    court bouillon, 201
    deglazing a pan with, 20
    making your own herb, 20
    in marinades. See Marinades
    types of, 20

Walnut(s):
    fish with, red onions, and pome-
        granate seeds, 68–69

oil, 19
    vinaigrette, 130
olive salad, 189
pesto, baked monkfish with, 64
sauce, salmon fillet baked with
    paprika and, 60
Watercress, 11
    butter, 214
    soup, 191
Weakfish. See Sea trout
Wehani rice, 165
Whitebait. See Smelt
Whitefish, 247–48
    with chipotle aioli, broiled, 83
    in mustard-scallion sauce, baked,
        91
    for smoked fish for Sunday
        brunch or supper, 138
    with two Texas butters, sautéed,
        92–93
White onions, 13–14, 15. See also
    Onions
White sea bass, 239. See also Bass;
    Black sea bass; Sea bass
Whiting, 245
    cold fish fillets Marseilles style,
        126–27
    rigatoni with eggplant, tomatoes,
        and, 82–83
    sautéed/stir-fried, 49
Whole fish, 4, 29
    à la Provençale, baked, 66–67
    baked in salt, 69
    buying, 1–3
    categories of, xiii
    cooking methods for, 29, 30
    cooking time for, 31
        testing for doneness, 31
    freezer storage of, 6
    with ginger and scallions,
        steamed, 65
    portion size, 5
    refrigerator storage of, 6
    with walnuts, red onions, and
        pomegranate seeds, 68–69
    See also individual types of fish
Wild rice, 165
    with scallions, 165

Wines, 20–21
  red:
    butter, 217
    court bouillon, 199
    fish braised in, 70–71
  white, court bouillon, 198–99,
    200

Yellowfin. *See* Tuna
Yellow onions, 13–14, 15. *See also*
  Onions

Yellow peppers salad, roasted, 187
Yogurt marinade, spicy, 212

Zucchini, 15
  fish en papillote with julienned
    leeks, carrots, cucumber
    and, 80–81
  fish soup with corn and, 146–47
  gratin, 178–79
  ratatouille, baked, 179
  removing seeds from, 15